Equity in Our Schools

Equity in Our Schools

Ensuring Marginalized Students Achieve at a High Level

GwenCarol H. Holmes

ROWMAN & LITTLEFIELD
Lanham • Boulder • New York • London

Published by Rowman & Littlefield
An imprint of The Rowman & Littlefield Publishing Group, Inc.
4501 Forbes Boulevard, Suite 200, Lanham, Maryland 20706
www.rowman.com

86-90 Paul Street, London EC2A 4NE

Copyright © 2023 by GwenCarol H. Holmes

All rights reserved. No part of this book may be reproduced in any form or by any electronic or mechanical means, including information storage and retrieval systems, without written permission from the publisher, except by a reviewer who may quote passages in a review.

British Library Cataloguing in Publication Information Available

Library of Congress Cataloging-in-Publication Data

Names: Holmes, GwenCarol H., author.
Title: Equity in our schools : ensuring marginalized students achieve at a high level / GwenCarol H. Holmes.
Description: Lanham, Maryland : Lexington Books, 2023. | Includes bibliographical references and index.
Identifiers: LCCN 2022054240 (print) | LCCN 2022054241 (ebook) | ISBN 9781475869064 (cloth) | ISBN 9781475869071 (paperback) | ISBN 9781475869088 (ebook)
Subjects: LCSH: Educational equalization--United States. | Children with social disabilities--Education--United States. | School environment--United States. | Language arts--Correlation with content subjects.
Classification: LCC LC213.2 .H636 2023 (print) | LCC LC213.2 (ebook) | DDC 379.2/60973--dc23/eng/20221206
LC record available at https://lccn.loc.gov/2022054240
LC ebook record available at https://lccn.loc.gov/2022054241

Dedication

This book is dedicated to educators everywhere who believe in the power of education to level the playing field for all students and who work day in and day out to make it so. Your relentless pursuit of equity provides a brighter future for our children, our country, and our world. For you, I am grateful.

To my incredible husband, daughter, son, daughter-in-law, and grandsons, I cannot begin to express how your love, encouragement, and support of my career and passion has fed my soul and provided the courage to continue to push forward in this work. The models provided by my paternal grandmother and my parents gave me a heart for marginalized peoples, especially children.

To the many of you that have mentored me through my career, you forever have my gratitude. Dr. Larry Vaughn, you taught me to be courageous and persevere in the face of skeptics. Drs. Robert Slavin and Nancy Madden, you taught me to be relentless in my work and to leverage the evidence from research. Thank you.

Contents

Preface	ix
Chapter 1: What Is Equity?	1
Chapter 2: Foundations of Equity in Schools	7
Chapter 3: Building Cultures that Support Equity	13
Chapter 4: Reading—The Basis of Equity in School	53
Chapter 5: Literacy in the Content Areas	77
Chapter 6: Highly Effective Instruction	97
Chapter 7: Student Supports	113
Chapter 8: Social Services: Why We Need Them	145
Chapter 9: Allocating Resources for Equity	165
Epilogue	185
Bibliography	189
Appendix A: Professional Learning Plans	203
Appendix B: Reflections and Next Steps	211

Preface

Rigorous Education for All

One of America's greatest gifts to the world is the idea of a free public education for all of our children. As with many of America's ideas, the vision is noble while the implementation is still a work in progress. Our educational system has been and continues to be improved time and time again over the years. The definition of "all" has expanded with time from white males of privilege to a slowly growing definition of all. We continue to strive for all of our children to be educated to the highest levels in a free public education system that embraces each of them for the unique and magnificent wonders they are.

The call for all of our children to be educated to the highest level will be realized only when we establish equity in our schools. Ensuring all students are educated to the highest level is not for the faint of heart. It takes the belief that it must and can happen, as well as the relentlessness to make it happen, by using what we know about how students learn from the ever growing body of high-quality educational research, honest examination of our own beliefs, and an understanding of educational systems.

I have been an educator for over forty years. I have been a teacher, a reading specialist, an educational service provider, a chief academic officer, and a superintendent. I have worked with and facilitated the development of hundreds of educational leaders working in schools all across our great country. I found that in whatever position I served, there were actions I could take to advance the cause of ensuring all students were educated to the highest levels.

This book shares the lessons I have learned about creating equity in our schools, both from the body of educational research and from lived experiences. It is my hope that what I have learned will add to your own professional growth and give you hope and encouragement that the vision of all students being educated to the highest levels can be achieved.

If you are an educator who strongly believes that all students can and must be educated to the highest level, this book is for you. We will examine the everyday actions we can take as educators—in our classrooms, our schools, and our districts—to establish equity for all our students. This book contains actions that classroom teachers, teacher specialists, department chairs, teacher leaders, principals, district directors, and superintendents can take to ensure that all of our students master rigorous standards.

Regardless of your position, if you only have the ability to influence what happens in your classroom or if you have the ability to influence school or district practices, you have the power to create a small pocket of equity in your daily work with students and other educators. If we all share our passion for educating all students to a high level by ensuring equity is the practice in our sphere of control, the results will transform our classrooms, schools, and districts across our country.

If you are an educator that strives to ensure all students, regardless of circumstances, graduate high school college and/or career ready, then join with your fellow educators as we take action in our classrooms, our schools, and our districts to remake the system for the success of all students. These are actions we can take regardless of district, state, or federal policies. Taking these steps will break from tradition, and that is not easy. However, if you are one of us who believes that all children must be highly educated, then you are already departing from tradition and know that our future as a country depends on educators ensuring the future of our children.

Educators working to create equity in our schools are the educators that Thomas Brown (1999) describes: "teachers who perceive themselves as the world's best hope for a brighter future reflect that perception through their relentless pursuit of excellence" (p. 2). Join the many before us that have been remaking public education so that every single child reaches their highest potential. Take this opportunity to reflect on your practice and commit to continuing the struggle to ensure every child is highly educated.

We will begin by defining equity and discussing the foundations of establishing equity: culture and systems. Chapter 3 will reflect on how to establish positive cultures that vanquish deficit thinking which keeps equity at bay. In chapters 4 through 6, we will discuss instructional systems that ensure the success of every student. Chapter 7 will look at special programs and how they can hinder the quest for equity. Chapter 8 discusses social services and why schools must be a partner in such services. Lastly, we will discuss how we can use the resources we have for establishing equity. Enjoy the journey. Our children are depending on us.

Chapter 1

What Is Equity?

Equity is more than access to a public education. While the United States of America has not established equity in its schools, there has been tremendous progress in the scope of public education in the United States. Recognizing the incredible strides that have been made in education across the country can encourage educators to relentlessly continue the effort to ensure all students are highly educated and graduate high school college and/or career ready.

Throughout the history of the United States, educators have expanded the reach of public education. Recognizing the accomplishments of earlier educators provides inspiration and encouragement to continue the work of ensuring all students succeed at the highest levels. The first more than two hundred years of the development of a public education system in the United States saw a continuous focus on widening the net to include more and more children: not just the white males of privilege, but all children regardless of gender, race, economic status, disability, or language. The focus was on providing *access* to school for all children.

Over forty years ago as our schools grew to serve a more diverse group of students the focus became "opportunity to learn" in an attempt to ensure all students were educated. Educators were expected to document when they taught each skill prescribed for their grade level or content area. For example, when the week arrived in first grade that the long "a" vowel sound was to be taught, teachers recorded that the skill was taught. They had fulfilled their obligation as a teacher by presenting the content required. It was considered that because the material had been presented to all students, educators had provided the "opportunity to learn" to all students.

There was no discussion about who had actually learned the long "a" vowel sound. The focus was entirely on what had been presented to the students, not what they had learned. Education in the late 1970s and 1980s was focused on access: ensuring all children had access to the content or an opportunity to learn. Educators were not yet systematically documenting who had learned (Elliott and Bartlett, 2016).

While the No Child Left Behind Act has been repeatedly and harshly criticized by educators and policy makers alike (and often justly so), there was at least one positive outcome from this legislation. It required that schools publish their data on student proficiency by a myriad of groups (race/ethnicity, language learners, students with disabilities, students qualifying for free/reduced price meals). This data made the glaring gaps in achievement from one group to another front and center.

While there were many efforts to explain away the gaps or even justify their existence, the fact remained that the education children were leaving our schools with at graduation varied widely, and there was still an incredibly strong bias in outcomes to those who were white and privileged. Access to an education had been provided to the vast majority of our children, but the outcomes had only minimally changed.

The data verifying that not all children were succeeding in school was not new; however, with the passage of No Child Left Behind, this data was much more public and widely published each year. It became a routine part of our educational landscape rather than the occasionally and sporadic outrage as was the experience with the publication of *Why Johnny Can't Read: And What You Can Do About It* (Flesh, 1955) or *A Nation at Risk* (National Commission on Excellence in Education, 1983).

This overview of American education history serves as a reminder of the actions earlier educators undertook to move us closer to the American ideal of all students educated to the highest levels. Now it is the turn of today's educators to take up the quest and continue the work of ensuring every single child graduates from high school college and/or career ready. The United States cannot allow another couple of hundred years to pass before we truly are educating all students to the highest level. This must be achieved now. Our children and our country's success depend upon it.

DEFINING EQUITY

The repeated publication of data under the No Child Left Behind Act illustrating the differences in outcomes for students was important for fueling the call for equity in schools. It was widely recognized that there was a wide disparity of the value of the education our students possessed when they graduated from school. This realization stoked the flames to continue to improve our school system for all children. This quest for equity in American schools continues through this day. As educators, we are learning and growing and pushing the system to become equitable so that all of our students graduate high school highly educated.

A quick illustration of the growing understanding of what providing equity in our schools really is can been seen in the following illustrations.

Figure 1.1
Source: A collaboration between Center for Story-based Strategy & Interaction Institute for Social Change. https://www.storybasedstrategy.org/the4thbox and http://interactioninstitute.org/.

Figure 1.2
Source: ©2017 Robert Wood Johnson Foundation. May be reproduced with attribution.

It is not uncommon to see some version of the generic baseball illustration used to convey the concept of equity and to help facilitate conversations about "equity" or the need to provide whatever it takes to ensure all students can be a part of the game (no boxes, one box, two boxes). However, the baseball illustration is not an illustration of equity, but rather a continued push for access for all with privilege still being central to the outcome.

Some viewers of the game have the privilege of being inside the stadium and in the stands. They get the full effect of the game. They have access to the hotdog vendors, doing the wave with their fellow spectators, and most importantly being completely welcomed at the game. The children standing outside the fence have access to the game in that they can see it, even if it takes a box or two to be able to see over the fence. However, they are not fully welcomed in. They are not fully included in the experience of the game. When the game is over, their experience is very different even though they had access to the game.

The bike illustration comes closer to conveying the concept of equity in education. Not only do all of the participants have access, but they have what they need to achieve the goal of riding a bike. They all are fully welcomed in, and they all are provided whatever each individual needs to achieve the outcome of riding a bike. The bikes are of various sizes and designs. Some of the bikes are more readily available and less expensive than others. However, that does not matter. What matters is that *all* are able to achieve the desired outcome of riding a bike because whatever it takes was provided to each individual.

The National Equity Project (n.d.) states: "Educational equity means that each child receives what they need to develop to their full academic and social potential." Equity can be defined as providing whatever it takes to ensure every child achieves at the highest levels, mastering the standards and graduating with the skills needed to pursue a large variety of opportunities in their adulthood: college and/or career ready. This way of defining equity helps educators understand what is expected of them.

Another way to consider the difference between access for all students and equity for all students can be found in the way the Center for Public Education (2016) distinguishes between equality and equity. "Equality in education is achieved when students are all treated the same and have access to similar resources. Equity is achieved when all students receive the resources they need so they graduate prepared for success after high school" (p. 1).

Treating all students exactly the same does not result in the same level of education for all. Our children, each a unique individual, come to school from a wide range of backgrounds and experiences. Their very individuality and varied backgrounds mean that they bring different strengths and abilities to the schoolhouse with them. Treating them all exactly the same says we expect them to all be the same with the same backgrounds. Treating them all the same is a failure to recognize and honor their uniqueness as individuals from a multitude of rich backgrounds.

The *Glossary of Education Reforms* (Great Schools Partnership, 2016) says that

> equity encompasses a wide variety of educational models, programs, and strategies that may be considered fair, but not necessarily equal. It has been said that "equity is the process; equality is the outcome," given that equity—what is fair and just—may not, in the process of educating students, reflect strict equality—what is applied, allocated or distributed equally. Inequities occur when biased or unfair policies, programs, practices, or situations contribute to a lack of equality in educational performance, results, and outcomes. (paragraph 1)

The push to provide equity within our system of education continues to gain momentum and is critical to our future. Understanding the concept of equity in our children's education is a part of education's continuous improvement journey. Through the dedication of educators and policy makers, over time, our schools have become more and more inclusive toward the goal of serving all students.

Children of all backgrounds, races, ethnicities, and genders; children with disabilities; children learning English as a second language; and children of all economic levels are all now served in our schools. They are not all served equitably, as is evident in the various levels of education or outcomes with which our children exit the schoolhouse. However, the quest for equity in education for all of our children continues.

Through extensive legislation and policy implementations, we have greatly improved access for all our students. However, access alone is insufficient for ensuring equality in outcomes for all our students. The "whatever it takes" actions that make equity happen and equality achieved are actions that take place in the classroom and the schoolhouse. State and national leaders and policy makers can support it. However, all the legislation in the world will not make it so. It is the actions of those working in and alongside the schoolhouse that will make equity happen. Educators provide the "whatever it takes" support for each individual child.

This book provides an overview and an opportunity for reflection on the ways that our current educational system is being or can be restructured to better ensure equity for all students so that all students are educated to the highest levels. It is hoped that those who read it take time to reflect on their own practice as educators, policy makers, and citizens and resolve, once again, to do all they can to continue to improve our educational system so that it does truly become a system that ensures all children are educated to the highest level. Our future as a country and as the human race depends upon all students being highly educated.

Chapter 2

Foundations of Equity in Schools

There are multiple approaches to establishing equity in schools: policy making, legislation including better funding formulas, establishing social justice education for staff, creating new systems that use equity practices, using research-proven instructional practices, and establishing strong positive school cultures. Numerous scholars have advocated for improvements as a part of establishing equity and closing the gap in outcomes for our students (Elmore, 2008; Hill, Campbell, and Harvey, 2000; Lezotte and Pepperl, 1999; Marzano and Waters, 2009; Marzano, Waters, and McNulty, 2005; McEwan, 2009; Tyack and Cuban, 1995).

This book is focused on what educators can do right now in their schools or districts to establish equity. Rather than have a long and overwhelming list of things to do to establish equity, the list is rather short. The work is hard, and the focus must be razor sharp. Educators must continuously improve the culture in their schools and the instructional systems in their schools, and focus on school culture and instructional systems.

Therefore, this book discusses (1) how schools and/or school districts can build cultures and belief systems that are focused on providing equity or whatever it takes for every child to graduate high school college and/or career ready, as well as (2) deconstructing instructional systems within their schools that deny equity and establishing systems that provide equity to all students.

Fien, Chard, and Baker (2021) put these two areas of control in focus when rephrasing Kendi's question regarding data from the General Social Surveys (2016) to be education explicit:

> Do students of Color have worse education outcomes than White students do mainly because of discrimination? An answer of no suggests that something is wrong with students of Color. An answer of yes suggests that institutional discrimination plays a role in creating and furthering racial disparities in education outcomes. (p. S106)

Both the beliefs upon which school cultures are built and the systems used to implement educational policies and practices are hurdles to establishing equity in schools for all students. These are two areas in which schools and districts can have significant impact, regardless of state or federal actions. School culture and systems go hand in hand. Establishing equity requires a sharp focus on both.

CULTURES THAT SUPPORT EQUITY

Schools that educate all students to high levels are often cited for being schools with strong teacher collective efficacy where teachers have high expectations for students and know how to help students reach these expectations (Donohoo, 2017; Hattie, 2009; Marzano, Waters, and McNulty, 2005; McEwan, 2009). Schools that have high expectations for students and teachers who believe they can educate all students to a high level are schools identified with strong and positive cultures. School cultures are not created overnight, but rather are a product of beliefs, customs, and behaviors over time that create the culture.

According to Fullan (2007), school cultures are the guiding beliefs and values exhibited in the school's operations. Deal and Peterson (2016) identify components of school culture such as artifacts, stories, celebrations, and history which maintain and communicate the values and beliefs of the humans that make up the school. Making changes to the culture takes intentional nurturing as new stories are told and retold, new traditions and celebrations started and repeated, and new artifacts identified.

It also takes time for the individuals in the culture to examine, reflect upon, and change, abandon, or revise their beliefs as a new culture is developed. The beliefs of the individuals within the school collectively create the school culture. That does not mean that everyone involved believes the same thing to the smallest jot and tittle, but rather they have overarching shared beliefs and actions. Their beliefs determine if it is a school where all students learn at high levels or if it is a school with a toxic culture and many students are marginalized.

UNDERSTANDING OURSELVES AND OUR STUDENTS

Individual beliefs are shaped by each person's understanding of themselves and the world around them. Each individual brings their own stories and experiences to the table. They bring their positionality, including their experiences with power and oppression, their orientation toward marginalized peoples, their inclination toward an asset orientation or deficit thinking, and their own understanding of history and race. These are core concepts in the field of social justice (Adams and Bell, 2016), but are also critical to the understanding of school culture.

These experiences, beliefs, and orientations shape the values and beliefs of each of the individuals within a school and therefore collectively create the culture of the school which is played out in the daily operations of the school, the stories told, the celebrations held, and the artifacts collected and revered. Therefore, when addressing school actions that can be taken to revise, modify, or solidify a school culture, school and district leaders need to help their colleagues examine their own positionality; understand power, oppression, and the concept of race in our society; as well as understand deficit thinking versus an asset orientation.

These actions or perspectives may be considered controversial to some in the current political climate. However, understanding the multitude of perspectives and experiences of the diverse educators and students in schools develops better educators and schools where all students know they are recognized for who they are. Understanding others' perspectives is not making individuals feel less or asking them to reject their core beliefs; it is only asking for awareness and understanding of other points of view.

Only when educators understand and are honest with themselves about these sensitive issues can they see how their beliefs and understandings are the bedrock of their school's culture for good or for bad. Ways in which educators can examine these social justice concepts in the context of their school must be found in order to help schools develop or strengthen cultures that support equity for all students.

Also critical to developing a strong culture are communication systems, rituals, celebrations, and daily and/or weekly actions that reinforce a school culture that holds high expectations for all students and the belief that the educators working there are fully capable of ensuring each child is educated to the highest level. School and district improvement plans, professional learning, and hiring the right people are powerful tools in creating positive school cultures.

SYSTEMS THAT SUPPORT EQUITY

Schools that educate all students so that they graduate high school college and/or career ready are inclusive schools that engage all students as learners at the highest level. These schools have high expectations for all students and do whatever it takes for each individual student to ensure they each are becoming readers, writers, mathematicians, artists, scientists, social scientists, problem solvers, critical thinkers, and ready to assume their full right of citizenship and create a better world for themselves and all humankind. They do not allow deficit thinking to reduce expectations for some students.

When students graduate from these systems, their future is wide open. The possibilities for their adult lives are numerous as they have proven to themselves that they are capable of college-level work while in high school. They are experienced collaborative problem solvers and critical thinkers, and have an expansive education from which to understand the peoples and issues of their world. Their futures are full of a multitude of choices of what they will do in their lives.

Systems that provide such an education are systems that ensure all students demonstrate sophistication in literacy as they exit the elementary grades. These systems ensure all students are mathematical thinkers who deeply understand how the mathematical algorithms they use function and can apply them in new ways. These students are able to examine issues from multiple perspectives before making conclusions and communicate their reasoning in well-crafted writing. As secondary students, they become literate in the various disciplines and are able to communicate as scientists, artists, economists, and so on.

Systems that educate all students to these levels are inclusive places that provide whatever it takes for each child to reach these levels. They actively work to ensure that there are no marginalized students and that the school's processes and procedures do not sort and track students so that students leave with great variance in the education they received. The high expectations are the same for all the students.

The supports that the students receive to reach these expectations will vary by child and by content area. Students with limited experiences and academic English may need additional supports in understanding a scientific text used in an advanced class compared to a peer who has a mother who is a scientist working for the Centers for Disease Control and Prevention. The school will provide these supports without marginalizing the student and/or putting them in a general education track with only basic science.

Systems that are designed to support equity devote attention to how students are grouped, curricula, instructional practices, interventions and/or additional supports, social services, budgeting, human resources, facilities, and accountability. Systemically changing school structures such as how a child qualifies for gifted and talented services or how reading is taught or who takes advanced math classes does not happen overnight. It takes time, just as changing school culture takes time. However, it can be done.

Changes in such programming or structures takes time for research and study, planning, communicating with stakeholders, implementing, and revising the implementation over time in order to achieve the desired results. However, despite the demands of making these changes, the future of our children is at stake. Educators must engage in this hard work relentlessly while also engaging in the hard work of creating a culture that accepts nothing less than the best education for all students.

SUMMING IT UP

Both cultural changes and systemic changes have to happen in order to have lasting change that truly impacts the educational outcomes for every child in the school or district. Schools and districts must address both cultural issues and system issues simultaneously. Gorski (2018) points out that as we work to reshape a school or district's culture, "we cannot wait for everybody to be on board" (p. 163). Students cannot wait for us.

Some systemic changes, such as requiring an advanced math class for all students, can be done through policy changes and mandates. However, without the accompanying change in the hearts and minds of the educators carrying out the changes or mandates, the results will not be robust. If the changes are made by educators who understand and abhor the common belief that "some students are not capable of advanced mathematics," then extraordinary measures are taken to ensure students develop the mathematical thinking and constructs to understand the advanced math and apply it to new situations.

If the educators implementing advanced math believe that some students just can't learn it or will not work hard enough to learn it, then many of the students will sit through the classes and squeak through with a grade of D or C– based more on their compliance in class rather than their demonstration of mathematical understanding. The advanced math class requirement will be met on paper. However, the student learning will not occur.

If the requirement for all students to have an advanced math class is occurring in a culture where deficit thinking prevails, many of the educators will engage in subtle resistance to such changes. Forms of resistance that might be employed include insisting they are incapable of teaching classes with diverse students so some other teacher should teach the class, engaging parents of privileged students to express their concern over such a policy as it might hinder their own child's education, and frequently complaining to administration that certain students in these classes don't want to be there and aren't even trying.

Secondary math departments either ensure all students successfully master an advanced math class or not. (You can substitute any other content or department in this scenario. It isn't exclusive to math.) Most likely, all of the members of the math department are not locked into deficit thinking and the belief that some students cannot learn the materials or will not work hard enough to do so. However, it takes incredible courage for educators who do believe, especially if the educator is in the minority, to stand up for these students and their rights in education.

School cultures often include unwritten norms of educators not wanting to be singled out for good or bad. They just want to fly under the radar and do their thing in their own classrooms. They just want to be nice and get along with their colleagues. DiAngelo (2021) is clear that niceness does not create the changes needed in our institutions. Niceness does not create schools and school districts that break through the privilege that some students are afforded and provide the equity that all students need. It takes courage to confront your own beliefs and actions as well as the group's beliefs and actions that are holding some students back.

It takes courage to admit to and make these changes. The norm of educator solidarity and protecting each other by not speaking up even when a colleague is blaming the student as lazy or unmotivated, as the reason they are not performing in class is often extremely strong (Williams, 2013). Only when educators have the skills and courage to tear down such deficient thinking can equity be established for all students.

As McGhee (2021) states when speaking about education since *Brown v. Topeka*, "When policies change in advance of the underlying beliefs, we are often surprised to find the problem still with us" (p. XVIII). When you have educators with courage who are willing to examine their own practices and beliefs as well as those of their colleagues, lasting changes can be made in reshaping the school culture while also making systemic changes in policy and practices. Leadership can provide the support needed for the educators who do recognize the inequities and want to be a part of creating a system that educates all students to high levels.

Chapter 3

Building Cultures that Support Equity

Schools and districts with cultures that support equity are inclusive places where students and families are valued for who they are and what they bring to the education process. They feel welcomed and secure in the school and know that only the best education will be received by each student. The educators in these schools believe that every student can learn to a high level and know that collectively, as a staff, they will make it happen through their relentless dedication to their students and continuous improvement of their own practices.

Staff are culturally proficient educators who value the students' cultures and teach students additional skills and ways of knowing so that they can fully participate in and enrich their community and our country. These educators are continuously learning alongside their students. Roland Barth (2001) describes learning-enriched schools as schools where both the students' and the educators' learning trajectories are on a steep upward climb. These positive cultures, where all students and staff thrive, do not happen by chance. Rather, they are carefully attended to and nurtured by educational leaders.

This chapter will discuss some of the factors that are critical components of establishing and nurturing a healthy school culture that is inclusive and ensures all students are learning to the highest levels. First and foremost, it is critical that the educators working in the school be fully aware of who they are and who their students are, individually and collectively. This involves some basic understanding of social justice concepts. Only then can educators make progress in achieving the American ideal of all students being educated to the highest level so that education is the great equalizer that Horace Mann proclaimed it to be.

This awareness of who they are and who their students are will serve as a foundation for educators as they work to create school and district cultures that support and sustain excellence. Communication in a myriad of forms, hiring the right people, and a climate of constant and rich professional learning are also key to creating and maintaining cultures that develop and nurture excellence. A strong, healthy culture is one where everyone on the team is learning, growing, reflecting, and willing to be uncomfortable when looking at the hard facts, confronting toxicity, and eliminating what is not working. It is hard work, yet also fulfilling and joyous work.

KNOWING WHO YOU ARE AND WHO ARE YOUR STUDENTS

Creating a culture that ensures all students are educated to the highest levels requires that the team working at the school and in the district have shared beliefs and values regarding student learning. Educational leaders frequently go down the path of developing a shared vision and mission statement, describing in detail what they will hear and see in the hallways, the classrooms, the teacher's lounge, and more, when their school is achieving as they envision. These exercises are intended to ensure that all staff are working together. However, when addressing school culture issues, leaders need to start further back.

It is fairly easy in a nice school culture to draft statements about the mission and vision for your school while some staff sit silently, not truly agreeing with the mission and vision because they do not recognize how their beliefs and systems marginalize some students. Staff who believe that not all children can learn to the highest level because of their life circumstances or perceived unwillingness to try create a toxicity that undermines the work of the school. This is not done with malice. It springs from their beliefs, current understandings, and unconscious bias (Fiarman, Kyles-Smith, and Lee, 2021).

Their knowledge is often limited to a view of life as they have lived it. Educators must start with an understanding of basic social justice concepts, including an awareness of where each member of the team is individually positioned, including themselves, in the many worlds or environments in which they operate day to day as well as the positions of their students in their many worlds or environments in which they operate. This understanding can help us expand our knowledge and see other viewpoints and experiences.

Educators ask students to consider other points of view when they problem solve in school. Educators need to do it as well. All school staff need to be involved in professional learning and reflection around their own positionality, the positionality of their students, understanding power and oppression, understanding the concept of race in our society and how it impacts their students, as well as understanding deficit thinking versus an asset orientation.

Too often schools have some educators who look through a lens of deficit thinking regarding students which then results in a school culture that educates some students to a high level and believes that others are not capable of learning to that level due to a multitude of reasons (Carter, 2000). This deficit thinking is often unconscious to those engaged in it. Deficit thinking is at the root for many of the reasons given for why students are failing to learn. This reasoning gives schools and educators a pass on why some students are not doing well in school.

TEXTBOX 3.1 EXAMPLES OF DEFICIT THINKING

- Their parents don't care.
- Their homelife is chaotic.
- They are not read to at home.
- They are still learning English.
- They are poor and have not had the experiences they need.
- They are not motivated to learn.
- They want to be the cool/funny kid.
- They are disabled, and life is hard.
- The elementary school didn't teach them to read.
- They started school behind.

Educators often do not even realize they are engaging in such thinking. The volume of work in schools is enormous and the pace frenetic; they often do not take the time to examine their own thinking or even listen to what they are saying. The relentless schedule of schools often does not provide the time needed for reflecting on their practices.

Deficit Thinking Undermines Our Best Intentions

An example of educators not recognizing their own deficit thinking is illustrated in the actions of a school leadership team after participating in an exercise that Dr. Luis Cruz (2019) conducted with the leadership teams in the district and a later district effort to make a change in the grading practices. The school leadership team was inspired by and latched on to the initial exercise that Dr. Cruz (who related that he learned this technique from Dr. Rick

Dufour) led them through and then went back and conducted it with their colleagues.

Dr. Cruz told the participants that there were four types of schools: (1) the Charles Darwin schools, (2) the Pontius Pilot schools, (3) the Warm and Fuzzy schools, and (4) the Whatever It Takes schools. The Charles Darwin schools believed in natural selection; some students did extremely well, some did poorly, and the majority performed at average (think Bell Curve). The Pontius Pilot schools had teachers that taught all the content they were expected to teach; if the students didn't learn, it was not because of the teachers. The content was presented and then the staff wiped their hands of all responsibility.

The Warm and Fuzzy schools had educators who knew that many of their students had numerous hurdles to overcome such as poverty, learning English, disabilities, and others. The staff in these schools felt so sorry for their students that they did everything they could to ensure that school was a warm and fuzzy place without expecting much of their students. They worried that too-high expectations would just increase the stress their students were under, so they tamped down expectations for students by several grade levels. They had language labs, reading labs, and general education classes for students that would be too burdened being in an advanced class.

Lastly, the fourth type of school, the Whatever It Takes schools, had high expectations for all of their students. They expected all students to perform on grade level or above and take advanced course work in high school. The staff in these schools made their high expectations clear to students, provided explicit instruction, as well as providing whatever additional supports were needed (both academically and socially) so that every student reached the expectations. They did not water down the expectations or the content. They did not make it easy for the students but worked with them until they succeeded.

After describing the four types of schools, Dr. Cruz asked participants to anonymously answer a series of questions including identifying which type of school they went to as a student. He also asked them to identify what type of school they would want their own child to attend. The anonymous data was tallied. Overwhelmingly, the participants had not attended a Whatever It Takes school, yet wanted their own child to attend a Whatever It Takes school. They recognized the difference and value of a Whatever It Takes school.

After this workshop with Dr. Cruz, the leadership teams returned to their buildings and conducted the same exercise with their colleagues. One middle school in particular was so excited by the experience, they were determined to make their school a Whatever It Takes school. Within the week, they had identified the students, by name, who were not meeting academic expectations and developed plans for what they would do to help these students meet expectations.

A year later, the district was changing the way students were graded. Staff fell right back into their old ways of thinking without even realizing it. The new grading practice was to be based on *demonstration* of what students had learned. Students were to have multiple opportunities to demonstrate their learning so if a student failed to master the learning at first, the teacher provided additional support. Student behaviors, homework or practice work completion, attendance, extra credit, and so on, was not to be reported as a part of the grade (the grade was a representation of what students could do), but rather reported separately.

A number of the staff in this middle school were against the new grading practices and were quite vocal about it. A meeting was held with the school staff, district administration, and a team of teachers from the high school who had helped develop and vet the new practices. The high school teachers reiterated the "why" for the change including establishing equity or a Whatever It Takes mentality. The staff raised objections such as how will these students learn to be responsible if they get a second chance or how will they learn how to do their work on time if homework isn't for a grade or some of the students won't do their homework if it isn't graded.

Administration then asked the staff present if this was the school that had decided to be a Whatever It Takes school. Had they committed to doing whatever it takes for each individual student to learn and meet expectations? Was this the school that realized that each student is different and may need different supports? Was this the school that realized each student comes to school from different circumstances and life experiences? Was this the school that believed all students could reach high expectations? Had they committed that they would do whatever it took to make it happen?

Even after this revisiting of their commitment to be a Whatever It Takes school, some staff still resisted and struggled with the new policy. However, many of the initial resisters saw how their actions were not supporting what they wanted to be as a school. They were willing to reflect on and work on their own practices to move their school closer to being a Whatever It Takes school. Change is hard, but this courageous staff persisted through the uncomfortableness to continue their journey to become a Whatever It Takes school.

Unpacking Our Hidden Beliefs

The previous example illustrates why it is important for staff to recognize their own positionality and privilege or lack of privilege as well as that of their students. Educators want to provide the very best for students. They care deeply about them. After all, that is why they went into education.

However, it is easy to fall back on old ways of thinking, habits, and traditions without even recognizing that they have fallen away from what they say they want to be.

Educators need time to frequently reflect on what they say about their students, their beliefs about students, and their practices as they work to educate students. Educators need to be courageous and identify when they are marginalizing students and cut these toxic habits out of their practice. Behaviors, both for the good and the not so good, are driven by beliefs. Educators must have the courage to dig in and unpack their true beliefs. It starts with some uncomfortable reflection.

Exploring these social justice concepts with honest and thoughtful reflection can help educators recognize their own deficit thinking, racism, classism, etc., and either own it and work to change it or dig in their heels. Hurtful actions are often subtle and not the ugly overt actions that come to mind, but they are still there. These actions say to students and parents that educators don't believe they can do it. This message is not at all what was intended.

However, educators are human and therefore imperfect, yet capable of improving their practice each day. Schools and districts need educators who own it and work to change it, to be the ones who are educating children. Needing to own it and working to change it is especially true for white, middle-class educators. The author is one of them, so she is especially aware of this need. White, middle-class educators are the largest staff group working with students in this country and so therefore are the ones most likely to engage in deficit thinking without even knowing it.

However, if educators do this work well, they will realize how deep internally held beliefs can sometimes raise their ugly heads, resulting in thinking less of a student or parent, marginalizing them rather than providing what they need for success. They don't do this intentionally, but they do it. This sounds harsh and may be hard for some educators to accept. However, if educators say they believe all students can learn to the highest levels, they will do this work. This is the only way educators will make the changes to the system so that all students are being educated to a high level.

The following are some terms and concepts (at a minimum) that are recommended for educators to unpack for a common understanding of what the terms mean and how they are manifest in their individual and collective professional practice. This is not something a building or district leader must facilitate for the group, especially if they do not have confidence in their competency in these areas. However, the work must be done so leaders should ensure that the right facilitators are found to lead the work while the leaders honestly and wholeheartedly participate in the work, reflecting on their own practice and doing the hard work of improving.

Please note that the recommendation is for educators to understand and reflect on these social justice concepts. It is not being recommended that students participate in this learning. What schools teach their students is determined by their state standards and their local school board. However, as adults, as the educators in the schoolhouse, having an understanding of these concepts can help them understand the values and beliefs that underlie their actions. This understanding can help them be more intentional in the actions they take to create a system that educates all students to the highest levels.

If a school or district leader does not feel comfortable facilitating this work, there may be other staff members who can facilitate these discussions and reflections or local university faculty or consultants. Dr. Robin DiAngelo has been known to present to staff very effectively (especially if the majority of staff are white) to develop understanding and reflection in these areas. Her visit to a diverse community was impactful. It gave fuel to quiet conversations that had been happening about the significant differences in outcomes between white students and Latinx students in the district.

Efforts had already been started in the schools to increase the number of Latinx students who took advanced classes, graduated, and moved on. However, after her presentation the conversations were no longer quiet and the number of educators pushing for changes in the system grew. A group of educators at a local high school started their own Equity Task Force, recruiting a local scholar to help facilitate their work. As a group of about thirty educators, they examined the data more thoroughly, read the literature, and began to make changes that accelerated the work of ensuring all students in their school were educated to high levels.

The role of the district administration was to reallocate resources to fund their work, encourage them in their efforts, and support their well-thought-out plans while providing them cover from other small groups of educators that did not agree with their work and spent time trying to impede their work. The educators on this task force were showing incredible courage in changing the culture of their school. The least the administration could do was support them.

Social Justice Concepts for Educators' Personal Reflections

Positionality refers to the social or identity groups in which an individual has membership; it is often involuntary. Each individual belongs to multiple groups and their memberships are multi-layered and fairly fixed, having been assigned to them by society and/or historical legacies. A person's positionality can change, but it is a slow process usually requiring intentionality. Examples of groups that impact positionality include race, socioeconomic status, gender, religion, profession, community where you live, club memberships or social circles, and more.

Some reflections on positionality:

- How would you describe your positionality, both as an educator and as a member of the larger community?
- How do your colleagues describe their positionality? What are the similarities and differences among your colleagues' positionalities?
- How would you describe the positionality of your students?
- What are the similarities and differences in positionality between your students and yourself?

Privilege refers to the advantages and/or benefits (as opposed to disadvantages or denied benefits) attached to the various groups of which an individual or an institution has membership or positionality. Privilege is not earned but is the result of belonging to a specific social group that has privilege that other groups do not have. The most pervasive form of privilege is white privilege. Although often unrealized, white people benefit for being the standard of normalization in our current society.

Examples of privilege include access to good health care, housing, and food; ease of travel (a person does not look like a security risk at the airport, or they aren't stopped when driving through the wrong neighborhood); and ability to be heard and acceptance of what they say by others without doubt when interacting with health care providers, the police, their child's teacher, and other members of the community. They normally receive excellent customer service, people do not shy away from them on the sidewalk or in an elevator, and they frequently see people like them portrayed in the media and holding positions of authority.

A reflection on privilege:

- When considering your positionality, what privileges do you receive? Ask a colleague, who is not in all the same groups as you, to help you identify some of the privileges you receive as a result of membership in these groups. If you have always received these privileges in your life, it is sometimes hard to recognize them. You might think that everyone receives these privileges, but your colleagues of another race, class, gender, and so on, can tell you differently.

Additional reflections on privilege:

- Which groups that you belong to, as identified in your positionality, provide you with the most privileges? Why do you think that is so?

- What privileges would you expect your students to have based on their positionality? What privileges would you expect their parents to have? Why do you think this is so?

Oppression refers to the disadvantages or denied privileges attached to the various groups of which an individual or an institution has membership or positionality. Social justice scholars identify six major forms of oppression: racism, classism, religious oppression, ableism, youth/age oppression, and sexism (Adams and Zuniga, 2007). Oppression is often experienced as microaggressions, or everyday slights, disrespect, and putdowns that are slight and almost unconscious but accumulate each day to cause an individual to experience stress just for belonging to that social group.

Examples of oppression could be misogynistic treatment of a female superintendent by male school board members, religious oppression or intolerance of religious dress, seeing few examples of people like you in the media or positions of power, being stereotyped such as being referred to as an "angry Black woman," being ignored or provided with poor customer service, being told you don't act like a (insert social group name) person, assumptions made about what neighborhoods you might live in and what type of career you have, and being referred to as "those people."

People of color often experience oppression in their daily lives as our society normalizes whiteness while all other skin colors are some degrees away from whiteness. Similar statements could be made about individuals with disabilities and those that do not identify as cisgender. They experience daily oppressions as society normalizes other ways of being that are different from theirs.

Some reflections on oppression:

- What oppression have you experienced? What microaggressions are a frequent part of your life?
- What oppression have you been a part of, even though unintentional? What did you do when you realized you had disrespected or slighted another person?
- What oppression have your students experienced based on their positionality? What microaggressions are a frequent part of their lives or their parents' lives?

Marginalization is when an individual or a group is treated as insignificant or peripheral. These individual or group identities are not taken into account or valued by the mainstream group. Some examples of marginalization include having your contribution to a discussion disregarded, not being allowed to ask your questions, and being ignored and/or being seated on the edge of the group.

Additional examples include having your concerns about your child dismissed by health professionals or educators, not being greeted when you arrive at a meeting or an event, not being asked for your opinion or thoughts, eye rolling by others when you express yourself, and receiving minimal customer service while others receive excellent customer service. This can include assumptions that you have no money to spend on a purchase and assumptions that a general education is enough for you or your child.

Students of color, language learners, and students with disabilities are often marginalized in our classrooms as they are often tracked, excluded from advanced opportunities, and allowed to sit on the edge of the classroom and not contribute to the class.

Some reflections on marginalization:

- When have you been marginalized? How often are you marginalized?
- What forms of marginalization do your students experience? Their parents?
- How do students group themselves in the lunchroom or on the school grounds? Who is left out of the groups? What groups occupy the least desirable locations?
- What have you done to reduce the marginalization your students experience?

Concept of race is socially constructed based on physical characteristics including primarily skin color. There are not biological differences that create race. Rather, it is a social concept that has changed over time. For example, Italian and Jewish people were once considered non-white in the United States, and today are considered white by the larger society. Race has a large impact on a person's experiences with positionality, privilege, power, and marginalization.

When educators fail to acknowledge the construct of race, they fail to acknowledge the impact of privilege, marginalization, and oppression on the process and practices within the educational system and society as a whole. When educators claim they do not see color in their students, they can miss the impact of their complicity in tracking and/or ability grouping, use of discipline, and the lack of trust in institutions that often stand in their way to achieving success with their students. When educators claim they do not see color in their students, it tells their students they do not see them.

Some reflections on concept of race:

- What do you think about the statement, "I treat all my students the same regardless of color"? Is it a position of strength, a problem, or both? Why?
- What percentage of your students, by race, are participating in gifted and talented programs, special reading programs, advanced classes, special education programs, behavioral programs, and basic math programs? Is the percentage similar to the overall percentage of this race in your school's population? Why or why not?

Further reflections on concept of race:

- How do your expectations for your students vary by race? How do you check yourself for implicit bias when planning lessons, grouping students, and delivering instruction?
- What races do your students see portrayed in the texts read in class? Are the races proportionately represented or is one more dominant? How are the different races portrayed?

Deficit thinking is the belief by educators that students who fail in school do so because of their internal, familial, or community "deficiencies" such as poverty, lack of English abilities, laziness, lack of motivation, lack of parenting, or immoral behaviors. Such thinking absolves the educators and the school of any responsibility for the student's failure. It is a blame the "victim" mentality. When lack of student success is blamed on the student's homelife or lack of English ability, that is deficit thinking.

Some reflections on deficit thinking:

- When you hear "the apple doesn't fall far from the tree" when talking about a struggling student, what do you do?
- When poverty is identified as a hurdle for your students, how does it impact your expectations and planning for improvement strategies?
- When a student's lack of motivation is blamed for their failure, what do you do?
- When you are unable to reach a student's parent by phone, what is your response?

Asset orientation is when educators view each student for their strengths and positive traits. Students and families are valued for what they bring to the classroom and the school. They are seen as capable learners that can contribute to the learning environment, rather than individuals that need to be fixed. Educators start with what students know, build on the student's culture and community to begin the learning, and then expand from there. Instruction focused on relationships and a sense of belonging, cooperative learning, place-based learning, explicit instruction, and building of cultural capital uses an asset orientation.

Some reflections on asset orientation:

- What strengths do your students bring to school? What strengths are in their community?
- When using cooperative learning, how do you ensure there is both team interdependence and individual accountability?
- Who talks the most in your classroom, the teacher or the students? Why?

Further reflections on asset orientation:

- How do you establish relationships with your students? Are some students left out due to lack of technology, their parents aren't in the right social groups, they are shy, etc.? What do you do about it?
- What student do you not have a good relationship with? Why? What are you doing about it?

Understanding these concepts and reflecting on how they impact our individual lives and our collaborative lives as educators in schools and districts allows us to then reflect on our individual and collective practices in order to continuously improve our practice and educate all students to the highest levels. Reflecting on these social justice concepts in relation to your positions as educators can help strengthen and improve our shared understandings and beliefs.

Books that Can Help Educators Reflect and Understand Other Viewpoints

Reading the work of a wide variety of social science authors can expand our understanding of other cultures and situations. Educators do not have to agree with every concept these books present. However, these books provide opportunities to work on understanding why the various authors make the points they are making. They provide opportunities for understanding different points of view. Educators and fellow citizens across our country will never completely agree with each. However, if educators can be open to listening to other points of view, whether they accept them or not, they will better serve our students from all cultures, races, and positions in life.

- *Antiracist School Leadership: Toward Equity in Education for America's Students* (2013), edited by Jeffrey S. Brooks and Noelle Witherspoon Arnold
- *Dismantling Contemporary Deficit Thinking: Educational Thought and Practice* (2010), by Richard R. Valencia
- *No Excuses: Closing the Racial Gap in Learning* (2003), by Abigail Thernstrom and Stephan Thernstrom
- *Caste: The Origins of Our Discontents* (2020), by Isabel Wilkerson
- *The Other Face of America: Chronicles of the Immigrants Shaping Our Future* (2002), by Jorge Ramos
- *The Dreamkeepers: Successful Teachers of African American Children* (1994), by Gloria Landson-Billings
- *Me and White Supremacy: Combat Racism, Change the World, and Become a Good Ancestor* (2020), by Layla F. Saad
- *Nice Racism: How Progressive White People Perpetuate Racial Harm* (2021), by Robin DiAngelo
- *The Sum of Us: What Racism Costs Everyone and How We Can Prosper Together* (2021), by Heather McGhee

COMMUNICATE, COMMUNICATE, COMMUNICATE

School and/or district cultures are reflections of the norms, values, and beliefs of the people who learn and work there. In turn the culture reinforces the norms, values, and beliefs in a continuous feedback loop. This continuous loop is what makes changing school and/or district culture, especially when it is toxic and dysfunctional, so difficult. Our values and beliefs are shared and reinforced through all sorts of communications.

The culture is expressed and reinforced through communication in a wide variety of direct and subtle forms including direct communication such as written and media pieces; stories and events; celebrations and rituals; symbols, mascots, and slogans; as well as through the daily actions and behaviors of those who are a part of the school and/or district community, including students, staff, and community stakeholders. The nurturing of school culture through communication happens every day in a school or district, whether done consciously or unconsciously.

Educational leaders in schools where all students are achieving at the highest levels are constantly tending to their culture, working to shape and nurture it as a positive force for accomplishing their goals. Communication that nurtures a school's or district's culture is found in its vision, mission, and goals; in its newsletters and publications; in its celebrations and traditions; in the symbols it uses; in its messages to staff; and in the way it includes parents.

Visions, Mission Statements, and Goals

In this age of increased accountability for schools and districts, the majority of schools have some type of improvement plan that is meant to guide their work as they strive to continuously improve outcomes for students. These improvement plans include things such as vision statements, mission statements, and goals and/or objectives with action steps for accomplishing the goals.

They are usually lofty and aspirational and speak to educating all students (plans typically do not say *most* students or *some* students) so that they become life-long learners and college- and career-ready, global citizens who are educated to the highest levels of achievement, inspired, engaged, educated, empowered, and so forth. The author's review of school mission and/or vision statements also noted how many of them mentioned an inclusive environment or creating an environment of respect and inclusion.

Amazingly, however, the actions the schools or districts plan to take in order to make their vision or mission become reality often include action steps that are just a continuation of what they are already doing (and not with the results that they need) or are actions that they expect families and students to take while they, the educators, continue to do everything the same, day in and day out.

For example, to improve reading outcomes, schools often include in their plans that parents will read with their children for thirty minutes every night and participate in parent and student book nights. Meanwhile, schools continue to provide reading instruction as they always have and send their students not reading on grade level down the hall to another room for remediation and below-grade-level instruction.

These type of action steps illustrate that schools often include actions in improvement plans that expose deficit thinking. The thinking might be something like this. *Educators are working hard and teaching the curriculum. There isn't anything that they are doing that could be improved so therefore they will just carry on. The students come to school far behind. However, if the parents cared more or if the students did their homework (reading at home) then they would achieve as needed.*

This is an example of a school or district blaming the students and parents for the lack of outcomes that are desired, and they don't even realize it. They are not taking the actions they should take if they really believed everything they wrote in their mission and vision statements and believe it is possible to get all students to proficiency in reading. This does not mean do not ask students to read at home. It is great if they can do so. It does mean do not blame the lack of desired outcomes on students who do not read at home. What is it that the school or district is doing that produces the outcomes received, good or bad?

Schools and districts often write mission and vision statements along with goals and then mismatch them with actions that reveal that their underlying beliefs are not what they need them to be. Educators are deeply caring and extremely hard working. Educators, like most human beings, aspire to be more than they often are. That is great! As professionals, they need to continue to aspire to be more while also working on their thoughts and actions to ensure all students are mastering rigorous standards.

That is why school and district educators need to first do the hard work of social justice learning so that each member of the team has a better understanding of who they are individually and collectively and who their students and their families are both individually and collectively. This awareness and opportunity for reflection can then provide the knowledge and fuel for developing improvement plans that actively work to develop a school or district culture that promotes and nurtures an environment where all students learn to the highest level.

Understanding who they are as educators and who their students are helps educators develop action plans to accomplish their goals that are rooted in redesigning the systems within schools and districts in order to ensure that all students are learning to the highest level (see chapters 4 to 9). It supports educators in developing action plans that do not, inadvertently, blame the students or their families for the lack of desired outcomes.

Schools and districts need strong, powerful mission and/or vision statements that help them paint a picture of what their educational environment will look like when this mission is accomplished and/or the vision is reached. Schools and districts are accountable for educating every student to the highest level. Each state has standards for literacy, mathematics, and many other content areas that are the expectations for all students.

So create those lofty mission and vision statements. Then with courage and honest reflection create the action steps that address the systems within your classroom, school, and district that marginalize some students to receiving a lesser education. This means that educators are taking actions that ensure all students are successful despite whatever circumstances our students come from when they enter our schools.

There is no blaming students and families and no tolerance for mediocracy in results by continuing to do what we have been doing. There is only courageous reflection on practices and the hard work to ensure every student succeeds. Many of the remaining chapters in this book will speak to systems in schools and districts and how they often times marginalize students. Use these chapters to help you reflect on your practices and systems and make changes where needed.

School or district continuous improvement documents should be used as powerful tools to help nurture a healthy school culture. As mission and vision statements are written and/or revisited, discuss as a staff what it means when you say all students will _____. Does that include the students that are learning English? How about the students of color? Does it include students with disabilities? If so, what evidence do you have that they are included?

How are the processes within your school or district changing so that all students are educated to the highest levels? Look critically at the actions your school or district plans to take to achieve your mission and vision. Do those actions change the status quo of how things are done now in your school or district? If not, what makes you believe that the outcomes will change?

Improvement plans or continuous improvement plans should be living and working documents. Schedule regular times throughout the year for staff to collectively review, discuss, and reflect on the school's or district's mission, vision, and goals. These opportunities are not for recreating the plan, but rather time to remember what the entire team has committed to and to reflect on what actions are working well, what has been forgotten, and what needs to be done better. Engage leadership teams in reviewing one single goal at a time with simple questions.

Questions for reviewing progress on improvement plans:

- Where are we? (in relation to one of the goals)
- How do we know? (quantitative and qualitative data/individual stories)
- Where do we want to be?
- So what do we do next?

Messaging in Everything You Say and Do

In addition to mission statements, vision statements, and continuous improvement plans, there are hundreds of ways in which the school or district cultures are messaged and reinforced through a myriad of communication opportunities. Many schools have slogans or some type of branding that help them communicate almost endlessly about what type of school they aspire to be. They put these slogans on clothing, walls, notebooks, pencils, magnets, banners across the top of newsletters, and anyplace else they can think of. They use these slogans frequently as they talk about the school and how the students and staff behave inside the school.

A Midwest school called themselves the Reading Place. It was on t-shirts, above the front door, on the walls, in the school song, and in the school celebrations. The school was a high-poverty school with the vast majority of the students from families that spoke a language other than English in the home. The school was reconstituted by the school board. As the new staff gathered to plan the goals and systems for the "new" school, it was decided that the primary focus would be on literacy.

The staff dubbed the school the Reading Place. There were pictures showing students of color reading that hung throughout the school. Students were issued school t-shirts that proudly proclaimed "The Reading Place" (thank you to the Junior League). A large library sat in the center of the school that was open and buzzing with students before, during, and after school. Quarterly celebrations were held schoolwide to celebrate reading that included the staff singing songs and performing skits about reading. Students charted their individual reading progress each quarter and celebrated their growth.

Each quarter all one thousand students and staff gathered in the multipurpose room. The staff dressed up in some theme and sang and danced about reading. One of the favorites was taking the song "Dancing in the Streets" and reworking the lyrics throughout to make it into "Reading in the Streets." Then twenty students sat facing the audience as students and staff prepared to find out where they were as a school in achieving the goal of each student reading on or above grade level.

The entire student body helped count by five to one hundred as the principal walked from one student to the next of twenty students sitting on stage to remind them what each student sitting up front represented (each student was an interval of five from five to one hundred). Then the principal asked the first student to stand, then the second, and so on until the number of students standing represented the new number of students reading on or above grade level. The first time the entire school came together they had two of the twenty students standing up (the rest remained in their chairs) or 10 percent of students reading on level.

Each time they gathered together they reminded themselves that they started with two students standing. Then the principal went down the row and asked additional students to stand up until the correct percentage of students were standing to represent how many students were reading at level now. For example, when they went from 10 percent to 25 percent, the principal had the two students representing their starting point standing. Then they asked the next three students to stand. The students and staff cheered, and the staff showered the students with confetti to celebrate. After five years, there were nineteen out of twenty representative students standing, meaning that 95 percent of students were reading on or above level.

One more note on this celebration tradition or ritual which the school formed: all staff, including the custodians, got to help throw confetti. After the celebration all staff who did not have students with them that period, including the principal, helped sweep up the confetti! The first time they

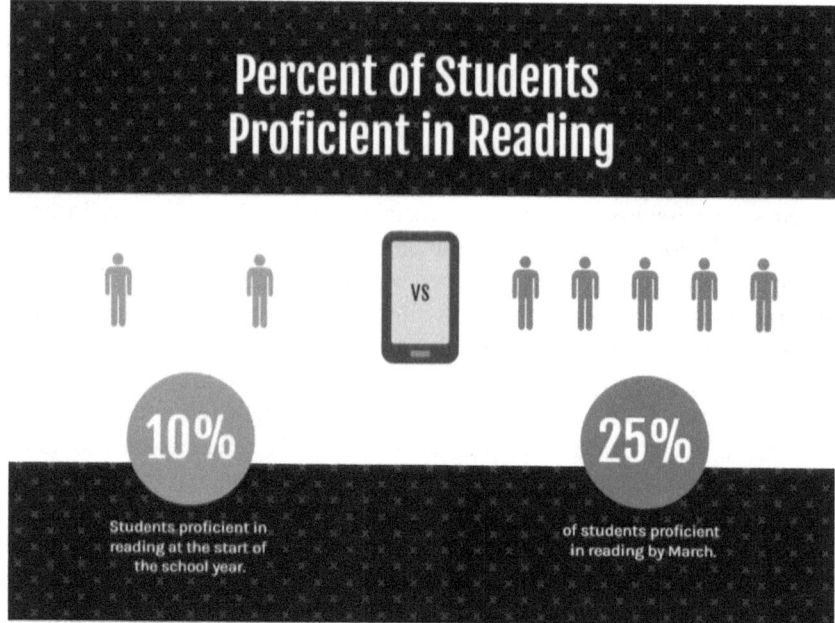

Figure 3.1

celebrated with confetti, they forgot to invite the custodians to join the celebration. Don't make that mistake!

Schools and districts are always messaging to their stakeholders either consciously or inadvertently. In order to reinforce and maintain a positive culture or to nudge a toxic culture toward positivity, it is critical that schools and districts thoughtfully and intentionally plan for ongoing communication that sends the messages that stakeholders need in order to support the school. Messages are sent directly through newsletters, video clips, and social media postings as well as through the graphics or symbols and slogans used throughout the school and on school paraphernalia.

Celebrations and/or rituals are critical to communicating and reinforcing the right type of culture in the school as well. These cannot be left to chance or to the once-a-year, end-of-school celebration. Calendar these events out for the school year to be sure they happen and then don't be afraid to add in another celebration or event as the year unfolds, such as celebrating your school's team winning the Battle of the Books contest or the physics class that successfully robotized cars and then, in collaboration with the power company, drove them into power poles to collect data on what were the best conditions for surviving a head-on crash with a utility pole.

Regular messages to staff can also serve to keep the focus on the goal as well as providing encouragement and celebrating what staff accomplish in pursuit of the goal. Building and district leaders can use daily and weekly bulletins or social media postings to highlight the great things happening throughout the school or district in addition to the regular announcements.

For example, an educational leader might write: *Enjoyed my visit to Ms. Smith's classroom yesterday. Her students were practicing their critical thinking skills as they debated how to tackle the lack of affordable housing. The students were using data to support their various positions.* Or *Thrilled to observe the students at Happy Valley School were using fraction models to show why when multiplying fractions, it works to invert and multiply. These students not only knew the algorithm, but could explain why it worked as well.*

Two cautions about this practice. First, not all educators like being in the limelight. Some just want to go quietly about their work. Second, there are educators who are offended if you don't give them a shoutout. Walking through classrooms and schools must be a constant for educational leaders. Only with a deep understanding of what is happening in classrooms can they be the supportive leader that educators need. Keep a list of staff or schools, and note when and why each individual or school is given a public shoutout. This helps leaders to be intentional in walking through different classrooms or schools regularly and celebrating all staff.

Also writing private notes to staff thanking them for something they have done or specifically noting something good that was observed in their classroom is another form of using communication to reinforce a positive culture. Notes can be sent via email; however, taking the time to write handwritten notes to individual staff members can be extremely powerful and an even greater sign of appreciation. Leaders cannot say thank you often enough to all of the team members. If you are an educational leader, schedule time each week to write a few thank you notes and express your gratitude.

The same concept applies to school boards. Seldom does a school district have the resources to pay their staff what they deserve for the time and effort they put in day in and day out to ensure all our students are highly educated. Even in districts that have some of the highest wages (usually accompanied by higher costs of living), a small expression of gratitude is appreciated. The board of education can take time at its meetings to honor staff and community members that have contributed to the success of their students.

One board had a long tradition of board accolades where they recognized staff contributions. A new board came in and, in an effort to streamline their meetings, eliminated the board accolades. Needless to say, it was not well received. The staff were offended by the board's actions. The board then found a way to reinstate the accolades without adding to the length of their meetings by having the accolades posted on the district's website.

Another example was a board that was disgruntled about a staff proposal to pay each certified and classified staff member (no administrators) a modest stipend for the extra work and stress they were undertaking to ensure that education was continuing despite all of the restrictions caused by the pandemic. The superintendent had called together a group of staff members (teachers and administrators) who met to draft a recommendation to the board on how to use some additional monies from the state because of the pandemic.

When this committee met, the district had already privately raised funds to connect families without internet connectivity to providers and pay the families' internet bills for up to eighteen months to ensure their children could participate in distance learning. The district had a robust technology program when the pandemic hit and was already in position with a one-to-one distribution of devices for students to use in connecting to the internet.

Additional funds from the state and Federal Emergency Management Assistance had been used to cover the costs of the additional health and safety modifications and precautions at the school buildings, and to pay principals and school secretaries for working additional time in the summer to prepare for dealing with the pandemic. The calendar had been reworked to provide additional time to teachers for training and working together to prepare for distance learning and the hybrid schedule required by the pandemic.

The district's finance department could not come up with an expense that had not already been covered. Therefore, the recommendation from staff was for a small stipend to certified and classified staff. The board did approve the stipend, but only after a contentious meeting where a large number of staff were watching to see if they would get a small stipend right before the holidays. The tone of the meeting and the attitudes expressed by board members inflicted a great deal of pain on the very staff they were depending on to ensure all students were being educated. The board missed a wonderful opportunity to graciously communicate thanks.

Another way to help keep staff focused on the goal, in the frantic pace of education, is a weekly brief message to staff such as a Monday Message. Effective leaders use these messages to keep everyone focused on the mission. It can be a short video recording or a written message with a standard banner across the top of the page sent as an email. It reminds staff of the primary focus such as Whatever It Takes (equity) or the Reading Place. These types of messages from the district leadership are important as well. They can provide a direct and focused message to all staff rather than relying on messages to trickle through the organization.

Figure 3.2. Sample Monday Message

In addition to taking every opportunity to keep staff focused, take every opportunity you get to thank staff for their efforts to ensure all students are readers, or all students are critical thinkers, for example. Little thank you messages with an apple and caramels in a small plastic bag, a balloon tied to each staff member's desk chair, a notepad embossed with the school slogan, muffins and coffee before school, or candies in a tin are good ways to welcome everyone back to school, celebrate education week, send everyone home for summer vacation on a positive note of gratitude, or just celebrate the middle of the year accomplishments of the staff.

Thomas Sergiovanni (1990) expressed the importance of many forms of communication in shaping culture when he stated:

> The behavior of successful leaders is often driven by a deep commitment to ideas and ideals they believe to be important. They speak often of the importance of perseverance and persistence—to hold the course, to keep trying again, and to try harder in pursuit of one's convictions. They communicate to others that good enough is okay for today but not good enough for tomorrow. They are constantly pushing themselves and others forward by their words, behavior, and deeds. (p. 10)

A good resource for helping educators reflect on the condition of their school or district culture and then intentionally develop plans and take action to shape and nurture the positive cultures needed for the student outcomes demanded is Deal and Peterson's (2016) *Shaping School Culture*. Leadership teams should intentionally plan the school's or district's communication effort to nurture a healthy culture.

Including Parents

The previous section talks at length about communicating with staff in order to grow and nurture a positive culture. In all of the efforts to communicate and celebrate what is important to your school or district, don't forget to include the parents in communicating and celebrating. Chenoweth's (2007) review of schools that succeed with marginalized children points out that these schools work side by side with parents. They recognize the challenges for many children and families. However, this does not deter them from ensuring that all students are achieving at the highest levels and developing a positive collaboration with parents.

Most schools use some type of school newsletter to send messages to parents about what is happening at the school and celebrate accomplishments made at the school. However, be ever mindful of your parents and their circumstances:

- Do parents work so many jobs that finding time to read a newsletter is difficult?
- Do all your parents read/understand English?
- If the newsletter is electronic, can parents access it?
- If read on a phone, how easy is it to read the newsletter in its current format?

Many schools and districts take great care to ensure the newsletter is not only in English, but in other major languages used by the families. This means a weekly newsletter is even more difficult to get out when it first has to be composed in English and then translated in several other languages. Maybe sending a newsletter every other week is more realistic for some schools. Set a specific schedule such as every Friday or every other Friday. Setting a specific schedule helps establish the routine of looking for information from the school on Fridays, etc.

Putting out a regular newsletter as well as putting it out in multiple languages is time consuming in an already hectic schedule. However, it is worth it. Think about the message it sends to families when the school or district regularly communicates with them. Think about the respect it communicates to families by ensuring messages from the school or district are accessible to them.

Using video clips is also another good way to make it easier for families to access the information. Just click on the language preferred and listen to the message. No reading needed. Using lots of pictures (especially pictures of students) and infographics is another way to ease the burden of reading a newsletter. A picture with a brief text message can often communicate the point and make it more likely that the message gets received than when parents have to read several long paragraphs.

In addition, when sharing a school's or an individual student's accomplishments, a graph works wonders for communicating between multiple languages. If the graph is going up, parents always quickly grasp that their child or the school is improving. Involve your students in helping you communicate. Older students can help you make the videos in multiple languages, translate brief written messages, and so forth. It is a great opportunity for them to practice their literacy skills in a real-life situation. Whatever you do, make sure to include plenty of information about what the students are doing at school. Parents love reading about their children!

You can also use school and district newsletters to communicate with other community stakeholders. Create a place on your website where these stakeholders can sign up to receive the newsletter in their inboxes as well. Add community stakeholders to your distribution lists so that the local police who help with school drop-off in the morning, the neighborhood senior center, local government officials, and all the rest of the community members with whom you interact are kept in the know about what is happening. The majority of community stakeholders love knowing the great things students are accomplishing in school.

Occasionally non-supporters call school or district newsletters propaganda when you continue to share student accomplishments. However, schools belong to their communities. They pay the bill for our schools. They deserve to know, and most often delight in knowing, the good things that are happening in our schools. Just don't forget to inform them about the not-so-good things that happen as well when they do occur and what you are doing about it. They should hear bad news from you before other media is putting it out.

If schools or districts are the first to share the bad news, it makes the school or district more credible and trusted by the community at large, even those that don't have children and aren't sure they like paying taxes for schools they don't use. Keep the community informed about struggles to increase graduation rates, bus accidents, and budget needs as well. Be sure your communication includes factors considered and why and how decisions are made.

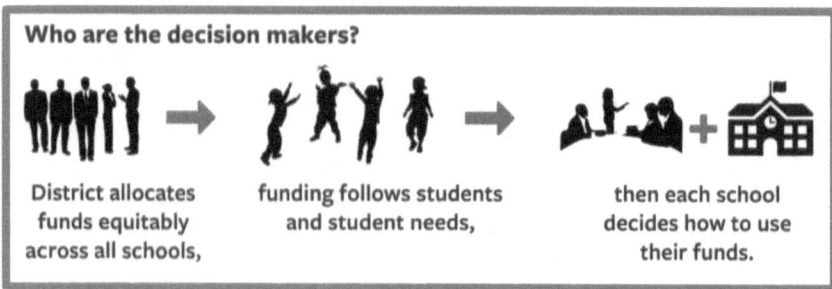

Figure 3.3

A school or district communication plan for parents should include more than a regular newsletter. Depending on your community, various social media applications can be a good way to share. In some places, Twitter is the preferred medium; in others, Facebook or a different tool is preferred. Make sure to include social media pages in the other languages spoken in the school or district in addition to English.

Social media is often the preferred platform for sending small tidbits of news so parents do not have a long piece of communication to read through. Many communities have neighborhood groups that communicate via Nextdoor, GroupMe, or a similar application. If you can use these sources to send information out from the school or the district, you are able to reach both parents and other stakeholders about what the school or district is accomplishing.

Newsletters and social media sites are not the only way that schools and districts should be communicating with parents. These are passive ways and depend on the parent reaching out and taking in the information. Communication is a two-way street, so it is important that there be plenty of opportunity for the school or district to hear from parents as well. These opportunities must be regularly scheduled, just like newsletters or postings.

It is critical that you reach out to and communicate with your marginalized parents. These are the parents who often felt uncomfortable in school when they were students or have never participated in the U.S. education system and are unsure about how it all works, or feel marginalized in society in general and therefore feel marginalized in the school. These parents, more than any others, need to know that the school recognizes them, desires to communicate with them, and will do whatever it takes to make it happen. These are the parents who most likely will not initiate communication with the school on their own.

A successful tool is home visits (porch visits) as a means of ensuring there is two-way communication with families. It isn't easy as there can be multiple languages to consider, and it requires going when parents will be home which is often not during the school day. One school with a diverse student body used home visits very effectively. They started with home visits before the school opened for the year. The vast majority of the staff were new to the school and to the families. The staff felt it was important that parents knew that their children were going to be spending the day with staff that cared deeply about them and had high expectations for them.

The staff decided before the school even opened for the year to make sure they connected with every family. The staff all dressed in bright blue school shirts with the school logo so as to be easily recognized as they walked through the neighborhoods. They doubled or tripled up and went in small groups. The list of families was divided up among the groups, being careful to ensure that one of the members of the team spoke the home language of the families they were assigned. They were working with five major languages throughout the school, so it required every teacher, administrator, and paraprofessional to ensure all the languages were covered.

The teams went knocking on doors during the evenings in anticipation that it would be easier to find families at home. They kept a list of who they contacted and who needed a second visit (like on a Sunday) to find them at home. They were relentless about it and before school started that August, every family had had a team of staff members standing on their front porch introducing themselves, telling them a little about the "new" school, and asking questions of the family to get them to share with them as well. They especially asked questions about each child in the home and what they are good at, what they like to do, and so on.

The home visits were a smash hit. The back-to-school social planned for the first week of school was highly attended. At the end of the first quarter, when parent-teacher conferences were being held, parents showed up in droves. Parents who did not come to the conference received another porch visit, this time about their children's progress in school. The continued effort to communicate directly with parents paid off. Parents came out in large numbers when parent-teacher conferences were held.

This same school continued to host numerous parent nights where parents could participate in English classes, cooking classes, student performances, and more. However, every time they hosted a parent night, they made sure to serve a hearty meal for the whole family. This school served families that struggled to make ends meet. Families attended in large numbers and as sharing a meal together often does, it helped create a sense of community between the families and staff and between the different language communities within the larger community.

Parent-teacher conferences should be a time of celebration and planning of next steps for the student. Each conference should start by celebrating what the student has accomplished. Many schools like to include students in the conference so that they are a part of the celebration and the setting of next steps or goals for the student. Schools often have students track and graph their own progress in literacy and mathematics. At conference time, those graphs are shared with parents. Having a graph makes it easier for parents to understand their child is making progress even if you are working with multiple languages.

Some schools even use student-led conferences, which allow the student to tell their parents what they have learned and what they need to learn next. It helps students take ownership of their learning and is another opportunity for clarifying expectations with students. Traditionally conferences have been scheduled during the school day. If parents were working and couldn't make it, that was that. However, many schools now schedule conferences in the evenings and other times that are more conducive to parents attending.

Some even hold conferences in churches or other places in the community that make parents feel more welcomed. In many of these schools, staff do a front porch conference on a weekend if that is what it takes to connect with the parents. They don't blame the parents if they are working three jobs and not able to get off for a conference without losing income. They just make the conferences happen at a time that works for the parents and send a powerful message to the family that they are a Whatever It Takes school and are committed to ensuring the success of every student.

Making sure every family is able to participate in a parent-teacher conference is quite a commitment. However, there are schools that go way beyond this to ensure that families are included in the communication loop and that students see the school and families working together. They make regular home visits or phone calls in between conferences to keep the communication lines open.

Many schools adopt procedures that expect every student's parent to receive at least one good news communication between conferences. This is not a certificate or a sticker sent home in the backpack that the student has to dig out and share with the parent, but rather a more direct communication with the parents. Teachers carefully log which families they have communicated with so that they do not accidently overlook a family. They make a home visit or a phone call or send a personal note through the mail addressed to parents to tell them something great their child has done in school.

A home visit or phone call has the advantage of allowing the parent to talk about something great their child has done at home as well. These visits are much easier these days as there are several different language line vendors or translation services that schools can contract with so that with a cell phone call you can easily include a translator in a conversation. Having a schoolwide subscription to language line services can also be a life saver when you need to communicate in a less common language and no one in the school speaks this language fluently. It can be instrumental in creating inclusive communication.

Another benefit of ensuring that schools regularly share good news about each student with their parents is that it builds trust. When there is a difficult circumstance that needs to be addressed with the parents regarding their child, parents and students are more likely to know that despite the difficult conversation, the school is on their side. The school's staff are cheering for them and expecting them to be highly educated.

A special reading teacher tells a great story that illustrates this point. One day the teacher called a new student's father to tell him how well his child had done in class that day. This student had been held back a grade multiple times in previous schools. He had just moved into the neighborhood around the school and had been enrolled a week and half in fifth grade. The teacher was struggling to engage him in class.

The student was considerably older than the rest of the fifth graders and had poor reading skills. He was much more interested in finding a girlfriend at school while the rest of the students wondered what was wrong with him as their hormones had not kicked in significantly at this time. The difference in interests was causing some difficulties on the playground as well as some showing off in the classroom.

The teacher called the father one evening to introduce herself and tell him that his son had done a great job in class that day, adding to the discussion on the different viewpoints of soldiers on both sides in the Revolutionary War. They were reading *My Brother Sam is Dead*. This student wasn't much interested in reading the book himself, but he would listen as parts were read and then struggled to do his part as his team worked through additional pages.

The day after the teacher called the father, the student came to class all excited about the call. His father had never received a good news call about his son. The student was proud that the teacher had repeated his comments to his father, valued his input in class, and had told his father about his contribution in class. The student wanted to know if the teacher would call his dad again that night to share some more good news. From then on, he knew it was his work to learn in class that got him recognition. He was attentive in class and worked very hard at improving his reading skills.

To provide him more support, he and the teacher began a project during recess where he was reading and studying to get his driver's license learning permit. He passed his written exam and got his permit. There was no stopping him at that point. The school was soon able to move him up a grade and get him closer to his aged peers. Before he left the school to go to middle school, he was fourteen and driving himself to school with his learner's permit. It was a little surreal having him park his car in the same lot as the teacher parked in each day at the elementary school, but also an opportunity to celebrate his accomplishments.

Another effort that provided great returns in engaging marginalized parents was getting them involved in the school's or district's work such as providing input on the budget or goal setting for a continuous improvement plan. A superintendent that did this quite successfully would always make sure she was careful to explicitly invite parents from various cultures and communities within the community so that the district would have broad representation on such development work.

However, despite the personal invitations, the district often lacked participation by parents from marginalized groups and had plenty of participation and feedback from the more empowered parents. Finally, the district scheduled a budget meeting for parents that was to be conducted entirely in Spanish. Several staff members who were well respected in the Latinx community facilitated the meeting all in Spanish. Speakers of other languages were welcomed to attend, but they had to wear a headset to hear the meeting translated into English and if they made a comment had to do so through a translator.

This was a complete reversal of meetings traditionally being in English and the need to wear a headset to hear the information translated into Spanish. All materials were in Spanish, and the notes taken on chart paper from participant feedback were written in Spanish. After the meeting those notes were translated into English for board members and the finance office. This all in Spanish budget meeting had more participants than the meetings conducted in English! Going forward, the district was careful to gather community input by not only making sure their surveys were in multiple languages, but that their meetings were as well.

This experience taught the district to ensure it offered information for parents in workshops that were also entirely conducted in their home language. For example, many immigrant parents or parents that didn't complete high school or attend college themselves did not understand the process that their children needed to go through to ensure they are ready for college and career.

On top of that, they felt uncomfortable coming to school to talk to a teacher or counselor about this process.

The district had always done parent workshops on preparing your child for college and career. The participants were primarily white, middle-class English speakers. The district started hosting "parent workshops" conducted entirely in other languages. They were offered at times when parents were most likely available: Saturday or Sunday afternoon or evening. The meetings included a meal, childcare, and a keynote speaker who was well regarded in their community, spoke their language, and knew how high school would be different for their children than what the parents had experienced.

This keynote speaker helped the parents understand the process and explained that it was important to ensure their students were taking advanced classes and not general education classes. They warned parents not to sign their child's enrollment papers if they were not sure it contained advanced classes, but rather to call the appropriate personnel at the school and ask. It was amazing how the course selections by the children of these parents changed. They wanted their children to be taking advanced classes and the children could no longer get by without doing so.

Parents of students in marginalized communities are often the hardest to reach in ways in which schools and districts have traditionally communicated. However, they are the parents that schools most need to communicate with. Educators need to communicate with them to let them know the high expectations they have for their children. Educators need to know what parents know about their children so that they can better support them. Schools need their students to see the school and their parents communicating and working together for their future.

Schools need to ensure when they are communicating with parents that they are valuing what they have to share with us about their children and not engaging in deficit thinking and telling parents if they would just supervise their child's reading at home or make sure their child completes their homework then all will be well. Parents know when schools are blaming them, and that does not create a unified effort between the parent and school.

Schools need to be flexible and ensure they are working to communicate with parents in their language and at times and places that do not take away from their ability to earn a living and provide for their family. To connect with families, take a cooler of bottled water to the soccer field on a Sunday afternoon and distribute the water as you talk with parents. Attend the local community festivals and spend time greeting parents, visit with them on their front porches, and wherever else they can be found. Go to them, and they will learn to trust the school.

Communication is a primary tool in establishing a positive school and district culture. If you want to be a Whatever It Takes school, you must constantly be communicating those high expectations to students, staff, and parents, as well as communicating the day-to-day happenings that make the school a Whatever It Takes school. This continuous communication helps shape the positive school culture that makes a difference for your students.

PROFESSIONAL LEARNING

Professional learning is another powerful developer of strong school and district cultures. Professional learning by the educators is a part of the fabric of schools where all students are achieving at the highest levels (Carter, 2000; Barth, 2001). Once again, it is not something that can be left to chance, but rather something that needs to be planned out over the school year or multiple years. Professional learning includes staff learning and growing together around district goals, school goals, and their own individual goals that *results in improved learning outcomes for students.*

Professional learning includes educators learning from experts and thought leaders, mentors, and their colleagues. It is ongoing and provides plenty of opportunities for reflection and practice of new learning. It is focused on instruction and support for improving student outcomes. In other words, professional learning has to be well planned with ample time allocated for it.

Professional learning happens at the districtwide level focusing on districtwide goals, at the school level focusing on school and instructional team goals, and at the individual level focusing on individual needs and areas of inquiry. When educators engage in professional learning, it should be clear that the goals are the student outcome goals expressed in the school's mission, vision, and continuous improvement plan. The professional learning is to provide the support and learning each staff member needs to ensure the process of instruction is highly effective and moves student outcomes toward the goals.

Time is precious in schools and districts, so it must be very clear how the learning is connected to the beliefs, values, and desired outcomes of the entire learning community. Professional learning must be tailored to the needs of the educators participating in it. It must be clear that the time and effort being expended is for the sole purpose of ensuring all students are learning at high levels.

Effective professional learning creates and reinforces positive school cultures and staff efficacy as educators collectively seek to better understand their students' strengths and needs, work to improve curriculum and the use of instructional strategies to best serve their students and hold each other accountable for having only the highest expectations for students. Odden and Archibald (2009) define effective professional development as that which produces change in teachers' classroom instruction resulting in improved student learning.

A team led by Linda Darling-Hammond reviewed the research on professional learning that improves student outcomes (Darling-Hammond et al., 2009). They found the following to be critical:

- Sustained and intensive professional learning, focused on teaching and learning
- Collaborative approaches to promote school change
- Substantial time to improve educators' skills
- Support for working with students with limited English or disabilities

A more recent review by Darling-Hammond, Hyler, and Gardner (2017) of thirty-five studies that confirmed the positive link between professional learning and student outcomes also identified the need for sustained duration in professional learning including weeks, months, and years. Odden and Archibald (2009) suggest that ongoing professional development requires many hours annually, from a minimum of one hundred to two hundred hours. These studies reveal the importance of educators engaged in active learning, collaboration, reviewing models of effective practice, and having ongoing support and opportunities for reflection.

Professional learning is not having a presenter come for a day and making everyone laugh or sending staff members to a national conference to bring back multiple ideas that are shared in a ten-minute presentation at a staff meeting. These types of activities can be valuable for keeping up with the research and current thinking in the world of education or adding to the learning a district or school is grappling with on an ongoing basis. They can be important for establishing knowledge that later can be accessed when needed. However, they are not, by themselves, the ongoing work that needs to happen to improve student outcomes.

Based on the identified goals in a school or district continuous improvement plan, professional learning needs to be planned so that it is ongoing and provide multiple times for educators to collectively and collaboratively engage around the learning. Districts need to have districtwide plans that keep everyone focused on districtwide goals and provides the overarching expectations with clearly defined outcomes. These districtwide plans should be developed in consultation and collaboration with educational leaders throughout the district and can delineate different paths for primary teachers compared to high school teachers.

In addition, each school needs to develop school plans for more specific areas of focus that are a part of achieving the student outcomes desired and expected by the district and their school. School plans also can be focused on all staff in the building or broken down to address specific needs of different instructional teams. Once again, they should be developed in consultation and collaboration with educational leaders throughout the school.

Many schools and districts also expect their individual educators to have professional development plans for themselves as well. Master educators and educational leaders are driven to improve outcomes for students and therefore are constantly examining and seeking to improve their practice. They are learners. Roland Barth (1990) defines schools that are improving outcomes for students as a community of learners in *Shaping Up the Schoolhouse*. They are a community of learners in that the students are learning, the teachers are learning, and the administrators are learning. They all are learning and growing together.

Barth (2001) further states that there are two types of schools:

> Ultimately there are two kinds of schools: learning-enriched schools and learning-impoverished schools. I've yet to see a school where the learning curves of the youngsters are off the chart upwards while the learning curves of the adults are off the chart downward. . . . Teachers and students go hand in hand as learners—or they don't go at all. (p. 22)

Learning is the business of educators. They should model learning for their students.

Weaving District, Building, and Individual Professional Learning Plans Together

Many schools and districts over the years have had goals around literacy. It is no wonder, considering literacy is crucial for success in academics. Consider for a moment that we are working in a school inside a district that is working to ensure all students are proficient in literacy. The district has considerable diversity in its student body in terms of cultures, economics, and languages. What might the professional learning plan look like in this situation?

At the district level, a three-year plan may map out ongoing efforts and opportunities to ensure all staff have high literacy expectations for all students aligned with the state standards. In addition, it might include actions being taken to eliminate tracking of students in literacy at all school levels. It might also expect that elementary schools use the science of reading and a research-proven program as their basis for literacy instruction.

Further, it might detail that middle schools ensure students are mastering academic language so that they can read and comprehend the increasingly academic texts that are a part of secondary learning. Lastly, it may include that high school students are able to use academic writing in multiple content areas and engage in logic and communication as the young scientists, historians, mathematicians, artists, and so on, that they are becoming.

The district does not control all professional learning nor even prescribe it. Rather, it provides the end goals, the what that the schools must achieve. Much of the work of how to achieve the goals will happen at the building level and the team level such as a grade-level team, a content team, or a professional learning community. Sergiovanni (1990) speaks to the balance between district-level and building-level actions when he notes that building-based decision making (or decentralization) only works when there is a central purpose and vision to the entire organization against which all plans and actions are measured.

The district defines the desired outcomes, monitors progress, and measures success. The individual schools and their educators create the actions that result in success. The plans of the district and individual building plans weave together learning and actions that improve student outcomes in literacy. The goals and objectives in district and individual school improvement plans are going to be very similar.

Where the conflict often comes is when the action steps identified for achieving the goals do not align. If you are not careful, the district can have a whole set of plans that are to guide the district's actions. Individual schools then have their own action plans, and they often go in different directions, even though they all are working on the same goals. Having conflicting plans does nothing but cause confusion and overload of work and stress, which results in poor implementation of the action steps and eventual abandoning of the work. Action plans between the various district and school efforts must be aligned. There is an example in Appendix A.

THE RIGHT PEOPLE SHAPE THE RIGHT CULTURE

A large, urban elementary school, where 80 percent of the students were classified as English learners and 99 percent of the students qualified for free and/or reduced-price meals was designated by the school board to be reconstituted. In April of that year, the superintendent and board of education named a new principal of this school as they designated that the school was to be reconstituted and reopened by August of that year. This was in the late 1990s and reconstitution for them meant everything about the school changed except for its students and its location.

The entire staff were to be reallocated to other schools in the district. If they wished to remain at the school they had to apply, interview, and be selected to work there. The new school was given a good deal of autonomy over how it spent its dollars, who worked there, the length of the school day and the school year, what programs and curriculum it used, etc. However, the school was still accountable for student outcomes on the district's benchmark assessments (this was before 2002 and the No Child Left Behind Act) and the Iowa Test of Basic Skills.

The principal began by recruiting and hiring a leadership team of teachers and support staff. This team immediately set to work to hire additional teachers and support staff as well as plan all the details of the reconstituted school. The story of this school is significant, because the progress made in changing student outcomes was exponentially more rapid than those of other schools.

There were multiple other schools within the district that brought in new programs, engaged in hours of professional development, and implemented massive improvement efforts. In five years, this reconstituted school went from one of the lowest achieving schools in the state to one of the highest. The other schools also made significant progress, but not nearly as rapidly as this school.

Staff credited their incredible gain to their opportunity to hire an entirely new staff. All members of the team were on the same page and had the same beliefs about the vision and mission of the school from the very beginning. The hiring was intensely focused on finding colleagues that had a passion to educate all students to the highest levels, believed they could do that, and were willing to examine what was working and quickly jettison what was not. Every member of the staff was all in and on board for the hard work.

This school's story reinforces how essential it is to have the entire school staff committed to creating a school where all children are educated to the highest levels: college and career ready. This creates a culture of high expectations, collaboration, and shared efficacy. However, the circumstances under which this school was created are not available to all schools. None of the staff who worked at the school before the reconstitution were let go from the district. They all received positions somewhere else in the district. It takes a large district to be able to absorb these staff members.

The staff who were hired signed on knowing they would be working outside of the contract. To do this, the teachers' association had to be a partner in this work and be willing to allow teachers who elected to work outside their contract do so. The district had to be willing to let the school reallocate its dollars in different ways so that the school was able to provide compensation to teachers who were working a longer day and a longer year as the leadership team decided to do. This situation provides a case study of what can happen in a school when there is a strong, united staff and a healthy school culture.

This experience illustrates Jim Collins' (2001) point about having the right people on the bus. Recognizing the power of school culture to impact the outcomes for students can give leaders the courage and strength to have difficult conversations when people are in the wrong seat. Recruiting the right people is critically important. The opportunity to fill vacancies should be treated with great care to ensure that a positive staff member is replaced by another individual who will be just as valued. At other times, filling a vacancy is an opportunity to excise a toxic individual and add a member who can make a positive contribution.

Many schools use an interview team comprised of staff members and sometimes parents. A team of staff that believe all students can learn to the highest levels are careful to select additional team members that will support this mission. Leaders are responsible for ensuring that the best educators are working with their students. If a school or district is in the process of building a culture that believes all students can and will succeed at high levels, the leader will want to carefully build the interview team to include like-minded educators. The team is to advise the leader regarding the candidates, but the final decision is with the leader.

Hiring opportunities are critical decisions. If done with great care and vetting, they can bring exceptional strength to the team and help propel a school or district forward. It is often better to delay filling positions if the right person is not immediately available and continue to search for the right person. This isn't easy because while looking for the right person, the rest of the team is continuing to fulfill their own positions as well as trying to cover for a vacancy.

However, hiring a person who is not going to be able to immediately strengthen the beliefs and culture of the team is catastrophic. They do not contribute to improving student outcomes. It often results in the sticky process of helping that person recognize the mismatch and move on to something else. This can cause all kinds of hurt feelings, disruption in the school culture, as well as legal hurdles.

Organizing the staff so that everyone is in a position where their strengths are maximized is critical as well. Sometimes a staff member is just in the wrong place or job function to be the highly competent contributing member they need to be. Reorganizing the team or giving new assignments to members of the team can also result in very difficult conversations. However, new assignments provide staff opportunities to bloom and become invaluable members of the team.

A principal tells the story of hiring a teacher at their school. A first-grade teacher from another school was needing a new home as the school where they had been working was anticipating fewer class sections the following year. The teacher came to interview for a first-grade position at the principal's school. Throughout the interview the principal was confused by what he was learning. There were many things said and examples given that made them believe that this teacher would be a great contributor to the school culture of relentlessly ensuring all students reached proficiency.

However, there were other things said that made the principal take pause. After reflecting on the interview, they realized that the things that made them take a pause were related to the typical behaviors and needs of first graders. The school was also in need of a fourth-grade teacher. The teacher was offered the fourth-grade position. They excelled as a fourth-grade teacher, contributed positively to the school culture, and went on to teach fourth grade until retirement. The teacher later confided to the principal that they did not want to teach fourth grade initially, but after doing so for several months realized it was a much better fit.

Another example of getting the right person in the right seat involved a principal who was mired in a school with a toxic culture. The principal was struggling mightily to lead the school. It was difficult for the principal to turn the culture around as they were unable or unwilling to confront the negative culture and things were going nowhere fast. However, this principal was an extremely intelligent person, fantastic with systems and an incredible advocate for marginalized students.

The principal was offered a director position that was in a department that desperately needed improved systems to ensure that students received the support services they deserved and needed. The principal excelled in this new position; the district was thrilled to finally have smooth functioning systems and dependable support from the district office. A new principal was found for the school who was able to collectively engage the staff in difficult conversations and help the staff create a new culture that they needed and deserved. This is an example of a fabulous educator being in the wrong seat and later excelling when in the right seat.

The hardest conversations of all, though, are those with colleagues when they are out of their element and working in the wrong field. Being an educator is hard work. It takes incredible determination and resilience to do this work. There are individuals who get into education because they like children, they like their content area, or they like having their "summers off." If they do not believe that all students can achieve to the highest levels and are determined to make it so, they are in the wrong field.

These too are very difficult but very necessary conversations. Educational leaders need to help these individuals understand they are accountable regardless of why they got into education and who their students are. These individuals need to move to a different career. Sensitive, caring educational leaders can help an employee feel valued as a person while also helping them to recognize that they are in the wrong field and will find much more satisfaction in another profession.

These conversations are delicate. It is important that the individual feel valued as a person and that they have a contribution to make to the world, while at the same time they need to see the misery that they cause by working outside of their wheelhouse. Helping individuals gracefully move on to another line of work where they can be a contributor is difficult, but necessary. An unfruitful school year for a student can never be redone. These individuals are still great people who are fun to meet for coffee or camp with in the summer, but they are not contributing to the work of ensuring all students are highly educated.

Schools mired in poor outcomes may try different programs year after year with no progress made, until the culture of the school begins to change. One school in a diverse district repeatedly told the superintendent how put upon they were. Prior to the superintendent's arrival, the district had opened a nearby magnet school and in doing so had moved staff and programs to their school.

The staff was adamant that their lackluster outcomes were because they had received the other school's language learners, students with severe special needs, and staff who were not going to be a part of the magnet program. This "poor us" attitude was reinforced by their principal. Hiring a new principal for the school, who put a good deal of work and mental stamina toward this cultural issue, was what it took to get a change started in the school's culture.

It became one of the most inclusive schools in the district. The school eliminated the silos of students learning English or with special needs being separated from the rest of the student body. Not only was getting the right principal in place key to this change, but the principal used every opportunity available to get staff in the right seats as well as encouraging some staff to retire or move to a profession more suited to them. The difficult conversations the principal had with staff helped them realize that these students were not a poor hand. He helped staff realize that they were going to be accountable regardless of who their students were.

Lastly, the principal spent hours working with individual staff members to help them improve their abilities or recognize that they were in the wrong seat or that times had changed and it was time to retire. This was intense work. However, the choices were to continue to get the poor outcomes they had with only the children who had multiple privileges finding success or change the culture and the systems of the school to ensure all students, regardless of position, were meeting standards and beyond.

SUMMING IT UP

School and district cultures are based on the shared values, beliefs, and actions of the people who learn and work there every day. Positive school and district cultures result in high achievement for all students. They are built on inclusiveness, constant communication around their high expectations for all students and staff, collaboration and continuous learning, and relentless and intentional nurturing and strengthening of their positive culture.

Educational leaders who create great schools develop strong, positive cultures that support and propel forward improvement efforts through continuous learning by students and staff. Attending to their school or district cultures, these leaders know who they are as educators, and they know who their students are and the incredible strengths they bring with them to the schoolhouse. They work to ensure no student is marginalized, but rather achieves at the highest levels.

They continuously communicate, in a multitude of ways, their beliefs and values in the worthiness and endless possibility of each of their students. They model learning to their students and colleagues while continuously working to improve their practice for even higher student outcomes. They search out, find, and bring on board like-minded colleagues who add to the strength of the team and improve the organization.

REFLECTION

There is a reflection section at the end of each of the remaining chapters of the book. It is intended to help you reflect on your school's and district's practices as well as your own individual practices. There is also a "Reflections and Next Steps" section at the end of the book that you may wish to use. It will allow you to make notes in one location regarding each of the chapters. This is to help you easily review your thoughts over all the issues raised throughout the book and then identify next steps to take in your own professional practice.

Reflections for chapter 3:

- Who are the marginalized students in your school? How do you know this? What are you doing about it? (In your classroom? In your school? In your district?)

- When a team of educators discusses individual students who are reading below level, what types of reasons are identified for this issue? When the student's home is blamed for their lack of reading ability, what do you say? How do you use the student's strengths to improve their reading abilities?

- What do the unspoken messages (symbols, celebrations, displays, etc.) say are the most important things or values in your classroom, school, or district? Why do you say this?

- What is your school or district's plan for nurturing a positive culture throughout the school year?

Chapter 4

Reading—The Basis of Equity in School

Educational equity in schools is defined as providing whatever it takes so that each child achieves the outcomes expected for all students graduating high school college and/or career ready. Equity is not merely the access to a possible education, but actually ensuring that all students are highly educated. The academic standards in each state define what students must know and be able to do in order to graduate. Being college and career ready means ensuring students at a minimum master these standards. Providing each student what they need to master the minimum standards is equity.

The standards for learning are defined in the United States as the standards each state sets for each of the content areas that will ensure students graduate from high school college and/or career ready. These standards are considered the minimum or the floor of what is to be learned. All states have benchmarks that students are expected to meet in at least the literacy and mathematics standards. Over the years the standards have become more rigorous, requiring all students to be critical thinkers.

Today's standards include more higher-order thinking than in the past. Teachers expect students to be analytical, critical thinkers, creative problem solvers, and life-long learners. The states are held accountable for student mastery in at least reading, mathematics, and graduation rates by their own laws and regulations as well as by the U.S. Department of Education as states submit their ESSA Consolidated State Plan (U.S. Department of Education, n.d.) that details their individual state's accountability plan and allows federal education dollars to flow to the state.

While each state sets their own standards and the assessments to be used to determine student proficiency or mastery of these standards, there is some commonality. Many of the states have drafted their standards based on the Common Core Standards. Contrary to frequent misunderstanding, the Common Core Standards were not developed by the federal government, but rather by the National Governors Association and the Council of Chief State School Officers (Common Core State Standards Initiative, n.d.).

It was an attempt by state and school district leaders to ensure, whether you were educated in Alabama or Wyoming or anywhere in between, that you graduated high school with skills and competencies comparable to your fellow students across the country. One of the major commonalities of the standards across the states is that they all require students to be able to read and comprehend complex, grade-level text in all content areas as well as apply mathematical thinking to new situations.

In turn, each state is also responsible for the development of assessments to measure student proficiency on these standards. There are also commonalities among these assessments, especially with many states, at least initially, using either the Partnership for Assessment of Readiness for College and Careers or Smarter Balanced Assessment Consortia to help them develop their assessments. These state-led assessment organizations developed and implemented tests aligned to the Common Core State Standards (Council of Great City Schools, 2014).

Despite all this work to align standards and assessments, there is still not a common measure to accurately determine if the children of Kansas who are deemed proficient in reading have similar skills to the children of Massachusetts who are proficient in reading. This is because each state makes their own modifications to standards and assessment items and sets their own cut points on the assessments for determining mastery.

The breakdown in commonalities among states, especially around what cut scores on the assessments indicate student proficiency, can be seen on the Institute for Education Sciences: National Center for Education Statistics (part of the U.S. Department of Education) table, "Estimated NAEP Equivalent Scores for State Grade 4 Proficiency in Reading: 2017," which maps state proficiency for reading and mathematics as measured by the National Assessment for Educational Progress (NAEP). The scores vary widely from one state to another, indicating that what is proficient in reading in one state is often not considered proficient in another state.

So, despite all of that, the best measure we currently have in the United States for determining how students in one state are performing compared to other students in another state is to use the results from the NAEP. This assessment is administered to a random group of students in all fifty states in grades four, eight, and eleven every other year, providing a measure to compare student outcomes across the country.

In 1969, NAEP began to collect data to provide insight, using a common assessment, regarding student achievement across the country. The early efforts involved a variety of assessments and content areas. In 1986, new assessments were developed to gather long-term trend data in reading, mathematics, and science. These new assessments were first administered in 1992 (National Center for Education Statistics, n.d.).

Years of administering these assessments show that the outcomes for students vary widely. Many students are not proficient readers, as measured by NAEP, and that is especially true for students of color, those impacted by poverty, language learners, and those with disabilities. In other words, while these groups of students have access to school and a free public education, the outcome for many of them is very different from the more privileged students. Equality in outcomes for students does not exist.

Many students are unable to read and comprehend complex, grade-level text in various content areas. They are unprepared to master the state standards, which is the baseline for graduating high school college and/or career ready. Their lack of reading ability becomes a barrier to their success. While most of these students had access to school, they didn't have whatever it took for them to become proficient readers.

While educators and politicians may take issue with the use of the NAEP assessments or state assessments to determine student proficiency in reading, a review of sample items from the fourth-grade NAEP reading assessments, included subsequently, indicates that it is not the most rigorous assessment that would demand the highest levels of critical thinking. Rather, it is a basic reading comprehension assessment requiring cognitive demands of minimal analysis and interpretation. These are skills that all of us would want at a minimum for our own children. If we want these skills and more for our children, wouldn't we want them for all children?

SAMPLE ITEMS FROM THE FOURTH GRADE NAEP READING TEST RELEASED IN 2017

After reading a six-page (four to five paragraphs/page) story based on a Turkish legend, "Five Boiled Eggs" retold by Laura S. Sassi, students are asked a series of multiple choice and short response questions. The questions are identified as medium level of difficulty and focus on student ability to interpret and integrate information from the text.

On page 3, the story says that the innkeeper was "eager to make a profit." This means that the innkeeper

   a. had a dishonest plan to make money
   b. thought a lot about how to make money
   c. tried to make money by raising prices
   d. really wanted to make money

Chapter 4

On page 3, the merchant mutters, "I'm ruined!" Explain what the merchant means when he says this. Use information from the story in your answer. *(Short written response expected.)*

What is the main reason Nasreddin Hodja tells the judge about corn?

    a. To suggest that the corn could be harvested
    b. To win the court case for the merchant
    c. To make the judge become even angrier
    d. To make the people in the courtroom laugh

Why does the judge decide that the merchant does not have to pay?

    a. Nasreddin Hodja shows that the innkeeper's demand is silly.
    b. The innkeeper finally agrees that the merchant is right.
    c. The amount of money the innkeeper wants is much too high.
    d. Nasreddin Hodja proves that he is a good friend of the judge.

After reading a six-page (three paragraphs/page and multiple illustrations) informational text about mummies, "Unwrapping the Past" by Natalie Smith, students are asked a series of multiple choice and short response questions. The questions are identified as medium level of difficulty and focus on student ability to interpret and integrate information from the text.

What is the article mainly about?

    a. Why the ancient Egyptians made mummies
    b. What the study of mummies can teach us
    c. Where an ancient Egyptian mummy was found
    d. How researchers unwrap mummies

In the last paragraph, what does Bob Brier mean by the phrase "to 'read' a mummy"?

    a. To understand the words written on a mummy
    b. To visit museum exhibitions about mummies
    c. To gather information by examining a mummy
    d. To make sense of the stories about mummies

Samples are from the NAEP Questions Tool where released questions from previous years and were retrieved February 18, 2021, from https://nces.ed.gov/NationsReportCard/nqt/Search.

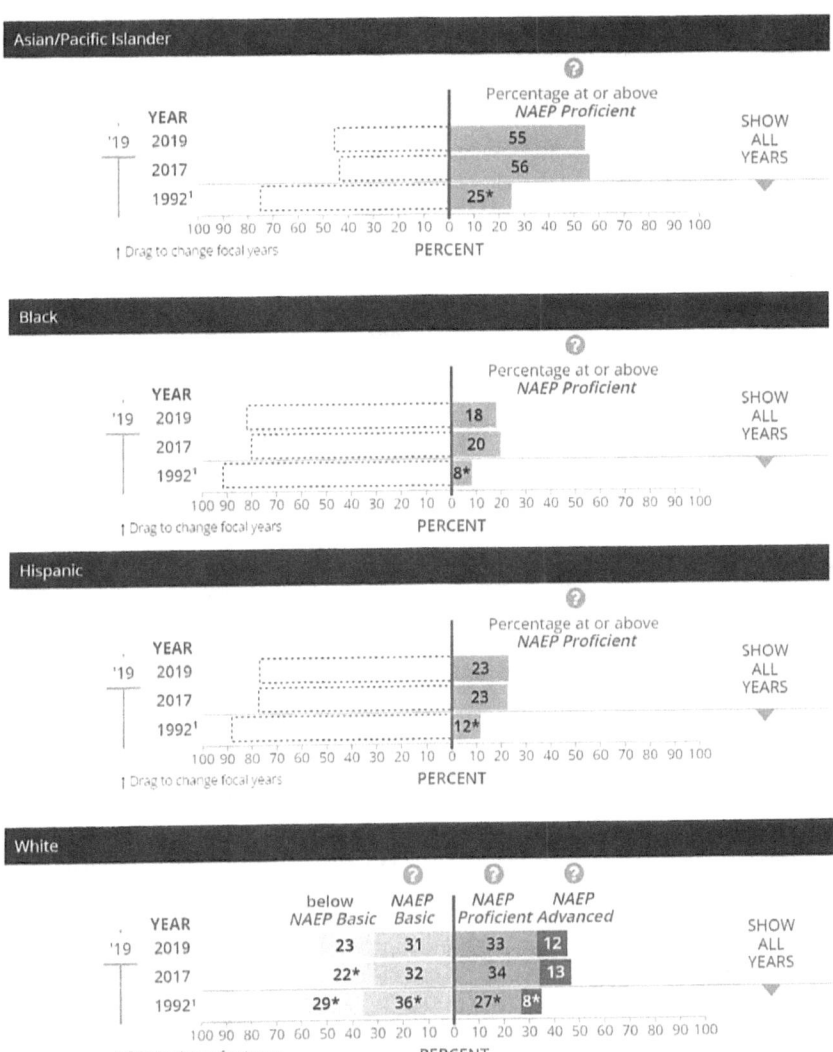

Figure 4.1. NAEP Fourth-Grade Level Achievement Results 1992 to 2019 by Student Groups
Source: Retrieved 2/19/2021 from https://www.nationsreportcard.gov/reading/nation/achievement/?grade=4.

Table 4.1 Estimated NAEP Equivalent Scores for State Grade Four Proficiency in Reading: 2017

State	Testing Program	NAEP Equivalent Score	Standard Error	Relative Error
Alabama	ACT	230	1.5	0.1
Alaska	NA	228	1.5	0.2
Arizona	NA	223	1.2	0.1
Arkansas	ACT	222	1.4	0.2
California	SBAC	224	1.1	0.1
Colorado	PARCC	234	1.6	0.2
Connecticut	SBAC	229	1.7	0.1
Delaware	SBAC	221	0.9	0.2
District of Columbia	PARCC	234	0.8	0.1
Florida	NA	226	0.7	0.1
Georgia	NA	231	1.5	0.0
Hawaii	SBAC	223	0.9	0.3
Idaho	SBAC	229	1.6	0.3
Illinois	PARCC	236	1.7	0.1
Indiana	NA	216	1.3	0.1
Iowa	NA	201	1.2	0.1
Kansas	NA	228	1.3	0.1
Kentucky	NA	227	1.3	0.1
Louisiana	NA	220	0.8	0.1
Maine	NA	225	1.7	0.1
Maryland	PARCC	235	0.9	0.0
Massachusetts	NA	238	1.2	0.1
Michigan	NA	229	1.1	0.0
Minnesota	NA	222	1.1	0.1
Mississippi	NA	234	1.0	0.1
Missouri	NA	214	1.5	0.2
Montana	SBAC	228	1.4	0.2
Nebraska	NA	224	1.3	0.1
Nevada	SBAC	224	1.4	0.2
New Hampshire	SBAC	-	NA	NA
New Jersey	PARCC	229	1.5	0.1
New Mexico	PARCC	238	2.0	0.3
New York	NA	234	0.9	0.3
North Carolina	NA	233	0.6	0.1
North Dakota	SBAC	230	0.8	0.3

State	Testing Program	NAEP Equivalent Score	Standard Error	Relative Error
Ohio	NA	217	1.0	0.1
Oklahoma	NA	231	1.1	0.1
Oregon	SBAC	225	1.3	0.2
Pennsylvania	NA	219	1.3	0.1
Rhode Island	PARCC	236	0.8	0.1
South Carolina	NA	228	1.9	0.1
South Dakota	SBAC	227	1.1	0.2
Tennessee	NA	234	1.1	0.0
Texas	NA	200	1.3	0.3
Utah	NA	238	0.9	0.2
Vermont	SBAC	232	1.0	0.2
Virginia	NA	201	1.8	0.2
Washington	SBAC	222	1.7	0.1
West Virginia	SBAC	224	1.5	0.3
Wisconsin	NA	229	1.3	0.1
Wyoming	NA	219	1.4	0.3

Source: U.S. Department of Education, Institute of Education Sciences, National Center for Education Statistics, National Assessment of Educational Progress (NAEP), 2017 Reading Assessments; and U.S. Department of Education Institute of Education Sciences, National Center for Education Statistics, EDFacts School Year 2016–2017. Retrieved February 18, 2021, at https://nces.ed.gov/nationsreportcard/studies/statemapping/table_2017a.aspx.

Note: The numbers reported in this table are rounded. Relative error is a measure of how well the mapping procedures reproduces the percentages reported by the state as meeting the standard in each NAEP-participating school.

New Hampshire was not included in the study because it did not use the same assessment for all students in grade four reading.

The results from the NAEP over the years illustrate that we have not achieved equity when equity in education is defined as ensuring all students have whatever it takes to at least master the baseline standards. Ensuring every student is proficient in reading is critical for ensuring all students are educated to the highest levels. Literacy is the basis for academic learning. Reading scores are rather stagnated on this assessment with way too many students having only marginal reading skills. There are glaring differences in outcomes for the various groups of students.

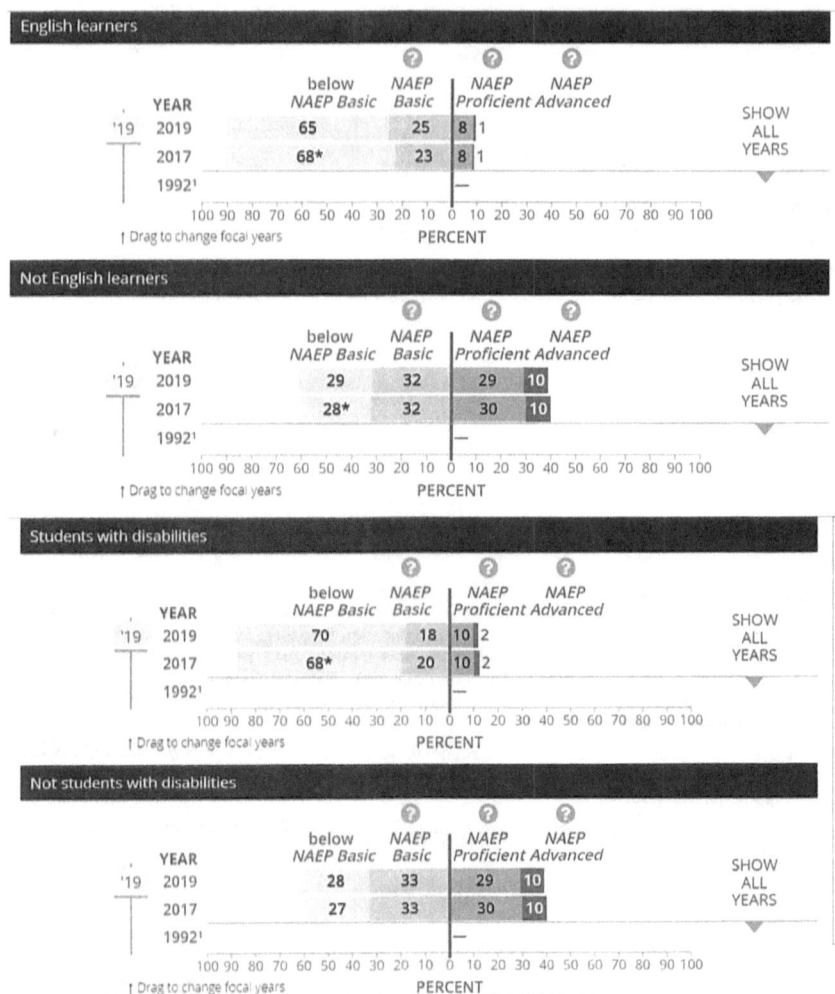

Figure 4.2. NAEP Fourth-Grade Level Achievement Results 1992 to 2019 by Student Groups
Source: Retrieved 2/19/2021 from https://www.nationsreportcard.gov/reading/nation/achievement/?grade=4.

EDUCATIONAL EQUITY STARTS WITH READING

Being able to read and critically analyze complex, grade-level texts in a variety of subject areas is the basis for all students mastering the standards and obtaining equality in academic outcomes (Carter, 2000; Cunningham and Allington, 1994; Gorski, 2018; Hill, 2017; Schmoker, 2018). Providing each student with whatever it takes to ensure they are proficient readers demands equity. Without proficiency in reading, students are much more likely to have a subpar education and are more at risk for increased difficulty in life.

Students who cannot read at or above grade level are destined to struggle in school and are seen as inferior to their peers who read at or above grade level. They are often provided reading instruction by being placed in small groups that are working below grade level, which reinforces an image of being an insufficient scholar and unable to excel in school, as well as exacerbating the gap as they continue to work below grade level.

Isabel Wilkerson (2020) would call this being identified as inherently inferior, the eighth pillar of a caste system described in her enlightening work, *Caste: The Origins of Our Discontents*. It is our educational system that allows them to work in below-grade-level groups, continuing the gap rather than doing whatever it takes to ensure all students are reading on or above grade level and closing the gap.

For years educators, policy makers, and political leaders have warned about the incredible difficulties children face in life if they are not reading on or above grade level by the end of their third-grade year. The research literature is heavy with warnings that the ability to read is fundamental to success in school. Students not reading on or above grade level by the end of third grade are more likely to drop out of high school, diminishing their life-long earning potential and their ability to participate fully in our nation's economy as well as avoiding and/or escaping a life of poverty (Fiester, 2010, 2013).

Educators need to expand this understanding that the results of a student not reading on or above grade level by the end of the third grade is not only highly impactful on the student but on the educators, who will serve this child and their peers learning alongside them through the rest of their years of public education. It continues to perpetuate the myth of these children being inherently inferior if we do not ensure they exit grade three as on level readers. It creates marginalized students.

Society often justifies that it just takes longer for these students to learn to read because of the poverty impacting their lives, their need for time to learn English, or whatever other reasons that can be assigned to them. Educators fall back to deficit thinking and justify that the students started school behind. However, these realities do not absolve professional educators from doing whatever it takes to ensure their success in school.

Ensuring that these students receive equity at school means ensuring they are reading on or above grade level by doing whatever it takes to make it happen. If educators allow these students to remain below-level readers, it becomes like the illustration of the children looking over the fence to view the game, previously referenced in chapter 1 and worth repeating. They have limited access to the action. They have not been fully welcomed into the game. They are marginalized.

The illustration of the children riding the bikes is closer to what schools should be striving for: all children reading. The goal of riding a bike is achieved by the children being provided whatever it takes for them to succeed at this goal. This is equity. It is not equal. If some children require more in order to be reading on or above grade level by the end of third grade, then schools have a moral imperative to make it happen.

Because reading skills are critical for success in school and success in school greatly increases the ability to succeed in life, ensuring that all students are reading at grade level or above by the end of third grade is an essential first step in providing equity for students in school. Schools must do whatever it takes for each student to ensure they are reading on or above level by the end of third grade. Failure to provide this for students is failure to provide equity for students. Failure to ensure students are readers is a failure to achieve our country's vision of a free and thorough public education for all students.

TEACHING EVERY CHILD TO READ

While it is daunting to do whatever it takes for each individual child to learn to read on or above grade level by the end of third grade, it is still amazing that schools do not routinely accomplish this with the knowledge we have. The fourth-grade NAEP scores show that a large number of children lack proficiency in reading. The percentage of students not proficient in reading is even greater for those students with disabilities, learning English as a second language, impacted by poverty, or of color. Despite these dismal numbers, there is a large and growing body of scientific evidence on what works in teaching *all* students to read.

We have the knowledge to ensure children are readers. Why has this not been accomplished? Education research has compiled a body of evidence of what skills and competencies students must master to be proficient in reading. These skills and competencies, or components of reading that enable all students to be successful readers, are referred to as the science of reading and has been widely acclaimed by the educational researchers and leaders in this area (Fien, Chard, and Baker, 2021; National Reading Panel, 2000; Seindenberg, Borkenhagen, and Kerns, 2020).

Embracing the evidence of what works in educational programs and practices is a growing best practice in the United States and throughout the world (Australian Society for Evidence Based Teaching, n.d.; Institute for Effective Education, n.d.; Slavin, 2017; Slavin 2020; What Works Clearinghouse, n.d.). We have evidence of which programs will provide instruction that will ensure the overwhelming majority of students master the skills and concepts needed to read. We know what interventions work when excellent, rigorous core instruction leaves only the smallest number of students needing additional support.

However, despite a large and growing body of evidence of what works in teaching all students to read, there are still untold numbers of classrooms and schools that do not adhere to following the evidence and do not use those programs and practices proven to work with the vast majority of students. Rather, these classrooms and schools base their instruction on tradition, how they were taught as students, what they have always done, or personal opinion and preference. This is a failure to embrace that teaching is both a science and an art and/or a surrendering to the lure of chasing the latest fads and glossy new materials and programs.

This is a systemic issue, not an individual teacher issue. Educators are genuine in their efforts to educate the students in front of them. However, they work in a system that is more focused on providing equality in process with the hope of achieving equality in outcomes. To obtain equality in outcomes, the educational system must be redesigned to do whatever it takes for each child. This will mean equity in process with equality in outcomes.

If equity in education is defined as doing whatever it takes to ensure all students achieve at high levels, then schools must follow the science and do what has been proven to work. They must put aside traditions, personal preferences, and prevailing instincts of educators to believe that every school must recreate the wheel because the circumstances in which each school finds itself educating children is completely different from any others. Educational coaches, consultants, and researchers who visit hundreds of schools and thousands of classrooms across our country assure us that our schools all have a great deal in common.

The entire school faculty and entire district faculty must be dedicated to eliminating traditional practices that have not proven effective for all students. Schools must stop the tracking of students into leveled reading groups with only fifteen to twenty minutes of explicit and rigorous instruction with the teacher while the rest of the reading block is spent keeping students busy as they await their turn for their reading group to meet with the teacher.

The goal must be to provide students, who are reading below level, instruction at grade level with all the additional scaffolding and supports needed to succeed. Remember, equity is whatever it takes, so when additional scaffolding to succeed at level is needed, do it. School teams must embrace and implement what the science of reading and the rigorous research on reading programs identify as programs that work for the vast majority of our students. Then practice equity by providing additional support for those who need it. Educators must shun programs that only work with some of the students.

Educators must follow the science. They must demand that schools and districts follow the science. If schools want to provide equity in education, they must ensure all students are reading on or above grade level by the end of the third grade. They must stop the tracking of students as soon as they enter school (Cunningham and Allington, 1994; Gorski, 2018; Hill 2017; Schmoker, 2018) by placing students in low-level reading groups that work below grade level and at a slower pace. When schools track students, they are exacerbating the problem! They must do whatever it takes to ensure all students are proficient readers.

This book addresses a multitude of areas for consideration when working to develop educational equity. It is not intended to be a book on how to teach reading. However, it might belabor the necessity of ensuring all students are readers as it is so foundational to their academic success across all of their schooling. Therefore, this book will include only highlights in the large and growing evidence of what works for teaching all students to read.

It will guide schools in creating the system for teaching students to read as well as provide resources on how to find those programs and practices that work. In additional chapters, this book will also highlight and discuss other components of the educational system that must be redesigned to have an educational system, including instruction and special programs, that ensure all students are able to read and understand complex, grade-level text.

WHAT WORKS FOR TEACHING STUDENTS TO READ?

In 1998, the Committee on the Prevention of Reading Difficulties of Young Children (a national panel of educators and researchers) published their report "Preventing Reading Difficulties in Young Children" (Snow, Burns, and Griffin, 1998). The committee stated in their report that the research on the teaching of reading had advanced sufficiently to find agreement on the results and conclusions of what works in providing reading instruction to young children.

They sought to present in their report the "optimal conditions" (Snow, Burns, and Griffin, 1998, p. 9) for ensuring young children did not develop reading difficulties in their first years of school. The committee found it "imperative that teachers at all grade levels understand the course of literacy development and role of instruction in optimizing literacy development" (Snow, Burns, and Griffin, 1998, p. 10). Even more telling, the committee concluded that "[a] large number of students who should be capable of reading well, given adequate instruction, are not doing so, suggesting that the instruction available to them is not appropriate" (Snow, Burns, and Griffin, 1998, p. 25).

We know what is proven to work and what programs ensure all students learn to read, so why are we not providing it? The committee found excellent reading instruction requires:

- an understanding of how sounds are represented alphabetically,
- practice to achieve fluency with different kinds of texts,
- background knowledge and vocabulary to make texts meaningful and interesting,
- ability to monitor comprehension and repair misunderstandings, and
- motivation to read for a variety of purposes.

What the committee found and advocated for every child was a solid core instruction based on the evidence of what works to ensure the vast majority of students become readers in a timely manner. They did not advocate for a host of supplemental programs with the idea that numerous children were going to need different programs to learn to read or that all students would naturally develop as readers if provided a literacy-rich environment. They advocated for solid core instruction in the skills or competencies needed for reading, now identified as the science of reading.

Regarding intervention programs, the committee stated,

> supplementary programs can neither substitute nor compensate for poor-quality instruction. Supplementary instruction is a secondary response to learning difficulties. Although supplementary instruction has demonstrated merit, its impact is insufficient unless it is planned and delivered in ways that make clear connections to the child's daily experiences and needs during reading instruction in the classroom. (Snow, Burns, and Griffin, 1998, p. 327)

High-quality core reading instruction for every student is essential.

A few years later, the National Reading Panel (2000) (a committee of researchers, educators, and pediatricians) reviewed the scientific evidence on the teaching of reading and compiled the implications found in their research. The science led them to conclude that reading instruction must include phonemic awareness, phonics, fluency, vocabulary, and comprehension. Time and again, they stated the evidence in their report that pointed the way to effective reading instruction.

Effective reading instruction includes:

- teaching students to manipulate phonemes in words across all the literacy domains,
- systematic phonics instruction with application,
- vocabulary development for comprehension, both oral and written, and
- comprehension taught so that there is the exchange of ideas between the reader and the text.

In addition, this committee also concluded that teachers need extensive training on how to teach reading and that professional development to improve teacher effectiveness in reading instruction is critical, especially in comprehension strategies. They summarized effective professional development as when teacher outcomes showed significant improvement and student achievement improved significantly as well.

A meta-analysis done by Johns Hopkins researchers (Slavin et al., 2009) found that programs that worked for all students included:

- changing the practice of teachers to follow specific teaching methods based on evidence,
- cooperative learning at the core,
- strong phonemic awareness and phonics instruction, and
- instruction in comprehension and metacognition.

The authors concluded that "what matters for student achievement are approaches that fundamentally change what teachers and students do together every day" (Slavin et al., 2009, p. 1453). Effective programs change practices, so that all teachers across the school embrace teaching methods based on evidence. The educators across the school are working together, rowing as a team, rather than each individual working in isolation and reinventing the instructional process.

Simms and Marzano's (2019) review of reading research is laid out in *The New Art and Science of Teaching Reading*. Their conclusion is that with high-quality teaching, all students can learn to read regardless of the point from which they started. Students made the gains needed in reading achievement if they had at least two consecutive years of high-quality reading instruction.

They advocate for a diagnostic approach to teaching reading: identifying what skills or strengths the student already has and filling in the additional skills needed for success in reading. The skills they identify as critical are very similar to those already identified in previous reviews:

- Concepts of print
- Word recognition (phonics)
- Fluency
- Vocabulary
- Comprehension

Simms and Marzano claim that at least two years of back-to-back highly effective reading instruction results in the reading achievement needed for students to read on level and aligns with Cunningham and Allington's (1994) and Darling-Hammond et al.'s (2009) findings on the impact that high-quality instruction year after year has on students.

These reviews all point to the same critical components: the science of reading.

- Systematic instruction on sound/symbol relationships and applying it to reading
- Building background knowledge and vocabulary to support the text
- Practices and procedures for students to monitor their understanding of text, make connections, and correct misunderstandings
- Continuous professional development for educators to follow specific teaching methods based on evidence that ensures high-quality instruction for every student

The science of reading has also been proven to work for students who are learning to speak and comprehend English while also learning to read English. Goldenberg (2020) reviews the literature on providing reading instruction in English to students who are simultaneously learning English in order to determine what is known about effective practices for this instruction. He notes that the evidence aligns with the science of reading for students who are learning to speak and comprehend English at the same time they are learning to read English.

Goldenberg finds that the foundational skills that English learners (ELs) need to be able to read in English are the same foundational skills that proficient English speakers need. However, he also found, in multiple studies, that ELs need English language development instruction along with the foundational skills to ensure that robust early literacy instruction was effective for ELs as well.

These findings align with previous reviews of reading programs in English that work for ELs (Cheung and Slavin, 2012). Goldenberg asserts that neurolinguistics support these findings as the more proficient ELs become in English the more proficient their reading skills become. He states, "In other words, ELs experiencing early reading difficulties need the same sort of instruction as non-ELs do, just more of it" (Goldenberg, 2020, p. S134).

In addition, Goldenberg (2020) also looked at what instruction was most effective for ELs beyond beginning reading instruction. In his review of the literature, he found that ELs need additional instruction and support in oral language development so that they can continue to achieve reading comprehension as the curriculum increases comprehension demands, both written and oral, at the middle grades and beyond. He notes the importance of developing academic language for ELs including connector words, discourse features, abstract words, and discipline-specific language.

Evidence of What Works

So how do busy educators go about finding the proven programs and practices that work for teaching students to read? Current federal law defines proven as "effective educational strategies supported by evidence and research" (ESEA, 2015). How do educators know what programs and practices have been proven to be effective without spending hours of precious time reading research studies?

As Seidenberg, Borkenhagen, and Kearns (2020) point out, the abundance of evidence from the science of reading informs us what skills and concepts students need to master to become readers. However, it does not provide much guidance on what instructional methods or strategies are most effective. There is a growing body of research on what programs or practices are most effective in teaching students to read. The most effective programs include ongoing professional learning so that educators are introduced to the instructional practices and have the support needed to implement and refine their use of these instructional models over time.

There are various websites that provide "consumer report" types of information to educators on educational programs. The following is a list of websites that address programs and practices available in the United States. (There are also websites for other countries such as the United Kingdom and Australia.) Each of these sites has slightly different criteria for what programs are rated as strongly effective and which ones are determined to be ineffective. However, the criteria are generally the same and include reviewing the research while looking for hallmarks of rigorous research and evidence of effectiveness.

Effective Educational Programs and Practices Websites

- Best Evidence Encyclopedia: https://bestevidence.org/
- Blueprints for Violence Prevention: https://cspv.colorado.edu/what-we-do/#blueprints
- Campbell Collaboration: https://www.campbellcollaboration.org/better-evidence.html
- Evidence for ESSA: https://www.evidenceforessa.org/
- Social Programs that Work: https://evidencebasedprograms.org/policy_area/k-12-education/
- What Works Clearinghouse: https://ies.ed.gov/ncee/wwc/FWW

Programs and practices that have evidence of effectiveness are ones that directly impact what students and teachers do in the classroom. There is no perfect textbook, computer program, etc. Rather, it is the instruction provided by the teacher that engages and ensures the student is learning and developing

TEXTBOX 4.1

Rigorous Research Evidence of Effectiveness

1. Does the research compare an experimental group to a control group? Are the groups randomly assigned or well-matched (quasi-experimental assignment)?
2. Is the study at least twelve weeks in duration?
3. Does the research involve multiple schools, teachers, and students in the treatment?
4. Does the research use fair, unbiased, reliable, and quantitative measures of skills for all groups?
5. Does the research find an increase in achievement for the treatment group more than the control group that is significantly positive?
6. Is the research conducted by outside reviewers and/or published in a peer-reviewed journal?
7. Is there more than one research study with similar results for the program/practice being reviewed?

as a proficient reader. If this is not happening for all students, then what the teacher does in the classroom will need to change. That is why the programs identified as highly effective are programs that include a great deal of professional learning and explicit guidance in how to teach reading.

Putman and Walsh (2021) in their review of teacher preparation policies note that "[m]ost states still do not verify that elementary, early childhood, or special education teacher candidates know the most effective methods to teach their future students to read" (p. 2). Using proven instructional methods to teach the components included in the science of reading is not a primary point in teacher preparation programs across the country. As schools and districts select proven practices and programs for ensuring all students learn to read at high levels, they must understand that professional learning will be a critical component of the process.

Every educator responsible for teaching students to read must be a master at teaching reading. Becoming a master educator requires ongoing significant amounts of professional learning, including on-the-job practice, reflection, and revision. This professional learning is ongoing and collaborative so that all educators responsible for ensuring children are readers become masters of literacy instruction.

The programs proven to work have commonalities including:

- instruction at grade level in the components identified in the science of reading,
- extensive time (more than ninety minutes) each day involved in *direct* reading instruction,
- explicit instruction of foundational and comprehension/metacognition skills,
- extensive reading, discussing, and writing to deepen comprehension, and
- monitoring of learning to ensure every student is mastering skills or immediate clarification and intervention is provided.

Unproven Practices That We Cling To

It is also imperative to note what was not mentioned as critical to highly effective reading instruction in these reviews of the research. Longstanding traditions in our current education system include the teacher working in isolation in their classroom and using leveled reading groups (sometimes now called literacy or book groups for reader's workshop) where the teacher divides the students into three or four reading groups based on the students' "reading levels" with some students working significantly below grade level (Cunningham and Allington, 1994; Gorski, 2018; Hill, 2017; Schmoker, 2018).

Though the classroom schedule may include a substantial reading block (more than ninety minutes), students only receive fifteen to twenty minutes of highly focused reading instruction while their group works with the teacher. The remaining time in the reading block is consumed by the students being engaged in independent or partner activities where they complete worksheets, read silently (or at least appear to read silently), do word sorts or spelling games, or engage in other activities that the teacher has created to keep the children occupied while the teacher works with a different group of students.

Also not found in effective reading instruction for all students is immersing students in a literacy-rich environment with the expectation that they will absorb the literacy or discover it on their own with little to no explicit instruction. We must also note that Goldenberg's (2020) review of the literature on teaching ELs to read in English also included cautions regarding the use of balanced literacy and whole-language techniques. The growth for ELs in these instructional models was not statistically significant.

The use of these models might be due to the assumption made by educators that these models promote oral language development, yet they were found not to do so for all students. Rather, they kept ELs from benefiting from instruction. ELs benefited from more explicit instruction. In addition,

Goldenberg cautions against using culturally appropriate instruction if this instruction fails to emphasize English language development and critical literacy skills.

Lastly, effective instruction does not include sending those students that may need additional support in reading to receive instruction from the reading teacher or the English language development specialist where the instruction is completely divorced from what is happening in the classroom. Please note that a review of what works in highly effective reading instruction does not include tracking students by putting them in small groups to receive only a limited amount of direct instruction in the regular classroom.

Effective reading instruction does not include putting students in groups that continue to highlight that some students are readers and some are inferior. These are practices based on tradition, often reflecting the way we as educators were taught when we were children. These practices do not provide for extensive explicit instruction and guided practice with gradual release of responsibility for students to learn the foundational skills and the critical thinking skills needed for reading. They do not provide rich student discussion in careful facilitated cooperative learning groups where students make sense of their learning.

Rather, they provide for limited explicit instruction with students then being sent away from the teacher to practice on their own, which often leads to reinforcing misunderstandings and bad habits regarding reading. While it may result in equality in the amount of time that students receive direct instruction from the teacher and then spend rotating through centers, it does not provide the "whatever it takes" for those students needing more support in learning to read. It does not result in equality of outcomes. It is not a whatever it takes or equity model.

One of the most damaging aspects of the tradition of reading instruction is dividing students into leveled reading groups for fifteen to twenty minutes of explicit instruction daily. It is most often highly damning as it relegates some children to lower-level groups to be lower-level readers for a lifetime and it relegates teachers to working in isolation with the expectation that they can be all things to all children. This is a system set up to fail many of our children. It is not individual teachers failing our children; it is the structure of the system.

Children reading below level need additional supports to succeed at grade level and reach the goal of being able to read independently at grade level in a timely manner. These additional supports, paired with grade-level instruction, may include additional instructional time, pre-teaching of background knowledge and vocabulary, and interventions or clarifications provided immediately during instruction as the teacher notes students not succeeding.

They do not need to have reading instruction slowed down by working in below-level groups year after year so that they fall further and further behind.

Every student is expected to make a year's gain in reading for each year of schooling in the elementary years. If a child starts the year below the standard for the grade level they just left, then they need to make more than a year's gain in order to close the gap and be reading on or above grade level as they exit third grade. These are the students that the teachers must rally around to ensure they make more than a year's gain in reading. They must provide whatever it takes.

It is shocking when some educators set goals for their students reading below level to make a year's gain in reading or even less. If they expect children who are behind in reading to only make a year's gain, then they are still behind at the end of the year because every other child also made a year's gain as well and so the gap continues. The goal for these students must be that they make more than a year's gain each year until the gap is closed! The gap must be closed to ensure all students graduate high school college and/or career ready.

Relegating students to work below level slows down their progress toward closing the gap, often resulting in these students being even farther behind at the end of the year. These are the students that must be the focus of the weekly teacher data team or learning community meetings as they work together to improve instruction. These students must receive the highest and greatest levels of coherent and explicit instruction. They must receive the additional time needed to ensure that they are grade-level readers. They need every moment of instruction they receive to be coherent and highly impactful. Equity is whatever it takes. It is not equal.

What About Pre-K

Preschool programs can be impactful for ensuring every student is reading on or above grade level by third grade. However, they do not eliminate the need for highly effective literacy instruction in grades kindergarten through third grade or ongoing literacy instruction in the content areas as students mature. They are not a blanket panacea. Like all programs of instruction, there are those that are highly effective and research proven and those based solely on theory or preference without evidence of effectiveness. Only programs proven to be highly effective should be used in schools working to close the gap for our marginalized students.

Evaluations of preschool programs, in general, find that these programs benefit children in terms of school readiness, especially for children in low-income households (Chambers, Cheung, and Slavin, 2016; Fischer, Keily, and Weyer, 2020; Meloy, Gardner, and Darling-Hammond, 2019; Meloy and

Schachner, 2019). Some of the programs reviewed have been found to have long-lasting positive effects while others resulted in more short-term results.

In addition, researchers have found that the monetary investment in preschool programs results in a greater return than the initial investment (Cannon et al., 2017; Fischer, Keily, and Weyer, 2020; Meloy, Gardner, and Darling-Hammond, 2019). Researchers and policy analysts call for the implementation of well-designed and well-implemented preschool programs that have long-term impacts (Cannon et al., 2017; Chambers, Cheung, and Slavin, 2016; Meloy, Gardner, and Darling-Hammond, 2019).

So which programs should schools and districts put their limited resources into to ensure their preschool programs put students on a path to literacy and overall success in school so that they graduate high school college and/or career ready? What are well-designed and well-implemented preschool programs? Let's look at the evidence from rigorous research.

Meloy and Schachner (2019) synthesized the essential skills that children developed in preschool that predicted later school success. These included social-emotional development, cognitive development, language and literacy development, mathematical and scientific reasoning, and physical development. Chambers, Cheung, and Slavin (2016) found that more intensive and extensive preschool programs had long-term impacts, especially for marginalized children. In contrast, they found that programs that were solely developmental constructivist approaches tended to have only short-term effects.

The more intensive and extensive programs that produced both short-term and long-term effects are a balance of explicit instruction in early literacy skills, language development, and socialization skills along with some use of developmental-constructivist model components. For example, these models include instruction in phonemic awareness, alphabet, writing, and mathematics while also including creative play, art, music, drama, and story time. A list of the most effective preschool programs and can be found on the Best Evidence Encyclopedia at https://bestevidence.org/category/early-childhood/early-childhood-early-childhood-education/.

Preschool programs are worth the investment of district and school resources. Schools that have huge growth in outcomes for the marginalized most often include preschool programs that are all-day programs (increasing the ability of children of working parents to participate) and use highly skilled certificated teachers (putting them on the teachers' salary schedule, often resulting in higher levels of qualifications), and research-proven programs that combine both explicit instructional and developmental-constructivist components.

More and more states are making preschool programs a part of their public education system, especially for marginalized families that cannot afford a private preschool experience for their child. Schools cannot allow the growth of preschool programs to be based on tradition, intuition, or personal preferences as was often the practice in early literacy instruction. Educators must advocate for and implement only those programs that have been proven to provide the long-term impact needed for our students, especially our most marginalized students who have limited opportunities for such preschool programs.

USING CULTURALLY APPROPRIATE MATERIALS WITH THE SCIENCE OF READING

Educators who labor to use the science of reading while teaching students to read can inadvertently fall into the trap of failing to connect with their students due to the texts selected for instruction. The science of reading and the Common Core Standards do not prescribe certain texts. Rather, they guide what skills and concepts should be taught, how they should be taught, and grade-appropriate levels. Excellent instruction also means connecting with your students and their backgrounds and experiences (Boykin and Noguera, 2011; Gay, 2002).

The literary experiences that educators have students engage in while developing their skills are important. Educators should be hypervigilant to ensure the experiences are ones in which their students can see themselves. Aukerman and Schuldt (2021) note that "literacy is socially, culturally, and historically situated, what counts as good reading is equally social, cultural, and historical" (p. S86). Students are more motived and engaged to read when the texts are meaningful to their lives and they see themselves in the text (Aukerman and Schuldt, 2021; Milner, 2021; Lindsay, 2010; Noguera, 2008; Guthrie, 2004; Krashen, 2004).

Some educators are not always the best resource for selecting texts or developing literacy experiences that connect with students that live in different situations from their own. However, excellent teachers are always looking for opportunities to identify texts and literary experiences that could add to their repertoire that will engage students. Good sources include colleagues (especially colleagues of other races and cultures), librarians, websites such as We Need Diverse Books (https://diversebooks.org/), and the students themselves.

Listening to students as they talk about their lives is a good way to identify literary experiences that are real to them. In addition, if a teacher has several texts that they are considering using with their students, let some of the students review the texts and tell them what they think. If students are engaged and motivated to read and see themselves in the texts that they read, they can build their self-efficacy as readers.

SUMMING IT UP

Educators have scientific evidence of what works to teach all students to read at high levels. They know that strong reading skills are critical for student success in academics. What, then, is keeping schools from ensuring that all students are reading on or above level at least by the time they leave third grade? Sacred traditions and theories for teaching reading which have not proven to be significantly effective with all students must be abandoned. Schools must stop the tracking of students from the day they enter by putting students in low, middle, and high reading groups in classroom after classroom.

Stopping the tracking is not impossible. The author was a first-grade teacher who used low, middle, and high reading groups when she first started teaching. It wasn't closing the gap, so she had to do the hard work to change what she was doing. It was her job to ensure every child left her classroom reading and ready to engage with grade two–level text. She discovered in her third year of teaching that she could teach all her students to read at or above grade level.

The previous spring, she had received a mini-grant for classroom books. She ordered multiple copies of *The Cat in the Hat*, *Little Bear*, etc. She put these books in the reading corner. It was one of the centers students were to rotate through while she was working with one of the small reading groups. Students could read a book of their choosing or practice from their reader the story that they working on in their reading group. There were also some books that were designed to provide stories for them to read while practicing the vowel patterns they were learning (controlled readers).

Mid-year, she noticed that every single student was working hard to read *The Cat in the Hat*, *Little Bear*, *Danny and the Dinosaur*, etc., and avoiding their readers and the controlled readers. Even the students in the lowest reading group were giving these titles a go. If they were working so hard to read these books, what was she doing having them work in a pre-primer reader? She moved every student to the top group! Now there was one whole class group that was working at or above grade level. That was a struggle for a while since there was one of her and twenty-four students, some of them struggling.

She learned, with a great deal of professional learning support, to use some cooperative learning strategies during guided practice, after providing explicit and interactive instruction and modeling, to help her ensure every student was responding to questions, reading, and discussing their reading during the lesson while she moved from student pair to student pair monitoring and providing additional support when needed. It was a wake-up call. She could ensure that all of her students left first grade as proficient readers and ready for second grade if provided the proper instruction. That was the end of having a bottom, a middle, and a top reading group in her class.

Educators must commit themselves to reading instruction that is rigorous and grade appropriate for all students based on what is proven to work. This includes extensive explicit instruction with lots of student practice combined with close teacher monitoring and clarification, and gradual release of responsibility. These are active classrooms with a good deal of student conversations as students discuss their reading. As they become readers together, the conversation will be rich.

Students will be able to encode and decode words; they will be able to read with fluency. The students' background knowledge and vocabulary will be continually expanding, and they will monitor their own reading for comprehension, repairing their reading when comprehension breaks down. In addition, their teachers commit themselves to ongoing professional learning to continuously improve the interactions in their schools between educators and students, ensuring that all students are readers.

REFLECTION

There is a reflection section at the end of each of the remaining chapters of the book. It is intended to help you reflect on your school and district practices as well as your own individual practices. There is also a "Reflections and Next Steps" section at the end of the book that you may wish to use. It will allow you to make notes in one location regarding each of the chapters. This is to help you easily review your thoughts over all the issues raised throughout the book and then identify next steps to take in your own professional practice.

Reflections for chapter 4:

- What fraction of children in your school/district leave third grade as below-level readers? Why? Be careful not to blame the children and their families. What it is about the system that causes students to leave third grade as below-level readers?

- How is reading instruction provided in your classroom, school, or district? Does it follow the science of reading and use proven programs? Why or why not?

- Is reading instruction in your building based on equality or equity? How do you know?

Chapter 5

Literacy in the Content Areas

Once a student is reading on grade level by the end of third grade, the importance of literacy development does not dimmish. Rather it continues as a foundational component of learning in all of the various content areas. Secondary students are expected to engage in and master skills in a multitude of content areas. There is a strong need for academic literacy in all of the content areas with students being expected to read narrative, expository, and argumentative text, while recognizing a variety of viewpoints and evaluating the validity of the information they encounter (Baye et al., 2019; Lee, 2012; Minaya-Rowe, 2012).

All students must be provided with continuing literacy instruction throughout kindergarten to twelfth-grade schooling so that they continue to develop sophisticated literacy skills. Literacy instruction in the content areas is even more critical for students who need additional support in mastering rigorous content standards. All teachers, including secondary teachers, need to be able to teach literacy in their content area. They need to provide explicit instruction in the vocabulary, language, and text structures used by the experts in their field. If you study economics, you need to understand how economists communicate. It is the same with all content areas.

The fact that the various content areas have language and text structures all their own was made very clear to the author early on in her career. Despite being a strong reader and a teacher, she struggled with English when trying to read texts used in law school. The words were primarily English. But the language structures and content were foreign to her. Early in her career, her husband required emergency eye surgery. As a part of the recovery, he was not allowed to read for several months as the back-and-forth movement of the eye while tracking text on a page would have been enough to undo the repairs done in the surgery.

It also happened to be his last semester in law school. His doctors advised that he sit out a semester and delay his completion of law school. That was not an option in his mind. However, he dutifully stayed home from classes.

Lectures in each of his classes were recorded, and she read to him from his law texts. Her fluency was lacking as she frequently stumbled over words and unfamiliar sentence structures. Thankfully, her husband had great background knowledge and legal academic language as he was raised in a family of attorneys. This allowed him to follow along despite her stumbles.

The author's experience of reading law texts to her husband gave her a deep understanding of the importance of teaching the literacy of whatever content area you are teaching to your students. She had a firsthand reminder of what many students experience when reading text for which they have no previous knowledge to rely on while reading the new content. She went back to the classroom much more focused on helping her students develop academic literacy, including an understanding of text structures in the various content areas in which they were engaging.

As she moved to principalships and district leadership positions, she was almost rabid at times to ensure that students were receiving literacy support in all content areas and that teachers had the skills they needed to be able to teach students the literacy of their content areas. Another tradition in education is being transformed for the better. Content teachers are not just teachers of chemistry or visual arts or geography; rather, they are teachers of both the science and literacy of chemistry and so forth.

ACADEMIC LANGUAGE AND CONTENT LITERACY

We often think of academic language as an area of support for students who are learning English as a second or third language. Much of the work around how to support students in learning the academic language of a content area has its roots in the work of Cummins (1984) who differentiated between conversational language or basic interpersonal communicative skills and cognitive academic language proficiency. Another way to think of academic language is to differentiate by content area and consider the host of disciplinary literacies used in academia.

State educational standards, the Common Core Standards, and standards set by various professional associations such as the Next Generation Science Standards (NextGenScience, 2013) all articulate the need for students to develop literacy in the various disciplines in order to engage in the higher-order thinking required by each individual discipline or content area. Each discipline has different ways of communicating to share knowledge in their field, from their way of thinking about the world, to gathering and understanding data, to organizing their learning (Zwiers, 2014).

McConachie (2010) defines academic literacy as "the use of reading, reasoning, investigating, speaking, and writing required to learn and form complex content knowledge appropriate to a particular discipline" (p. 16). Therefore, educators in the various content areas must all be literacy educators for their content area. They must ensure that students are able to engage in and use the literacies of their discipline or content area (Lent, 2016).

Students that have the skills and abilities to navigate the literacy of the various disciplines are able to participate and engage in that discipline. They become budding scientists, economists, mathematicians, historians, artists, etc. Students learn how to use information and create new knowledge within the various disciplines. They will not develop master-level status in each content area in high school, but they will develop the necessary understandings for becoming productive citizens while also finding those content areas that so deeply engage them that they continue their learning in these areas after leaving high school.

Just as the author struggled to read a law text that was written in English, despite being a fluent English speaker, educators must always be conscious that our students come from a wide array of backgrounds—even the students who speak English as a first language. Speaking English as a first language does not mean that you speak the English of law or economics or mathematics or music. These are specialized content areas. Our students are in school for the very purpose to learn the various content areas from each of us as experts in our content.

Educators must teach students to speak, read, and write the language of their various content areas. Some students will come with much more information in biology than others because of their backgrounds, while others will bring knowledge of music or Southeast Asia or a multitude of other content areas. Remember that the task is to ensure that all students are educated to the highest levels and that requires that educators do whatever it takes for each student to master that content area. That is equity.

PROVIDING INSTRUCTION FOR CONTENT LITERACY

The teaching of content literacy and/or academic language has not been a given in the hundreds of secondary classrooms. The teaching of vocabulary words specific to the various disciplines has been a constant. The assigning of chapters to read and questions to answer is also often a part of a content class. However, examining the literacy used in a specific content area such as how scientists reason and then structure their writing to share their reasoning and learning is not always a part of secondary instruction.

It is often assumed that the English teacher is responsible for any instruction that involves writing. English teachers are experts at English literacy. They are not scientists. The lack of consistency in providing explicit instruction in the literacy of the various disciplines is once again a system issue. Secondary teacher preparation programs stress the acquisition of the knowledge and skills needed for the specific content area of biology, chemistry, calculus, or world history, etc. Educators in each of these disciplines are experts in their content.

They are so steeped in it that they often do not recognize that they are speaking a different language than the rest of us when engaging in discourse about their content area. Meanwhile, students are having experiences similar to what the author had when she tried to read law textbooks to her husband. Secondary teacher preparation programs vary widely in the support they provide to preservice teachers to understand the need for and to know how to develop content literacy in their discipline with their future students.

The principal of an elementary school that sat adjacent to a middle school was making an effort to develop a better working relationship with the middle school. She had invited their leadership team to meet with her leadership team to discuss ways that they could better support each other. Early in the discussion, an eighth-grade biology teacher stated that if they would just teach the students to read so that they could read the biology textbook, he would be happy.

After biting back her initial thoughts about this statement, the principal asked if their fifth-grade students were reading on grade level when they left them to matriculate to middle school. The majority of staff (from both schools) involved in that discussion thought that students were reading on level and the assessment data supported that belief. So then she asked how did they propose that students reading at a fifth-grade level when exiting elementary school be taught to read an eighth-grade level biology textbook?

Long story short, the conversation concluded that sixth-grade teachers needed to ensure students were continuing to develop their literacy skills in all content areas, and then seventh-grade teachers needed to do the same. Then, finally, when students reached eighth-grade biology, the students needed to have instruction that supported them learning to read a biology text at this level. In other words, developing literacy skills does not stop at the end of elementary school.

Educators do not expect students leaving the elementary grades to have all the literacy skills they will need for secondary school and college. Rather, they expect them to continue to develop their literacy skills. As educators, it is their obligation to ensure that they continue to support the literacy development of students, especially in the content areas in which they are the experts. Educational standards clearly articulate the expectation that students grow in their ability to read, write, and think critically in the various disciplines.

As educators, it is imperative that instruction in content literacy and/or academic language be a part of each secondary course. Leaders must ensure that these expectations are clear and included in curriculum maps and documents. Leaders must expect to observe students reading a variety of content-specific texts and writing content-specific pieces that give students opportunities to practice and develop their literacy skills in the various content areas.

Educators must also be sure that they have clearly communicated with their students that they expect them to learn to read and write like scientists, mathematicians, artists, social scientists, etc. The goal must be clear for students as well as for educators. The good news is that there is evidence that instruction in content literacy improves student mastery of the content as well (Goldman et al., 2019; Lee, 2012; Minaya-Rowe, 2012; Reisman, 2012).

We must ensure that educators have the time to work together, by content area, to identify the content literacy skills and academic language that they need to explicitly teach in their classrooms. Working collaboratively with their peers that teach the same or similar content areas, educators need time to reflect on what literacy skills are specific to their field. How do scientists approach a piece of professional text? Once this is identified, educators need to work with their peers to determine how to best teach and assess these skills to engage students as critical thinkers, readers, writers, and speakers specific to their content area.

They can also work together to find a variety of text sources they can use in their instruction that gives their students experience with the literacy of the discipline through reading research reports, peer-reviewed journal articles, technical manuals, blogs, data sources, etc. Educators need to work together to clarify or even practice how they will model for their students how to reason, read, and write like a scientist. Content teachers must guide their students in developing abilities to reason, read, and write like a scientist, etc.

If you need help in getting started on thinking about the literacy specific to your content area, check out Lent's (2016) great tables that list characteristics of how scientists, mathematicians, historians, and social scientists approach reading and writing in chapters 2 and 3 of her *This Is Disciplinary Literacy: Reading, Writing, Thinking, and Doing . . . Content Area by Content Area*.

English language development educators are great resources for content teachers who need support in determining what and how to teach the literacy of their content area. These experts can examine text and help their colleagues identify skills and knowledge that need to be explicitly taught to develop literacy in that specific content area. English language development educators working alongside their content educator peers can be a source of information and support in developing lesson plans as well as co-teaching in their classrooms.

The co-teaching experience provides on-the-job professional learning opportunities as content educators observe language experts providing explicit instruction and support to students on the specific literacy needs of the content area. English language development educators focus on ensuring students learning English acquire the academic language while content teachers simultaneously ensure they master the content. The skills and strategies they employ can be useful for all students (regardless of first language) as all of the students are developing their literacy skills in a new content area.

World-Class Instructional Design and Assessment (WIDA), a consortium of more than forty states and territories, supports educators in developing their abilities to support the language development of their students. WIDA (2020) includes academic language in their standards for supporting students in language development. Academic language includes vocabulary such as technical language, nuances of meaning, and idioms. However, it is much broader than this. It also includes such items as language forms, types of grammatical constructions, and density of text. WIDA identifies three components of academic language: vocabulary usage, language forms and conventions, and linguistic complexity.

Teaching specific content vocabulary in isolation or just reading textbooks is not sufficient. Academic language or content literacy instruction should be rich in actual texts from the specific field such as primary documents, infographics, personal communications, journal and magazine articles, research papers and summaries, news briefs, handbooks and manuals, field notes, raw data, tables, graphs, etc. Students need to observe scholars modeling how they engage in the literacy of their content and receive explicit instruction as they begin to engage with authentic text from the discipline.

Academic language or disciplinary literacy must be a part of all content area instruction regardless of students' first languages. Students are not expected to show up at the schoolhouse door as scientists, mathematicians, artists, etc.; rather, it is the educator's job to help them learn the ways scientists, mathematicians, artists, and so forth think and communicate. That includes learning the languages of these disciplines so that students may fully participate in the joy of learning in each of these areas.

Educators must teach and expect their students to read discipline-specific pieces and be able to analyze and synthesize the information. They must teach and expect our students to write discipline-specific pieces that are constructed as the experts in this discipline expect. This can be difficult when you are so deeply embedded in the content as an expert. It is hard to step back and see all of the specific steps of how an expert in your field reasons, investigates, and shares their learning through spoken and written text.

In addition to accessing the expertise of educators who are English language teachers, think about the colleagues with whom you work. What educators do you work alongside that have students reading journal articles or primary source documents with great success? What colleagues have students

The Features of Academic Language in the WIDA Standards

The Features of Academic Language operate within sociocultural contexts for language use.

Dimension	Performance Criteria	Features
Discourse	Linguistic Complexity *(Quantity and variety of oral and written text in communication)*	• Amount of speech/written text • Structure of speech/written text • Density of speech/written text • Coherence and cohesion of ideas • Variety of sentence types to form organized text
Sentence	Language Forms and Conventions *(Types, array, and use of language structures in communication)*	• Types and variety of grammatical constructions • Mechanics of sentence types • Fluency of expression • Match language forms to purposes/perspectives • Formulaic and idiomatic expressions
Word/Phrase	Vocabulary Usage *(Specificity of word or phrase choice in communication)*	• General, specific, and technical language • Multiple meanings of words and phrases • Nuances and shades of meaning • Collocations and idioms

The sociocultural contexts for language use involve the interaction between the student and the language environment, encompassing the...
- Register
- Genre/Text type
- Topic
- Task/Situation
- Participants' identities and social roles

Figure 5.1. The Features of Academic Language in the WIDA Standards
Source: © 2014 Board of Regents of the University of Wisconsin System, on behalf of WIDA—www.wida. us. Retrieved August 16, 2021 https://wida.wisc.edu/sites/default/files/resource/2012-ELD-Standards.pdf (p. 8).

writing papers that would stand up as excellent writing in college classes within the field? These master educators can be a rich source of collaborative professional learning. Engage in lesson studies with them, visit their classrooms, and work together to plan instruction.

If you find that these master educators are the advanced opportunity teachers (advanced placement classes, dual-credit course, etc.), have you considered providing the professional learning opportunities these instructors have access to for all educators at the secondary level? What if every teacher taught their content class as an advanced opportunity class? In our quest for equity, should we not have the same high expectations for all students?

One way to ensure that there are high expectations for all students is to ensure all educators have the knowledge and skills to teach advanced-level courses and then teach every course as an advanced-level course. Stop the tracking where some students are expected to reason, read, and write like scientists in advanced classes and other students get by in a general science class that uses simplified textbooks, little to no writing, and assesses students only on factual recall of information.

Schools and districts can also provide opportunities for content teachers to take courses toward earning their English as a second language credentials.

This is not to expect them to leave their content classrooms and become English language teachers, but rather to become even more effective content educators as they add to their skill set and become better teachers of academic language, especially the language of their content expertise.

If the school or district pays for the tuition for these classes, provides classes within the district, and encourages a cohort of educators to engage in the work together, it can be a win-win. The school or district gains even more highly skilled teachers that can serve their diverse students, and the educators gain additional skills and graduate credits that move them up on the salary schedule.

Summing It Up

Developing literacy is a life-long pursuit, especially in the current age where knowledge is rapidly multiplying and being distributed at ever increasing speed. Educators must ensure their students develop literacy competency in multiple disciplines. Instruction and support for students in developing literacy across the disciplines communicates to students the high expectations their teachers have for them. They expect them to be able to engage with scientific knowledge, mathematical knowledge, and other disciplines as well.

Developing content literacy in students begins by setting clear expectations and helping students understand that there are different ways of communicating in the different disciplines. It requires explicit instruction and modeling how professionals in the different disciplines read and write. Students must be exposed to a wide variety of authentic texts and documents within the different content areas and not rely solely on the course textbook.

Students must also be expected to write or produce a variety of texts within the various content areas as well, such as technical pieces, charts and graphs, observations, journal articles, research summaries, biographical reports, argumentative essays, news articles, etc. As educators guide their students through the variety of texts in their discipline, they must provide explicit instruction in the academic language students will need to thoroughly comprehend what the author is saying. This includes vocabulary, language forms and conventions, text structures, and how the text is organized.

As always, the components of effective instruction apply (more about this in chapter 6) including clarity in expectations or learning outcomes, understanding the why, modeling, guided practice with close teacher monitoring and immediate revision in instruction when understanding breaks down, as well as opportunities to apply the learning in new and different ways. The strategies and tactics that work in helping English language learners to understand the content presented in English also work very effectively for all students. Use those same strategies for teaching literacy to all students.

Lastly, teach every class as if it were an advanced class, as if every student was a scientist, mathematician, social scientist, artist, etc., in the making. Do whatever it takes for each student to achieve at the highest levels. Use those programs and practices that have proven to be most effective in helping the vast majority of students develop academic literacy. Each school year is gone at the end of the year. We do not have the ability to call it back and redo it. We must ensure every student is learning at the highest levels. They are our future. Some additional resources that can help educators teach content literacy are listed here.

Resources for teaching content literacy:

- *This is Disciplinary Literacy: Reading, Writing, Thinking and Doing ... Content Area by Content Area* (2016), by Releah Cossett Lent
- *Developing Readers in the Academic Disciplines* (2011), by Doug Buehl
- *Focus: Elevating the Essential to Radically Improve Student Learning*, second edition (2018), by Mike Schmoker

Websites for finding proven programs:

- Best Evidence Encyclopedia: https://bestevidence.org/
- Evidence for ESSA: https://www.evidenceforessa.org/
- What Works Clearinghouse: https://ies.ed.gov/ncee/wwc/FWW
- WIDA: https://wida.wisc.edu/

MATHEMATICS

While there is not enough time to discuss each content area specifically in terms of supporting student literacy, this section will speak to the specific content of mathematics. Mathematics is a unique language. Just as reading on grade level or beyond by third grade is critical to students' learning at a high level, so is the mastery of mathematics on or above grade level including all students participating in a high-quality mathematics pathway and developing algebraic thinking at the high school level. It is critical to success on the road to being highly educated and able to pursue any number of future opportunities upon graduation.

Advanced high school mathematics empowers students and expands their professional opportunities after graduating high school (Checkly, 2001; National Council of Teachers of Mathematics [NCTM], 2018; Rech and Harrington, 2000). National Assessment of Educational Progress scores in mathematics indicate that we have as serious or an even more serious issue than reading with the number of students not demonstrating proficiency in mathematics in our kindergarten to twelfth-grade system.

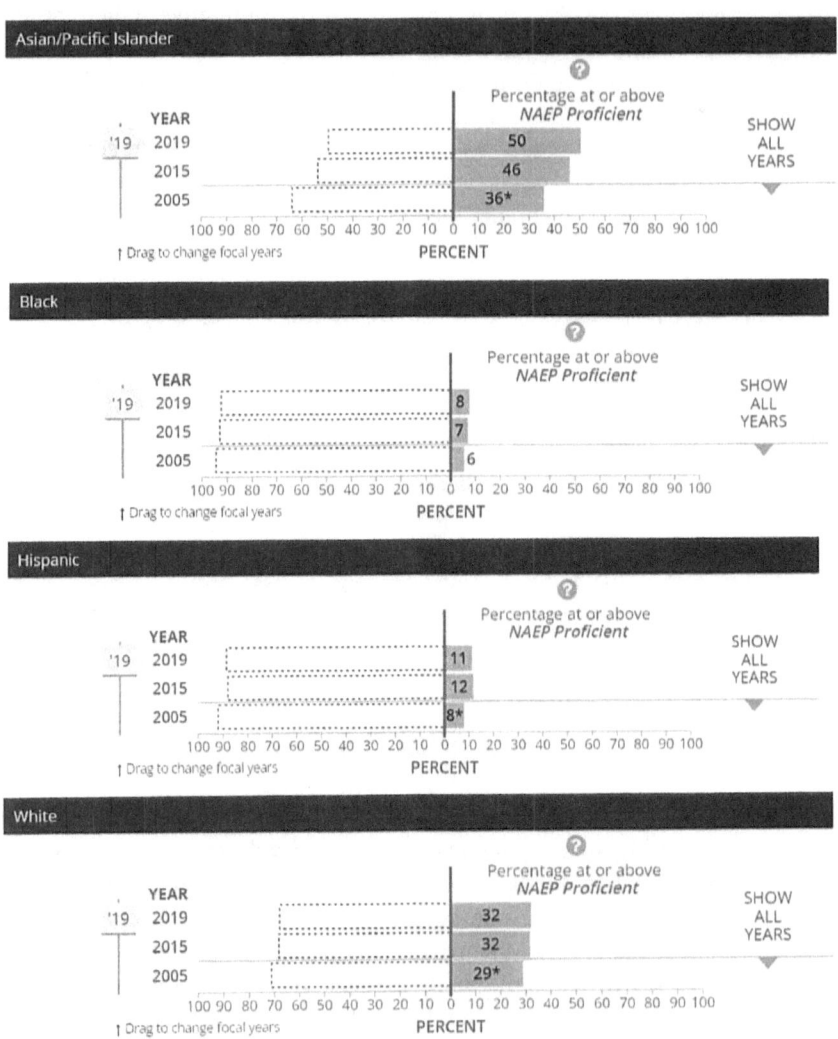

Figure 5.2. NAEP Twelfth-Grade Mathematics Level Achievement 1992 to 2019 by Student Groups

Source: Retrieved 11/28/21 from https://www.nationsreportcard.gove/mathematics/mation/achievement/?grade=12.

NAEP Twelfth Grade Mathematics Level Achievement 1992 to 2019 by Student Groups

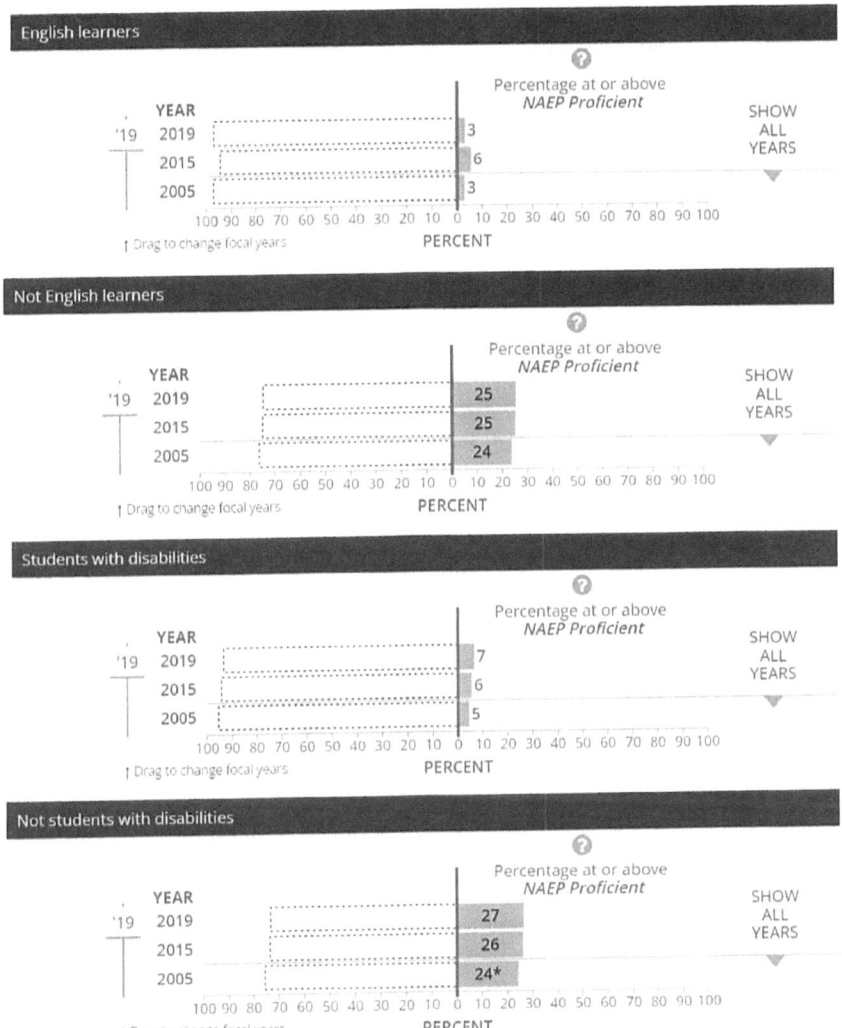

Figure 5.3 NAEP Twelfth-Grade Mathematics Level Achievement 1992 to 2019 by Students Groups

Source: Retrieved 11/28/21 from https://www.nationsreportcard.gove/mathematics/mation/achievement/?grade=12.

Schmoker (2018) presents the case that nearly three-quarters of our students matriculating to community college fail the required college algebra course, with most of those students then dropping out of college. Schmoker states that this is alarming as the primary cause of students dropping out of high school and/or college is failure in mathematics. Just as reading is critical to student success in school, so is advanced mathematics.

The NCTM (2018) points out the extent to which our society is dependent on mathematics in their *Catalyzing Change in High School Mathematics* as they identify the never-ending use of mathematics in everyday life through polling and data mining, algorithms to drive social media, advertising, knowledge searches, and financial models that drive investors and guide business development as well as government leaders. The role of mathematical proficiency in determining what pathways are available to students after high school makes it critical that all students are literate in advanced mathematics.

The NCTM sums it up by stating:

> Everyone involved in the mathematics education of high school students must be committed to ensuring that each and every student has the opportunity to learn the mathematics necessary to be well prepared for whatever the future may hold for his or her educational, professional, and personal lives. When the potential of so many students is squandered, the loss is not only to individual students but also to society at large. (p. 3)

These efforts begin with effective instruction. Slavin, Lake, and Groff (2009) found in their review of effective secondary math programs that educators should focus more on what happens in the classroom to engage students in learning mathematics than choosing one curriculum or textbook over another. They state "that the programs that produce consistently positive effects on achievement are those that fundamentally change what students do every day in their core math classes" (Slavin, Lake, and Groff, 2009, p. 887). The evidence supports programs that include cooperative learning and a focus on teacher instructional methods.

Effective instruction begins by eliminating tracking of students. Placing students on various tracks for mathematics instruction is unfortunately very common, especially at the secondary level (Lambert, 2021; NCTM, 2018). While the majority of students in grade 9 may be enrolled in Algebra I, the differences between the various Algebra I classes such as advanced or honors, general, and adjusted or remedial are substantial in student outcomes and instructional content.

The NCTM notes that Algebra I classes on a high track are often focused on conceptual understanding and problem solving, while the low track is focused on rote procedures. Students on the low track are on a dead-end pathway as they fail to truly learn algebra and are unable to pass exams later, which relegates them to remedial math rather than admit them to College Algebra in their post-secondary education. NCTM recommendations include that all Algebra I classes be equal in content and expectations and student representation.

Students who need additional support are provided additional time (in the same semester/school year) for instruction that is focused on the content that is connected to their Algebra I class rather than removing them from rigorous expectations and instruction. Schmoker (2018) questions the need for tracking students in mathematics by noting that whole-class, teacher-directed instructional approaches work at all levels in Singapore, a model which many U.S. schools identify as highly successful in mathematics.

A high school that was well regarded by many parents had an Algebra I track that took two years for students to complete. They spent the first year learning the content the rest of the students learned in the first semester of Algebra I and the second year learning the material from the typical second semester. Most of the students in these classes were marginalized students and those whose parents often had not completed high school themselves.

If you started this Algebra I class as a ninth grader, you would not complete it until the end of your sophomore year. Now, as a rising junior, you still have to take at least Geometry and another math class to graduate. Do you need two years for each of these courses as well? It was a pathway to failure and dropping out. After much angst and gnashing of teeth, the principal and the math educators decided to eliminate that two-year, one-class track and provide additional time to students needing it with a second math period each day instead so that Algebra I was mastered in one year.

Once they started, they found that they didn't have near as many students as they thought that needed the extra time. In addition, the graduation rate for their marginalized students increased significantly. These students increased their participation in advanced classes during high school and increased their participation in college or technical courses after high school graduation.

The NCTM (2018) cautions against tracking math teachers as well. This practice often results in the more experienced or effective teachers assigned to the advanced courses with the newer or less effective teachers assigned to teach the lower track classes. Teacher assignments should be balanced out so that all math teachers have high-achieving students and students who need additional support. This helps develop collaborative teams where all teachers are responsible for all students and expectations for all students are the same.

Stopping the tracking of students in mathematics (as in reading) is critical to establishing equity and closing the achievement gap. Educators solidify the achievement gap when they track students into basic math versus advanced math. The expectations, the content, and the rigor is all highly impacted and greatly different between a basic math class and an advanced math class.

Many schools have grappled with their systems to end tracking in mathematics at the elementary, middle, and high school levels. One high school that found success was very large. Its student body was comprised of well-to-do students who had grown up speaking English and living in the United States as well as students whose first language was not English (125 different languages in that school), whose parents worked multiple jobs to provide the basics for the family, and who were often newly arrived in the country.

This school had so many math teachers that they didn't even know all their colleagues other than by name. They also had so many different types of Algebra I classes that the teachers were not even aware of all their department offered. However, under a new principal the entire school was intensely focused on ensuring all students graduated college and career ready. This meant that all students had to master Algebra; no more basic math.

The teachers who were committed to ending this tracking agreed to teach Algebra I and be a part of the Algebra I learning community. They spent the summer learning more about cooperative learning, identifying essential standards, developing performance assessments, and planning their initial lessons. They enlisted English language development teachers and outside experts on cooperative learning and English language development to help them. They eliminated basic math classes and developed an Algebra I course that was for every student.

Advanced Algebra I was folded in and now a part of every Algebra I class. Students knew what they had to do to demonstrate proficiency in each concept taught in the algebra class. Students worked in cooperative learning groups closely monitored by the teachers to ensure that the teams maintained the interdependence and individual accountability critical to successful cooperative learning. If students elected, they could go beyond proficiency and demonstrate advanced understanding of the concept as prescribed by the course materials.

Students that demonstrated advanced understanding for at least 80 percent of the advanced content were rewarded by having "advanced" notated on their transcript. These students were not in separate classes, but rather in the only Algebra I class offered at this large school and functioning as a part of the cooperative learning teams in their classroom. The excitement the students and teachers shared as students with limited English earned their "advanced" notation on their transcript was incredible to witness.

The success of this professional learning community of teachers and their students was observed by their colleagues. Their practices began to spread to middle school mathematics and to additional high school courses of Geometry and Algebra II. After several years, the English department followed suit by eliminating honors English and creating English I and II classes that were the same for all students with the opportunity to demonstrate advanced proficiency and have it so noted on their transcript.

In addition to avoiding the tracking of students and teachers, other effective practices are identified in the literature. Schmoker (2018), in his *Focus: Elevating the Essentials to Radically Improve Student Learning*, discusses in detail effective teaching practices that he attributes to all students developing proficiency. These include clarity of goals/objectives, chunking the learning into small pieces (which he re-emphasizes in his discussion on mathematics in chapter 7), and providing guided practice with close teacher monitoring and immediate modification of instruction if needed.

Schmoker also notes that there is work to be done on the Common Core Standards and similar state standards for mathematics. While the intent of the Common Core was to focus on the most essential learnings, this did not happen with the development of secondary mathematics standards. The standards (Common Core State Standards Initiative, 2010) for the elementary grades do reflect a reduction in breadth of content at each grade level with a focus on going deep into a limited number of concepts per grade.

The amount of content expected per course at the secondary level makes it difficult to achieve the outcomes of deep understanding and rich engagement with problem solving. Schmoker strongly recommends a narrowing of the focus to only the most essential skills and knowledge. This aligns with the NCTM's (2018) recommendation to focus on essential concepts only for improving high school mathematics. They state what is truly essential learning in secondary mathematics is concepts of number, algebra and functions, statistics and probability, and geometry and measurement.

Mathematics is a tool for problem solving, interpreting the outcomes, and using the knowledge to move forward (NCTM, 2018). Therefore, problem solving should be the beginning and core of building new mathematical knowledge. In order to include the "why" in mathematics instruction or real-life application, Schmoker (2018) recommends starting with problem solving to introduce the formulas and algorithms.

Involving students in mathematical modeling is another way to engage students in real-life mathematics. Developing multiple mathematical scenarios/problems to provide data for use in problem solving is time consuming. However, if problem solving is the launch pad for mathematical learning and only the most essential concepts are given instructional time, classroom time will be dedicated to the real-life, hard work of mathematical problem solving.

Development of mathematical models involves mathematical thinking. Educators who teach mathematics through the lens of mathematical thinking (rather than rote algorithms) develop students who understand the "why" or how mathematics works and the interconnectedness of mathematical concepts so that they are able to use their learning in new and different situations (Brendefur et al., 2013). The NCTM's (2018) review for improving secondary mathematics recommends that each and every student develop deep mathematical understandings.

Using multiple representations or models builds conceptual understanding, procedure fluency, opportunities to apply mathematics in new situations, and practice in explaining mathematical thinking. Developing these understandings enables students to identify, interpret, and critique information and assertions presented in life from the sciences, business sectors, political organizations, and social media.

Mathematical thinking is further strengthened through engaging in mathematical literacy, reading, and writing. The highly respected thought leader on mathematics instruction Marilyn Burns (2004) stated, "I can no longer imagine teaching math without making writing an integral aspect of students' learning. It requires students to organize, clarify, and reflect on their ideas" (p. 30). Lent (2016) also notes that students deepen their mathematical understanding through engaging in mathematics literacy: reading and writing like a mathematician.

Mathematicians are looking to solve problems, so when they read, they are looking for patterns, relationships, connections to other mathematical concepts, as well as looking for what is missing. Schmoker (2018) encourages educators to engage students in mathematical thinking through the development of arguments, reports, and proposals that mirror real life. He argues that writing in mathematics helps students deepen their understanding and learn to communicate effectively about quantitative topics, a trait highly desired by employers.

As noted by Slavin, Lake, and Groff (2009), practices and programs with evidence of effectiveness deviate from tradition and completely change the interactions between students and teachers in the classroom. If we expect educators to move from the traditional mathematics instruction focused on memorizing algorithms with lots of rote practice to instruction that primarily consists of problem solving, mathematical thinking, and application of learning, then we must provide educators the support they need (NCTM, 2018; Slavin, Lake, and Groff, 2009).

Critical to providing educators the support they need includes time, professional learning, and research-proven programs. Learning and collaborating with peers takes time. There is never enough time in schools and districts to meet all the demands placed upon them. Despite this reality, educational leaders need to set aside time specifically for professional learning where educators can work together to improve their practice and outcomes for students. Educators also need to be paid appropriately for this time.

This means educational leaders need to continue to help all stakeholders understand the importance and value of professional learning so that the time and funds needed for professional learning are more readily accepted by the community. The professional learning that is a part of the research-proven programs identified by Slavin, Lake, and Groff (2009) is not a one shot and you are good to go. It is intensive and ongoing.

The professional learning in these programs is ongoing with educators learning from content experts (both external and inhouse). They collaborate together to review student data to identify strengths and needs, plan for changes in the system to meet the student needs, identify and unpack essential standards, plan lessons and work together to develop real-life problem-solving scenarios to engage students, participate in lesson studies, observe and learn from each other, and the list goes on.

The need for educators to work together to develop real-life problems for students to solve as the core of math instruction is specifically pointed out here. If instruction in mathematics needs to start with and be centered around real-life problems to solve, educators need time and support to develop these scenarios so that the problems connect with the students' lives and are rich, meaty problems.

Brendefur and Carney (2016) note that high school math teachers may have high levels of math content knowledge, but often limited knowledge of how math concepts are applied in real-life situations. Therefore, there is a need for educators to collaborate on developing real-life problems that resonate with their students and engage them in the "why" of learning mathematics. The preparation that needs to be done in order to provide instruction that ensures every student mastering mathematics is extensive. It is critical to find the time for professional learning teams to do this most important work.

One very successful school created time for educators to engage in professional learning in their daily schedule. It was a prekindergarten to fifth grade school. They reallocated funds in order to be able to hire a couple of additional teachers than what were typically on staff. Then they restructured what grade level teachers were expected to teach to include literacy, mathematics, and social studies. This reduced the number of areas in which these elementary educators had to plan for, teach, and assess. Science, art, physical education, and music were all taught by educators hired to teach one of those single subjects.

The science educators were set up in lab classrooms to ensure the bulk of science instruction was happening in a lab format. Grade-level classes had two forty-five-minute "specials" classes (science, art, music, physical education) each day back-to-back rotating between two of the four classes each day. All the classes in a grade level were engaged in these "specials" classes at the same time. This provided a ninety-minute block for the grade-level teachers to work and learn together. Two days a week were formalized professional learning community times. The other three days could be used as the team decided.

Similar time was provided for the specials teachers to have professional learning time as well. The teachers in these communities became very tight teams and often chose to work together almost every single day rather than working in isolation during their ninety-minute professional learning and/or lesson development time. The school served primarily students living in poverty and learning English as a second language, yet they had some of the highest literacy and math scores in the state.

Summing It Up

Mathematics is a gate keeper for students leaving high school and entering post-secondary education and careers. Students who do not develop proficiency in advanced mathematics in high school are relegated to lower paying jobs and/or struggling with remedial math classes at the community college or university which cost them time and money, but provide no credits toward a degree. We must stop tracking students in mathematics and do whatever it takes to ensure that all students graduate high school with proficiency in Algebra I and II and Geometry.

Our world needs problem solvers and critical thinkers that can analyze the claims presented every day in the news and on social media regarding the environment, the government and political systems, advertising, health care, education, space, and a host of other issues and developments. We can ensure all students are proficient mathematicians if we teach them to think mathematically and solve complex problems. We can do this by creating systems that set high expectations for every student and use those programs and practices that have been proven to work.

REFLECTION

There is a reflection section at the end of each of the remaining chapters of the book. It is intended to help you reflect on your school and district practices as well as your own individual practices. There is also a "Reflections and Next Steps" section at the end of the book that you may wish to use. It will allow you to make notes in one location regarding each of the chapters. This is to help you easily review your thoughts over all the issues raised throughout the book and then identify next steps to take in your own professional practice.

Reflections for chapter 5:

- How many different types of Algebra I classes are taught in your school? Why?

- What will you do so that all students graduate from your school proficient in algebra?

- How do you support mathematical thinking throughout your school?

- How do you help students learn the characteristics of literacy in your content area?

- Is the rigor in your classroom what you want for your own child? Why or why not?

Chapter 6

Highly Effective Instruction

What is highly effective instruction? Highly effective instruction ensures all students are performing at high levels and closes the gap for students not achieving on or above level. In previous chapters, the need to ensure all students are reading on or above grade level by the end of third grade was addressed. Also, the need for all students to successfully complete rigorous high school mathematics has been discussed. Failing to achieve these benchmarks puts the student even further behind with a widening of the gap. It is imperative that students be provided grade level and above instruction.

The reality is some students are below grade level and providing instruction at grade level will require additional scaffolding and support for some students until the gap is closed. No longer can we tolerate assigning students to below-level reading groups for fifteen to twenty minutes of direct instruction per day from the teacher and think we will ever close the gap. Continuously providing instruction that is below grade level continues and exacerbates the gap.

Math, like reading, is another gate keeper. If students cannot engage in mathematical thinking and solve rigorous real-life math problems requiring algebra and geometry, they will not graduate high school college and career ready. Yes, for some of our students it will require scaffolding. Enrolling some secondary students in basic math classes or an Algebra I class that takes two years to complete puts them even further behind, widening the gap. No longer can we tolerate students receiving below-level instruction in mathematics.

Students do not graduate high school college and career ready if they cannot read, write, and critically think in the various disciplines of mathematics, science, social studies, the arts, etc. This chapter discusses highly effective instruction that allows below-level students to learn along with their classmates and close the gap. There is a robust body of research on what works and what does not. This chapter explores what the evidence tells us is the most effective way of ensuring all students are learning and grappling with rigorous, grade-level content in all academic disciplines, as well as the hallmarks of exemplary instruction.

HIGH EXPECTATIONS AND STUDENT RELATIONSHIPS

High expectations for each individual student are critical for ensuring all students achieve at the highest levels. They are the beginning point for improving student achievement (Ferguson, 2007; Gorski, 2018; Hattie, 2009; TNTP, 2018). It is not enough to expect a group of students to achieve overall. We must expect each individual student to achieve. Some students will need more support in meeting these expectations. Good instruction provides that support or scaffolding in the moment so that students continue to move forward to mastery. High expectations include mastering grade-level content and applying it with higher order thinking skills.

High expectations are communicated to students by the level, rigor, and quality of instruction we provide to them (Hill, 2017; Schmidt et al., 2015; Schmoker, 2018; TNTP, 2018). If educators provide instruction that is on or above students' grade level, is connected to students' lives, and demands that they work hard to grapple with their learning, then educators are saying to students that their learning is important, they believe they can do it, and they are there to help them.

High expectations are also communicated to students by the relationships educators have with each of them (Boykin and Noguera, 2011; Gorski, 2018; Hill, 2017; Peters, 2006). This can be a bit daunting for secondary educators who teach 125 to 150 students or more each day. It can be daunting for the elementary physical education teacher that teaches all five hundred elementary students in their building over the course of the week. A smaller student-to-teacher ratio can help, but it is not a guarantee of strong student-teacher relationships. Strong student-teacher relationships take deliberate effort on the part of educators.

Strong student-teacher relationships are built on an educator's ability to see each individual student: their strengths, the cultures they navigate throughout each day, and the various positions they occupy in the school, the home, and the community. If you believe you see all your students the same way (I don't see color, etc.) and treat them all the same way, you have most likely failed to develop individual relationships with each of your students (Boykin and Noguera, 2011; Jean-Marie and Mansfield, 2013; Landson-Billings, 1994; Peters, 2006). Review the social justice concepts in chapter 3 once more.

Each student is unique with differences in their personalities and positionality. Educators need to take the time and effort to get to know each of their students: what are their hopes and dreams, their fears, their strengths, and their challenges? Students need to know that their teachers see each of them individually, that they welcome them to the group and are there for them in both the good and the bad times.

A young teacher was made acutely aware of the importance of relationships when she started teaching midway through the school year in a first-grade classroom. This meant that she was walking into a classroom of students that had been together since August and were halfway through their first-grade year. The teacher that she was replacing had resigned for health reasons, and the students had had a dizzying array of substitute teachers over the first semester.

When she arrived for her first day, she found a refrigerator box that had one of the four sides cut out. It sat in the back of the classroom with a child's desk and chair inside. The graffiti on the inside of the box clued her in that some student had spent a considerable amount of time inside the box and had some literacy skills, especially with words not generally acceptable for use at school. When she asked her neighboring teacher about the box, she was told that this is where Robert sat and that it was the only way to keep him from constantly disrupting the class. By the time the students arrived, the box was gone, and Robert's desk and chair were up in the front row.

Robert and the rest of the students were confused by this change, but they accepted it with some hesitancy. Now, just because she had moved Robert out of the box and to the front row did not mean there were no more disruptions by him. It was a process of constant teaching and reinforcing expected classroom behaviors. She spent a good deal of extra time with Robert on the playground, in the lunchroom, and after school. Robert knew that she saw him for all that he was and wanted to include him.

Over the course of that second semester, Robert and the young teacher built a relationship where he knew he was valued. She expected him to contribute to the learning rather than disrupt the class, and she wasn't giving up on him. Their relationship was the basis of their work together to help him become a respected and welcomed member of the class. The teacher was learning that semester as well. She learned that one of the strongest tools she had in her teacher toolbox was an individual relationship with each student. She also learned that for some students it took more time and investment. She learned about doing whatever it takes for each student.

The vast majority of educators pride themselves on their relationships with their students. One of the reasons they went into education is their enjoyment of children and adolescents. They chose to work with our youth. However, there are always some students that do not click immediately with their teacher. They might be shy and try to stay out of sight, or their exuberance is almost more than the teacher can handle at times. It takes a concentrated effort on the part of educators to develop individual relationships with each student.

The staff at a high school, one that was well recognized for student accomplishments and was the pride of the community, took their superintendent to task for suggesting that they needed to work on their student engagement, starting with their relationships with their students. They were very proud of the fact that many of their students had their phone numbers and would call them after hours if they had questions about assignments. They knew the parents of many of their students and even socialized with some of them outside their job. The staff wrote personalized letters of reference for their students and encouraged them in their extracurricular activities.

However, when their student survey results were reviewed by different demographic groups, it told a very different story. Students from white, middle- to upper-class families generally felt that their teachers cared about them as an individual. Students from lower-income families, homes where English was not the primary language, and predominantly families of color did not generally feel that their teachers cared about them or even saw them. These were not the students that had a teacher's phone number to call after hours or the children of parents who socialized with the teachers outside school.

These teachers had incredibly strong relationships with *some* of their students, and it blinded them to the fact that they did not have these relationships with *all* of their students. Some of their students were being marginalized, without intention, and the teachers didn't even realize it. Strong individual relationships with each of our students is an incredible force in supporting student success.

Take time to think about your students who are most often marginalized. What strengths do they bring to the classroom? Do they know what strengths you believe they bring? Do they reach out to you when they need further help with their learning? A strategy that schools have used with great success is identifying their most marginalized students who need additional support. Teachers of these students focus on establishing strong relationships with them.

In addition, other staff in the building are assigned to work on establishing a strong relationship with one of these students so that each identified student has an additional adult in the building looking out for them. These staff work to establish relationships that tell students they are seen and valued. They greet the student each morning, check in at the end of each day, and spend short amounts of time with the student in any way they can find. There is not an expectation for this additional staff member assigned to the child to do any tutoring, etc., but rather just be another adult who sees them for who they are and values them.

Two examples of effective pairings of a student and staff member, who was not one of their teachers, were a custodian and a principal. In the first case, the head custodian offered to be an additional adult friend to a fifth grader who was struggling mightily in school. The custodian was very aware of this child's struggles as the custodian often encountered him sitting in the hallway or, worse yet, had to help put the room back together after the student had an outburst. Over several months, the custodian got to know the student: his strengths (he was a great comedian), his fears, and his hopes.

The student learned when he was feeling pressure, he could go visit Mr. Vince and have a few minutes to destress and recompose himself. He could try out his latest jokes and impersonations with Mr. Vince without disrupting class. He knew Mr. Vince cared about him on both the good days and the tough days. Mr. Vince was critical to this student successfully mastering fifth-grade standards even though he wasn't responsible for any academic instruction. His care and attention enabled this student to stay in class and learn. Mr. Vince was the custodian. He also made an incredible difference in the success of students each and every day.

The second example was a principal in a school with many students from homes that were struggling to keep a roof over their heads and food on the table. In addition, there were a significant number of families that were grappling with mental health issues with very little medical support. There was a student from one of these families that was quickly becoming a frequent flier in the principal's office as he was often sent out of class because he was so disruptive. The principal got to know this student as an individual. He learned that he had a huge interest in and talent for working on cars.

A visitor to the principal's office was startled to find a car transmission sitting in pieces on a cart. Over the course of that year, other parts and pieces of a car engine came and went from the principal's office as the student and the principal worked on them. The student also learned how to manage himself successfully in class and went on to finish as a strong student, mastering the academics in class. This principal worked hard to develop individual relationships with his students and their families and demonstrated to his colleagues the ability to do whatever it takes to ensure each student's success.

WHY WORRY ABOUT STANDARDS

Each state has standards that define the expected learning for students in schools within the state. These are the academic benchmarks to which schools are held accountable. Schools that ensure all students achieve to the highest level expect and support each student in mastering their grade-level standards. Teaching some students only standards below their grade level continues and widens the gap.

Most states have standards that are either based on the Common Core Standards or are the state's variation of these standards. The 1990s saw a movement toward grade-level standards across the country (Hurst et al., 2003). The release of the Common Core Standards in 2010 resulted in the majority of states significantly revising their standards (Common Core State Standards Initiative, 2010). As standards were revised, there was a trend toward greater rigor and more complex thinking skills.

For example, the May 2000 English-Language Arts Content Standards for California Public Schools included the fifth-grade standard for informational text, which required the identification of types of statements:

Expository Critique
2.5 Distinguish facts, supported inferences, and opinions in text. (p. 29)

California Common Core State Standards (2013) for informational text for fifth graders now includes the standard that includes identification of types of statements as well as the integration of knowledge and thinking about how the text was used:

8. Explain how an author uses reasons and evidence to support particular points in a text, identifying which reasons and evidence support which point(s). (p. 16)

Teaching so that all students master the grade-level standards helps to ensure that educators are not unintentionally teaching below-level content to students and thus perpetuating the gap.

Educators should not only identify which standards they are teaching in their lessons but also analyze what they are asking students to do in their lessons to ensure they are teaching to the standards and at the appropriate high level of thinking. Assignment analysis is a good way for professional learning teams to learn and grow together while gaining greater insight into the standards. Take the two sample standards previously mentioned. The first standard from 2000 could easily be assessed by asking students to read a brief paragraph and underline the facts, circle the inferences, and box the opinions. A very basic comprehension activity.

The second standard from 2013 could be assessed by asking students to read a text and identify what points the author is making. The students would be asked to explain what reasons the author provides for each point and/or the evidence for each point, distinguishing between positions and evidence. When explaining the reasoning provided as evidence, students would have to be able to identify facts, opinions, and inferences. Finally, they would have to share the author's points and explain the author's reasoning for each either orally or in written form that shows they are able to identify the points and analyze the support for each point.

Meeting these standards requires more complex thinking than the standards from 2000. Educators working together can help each other create lessons that include the depth and complexity called for in today's standards. Analyzing the assignments given to students by a team of teachers helps educators unpack the level of thinking they are expecting of students. Together, assignments can be developed or revised to ensure students are being asked to engage in higher-level thinking and meet the expectations of the standards each and every day.

It is demoralizing to see student work that demonstrates that what they were being asked to do was not addressing the standards, did not include high-level thinking, or was even appropriate for their grade level. This failure to teach to the level expected for that grade level is what perpetuates the gap. One middle school in a very large northeastern city had all the sixth-grade hallways filled with student colorings of a haunted house scene that had been duplicated on the copy machine. There were approximately 250 sixth graders, and 250 haunted houses were colored and hung on the wall.

The teachers were asked by a visitor what the standard was that they were teaching with these pictures. They could not identify one. When asked what thinking the students had to do to color the pictures, they replied the students had to choose which colors to use. It was not a lesson we would want our own children to be involved in as a sixth grader. It was not a lesson any sixth grader should have been involved in.

Another example, in the same district, was the tenth-grade hallway in a high school. The walls were lined with large sheets of construction paper that were divided into two parts with a line drawn down the center of each sheet. On one side of the sheet the name of a character from the literature that the students had read was written in black marker and the name of another character from the same text was written on the other half of the sheet. Below each character's name were several pictures cut out from magazines.

Again, the teachers were asked what the standard was that was being taught. They replied they were working on comparing characters in a text. The pictures were to represent the traits of the two different characters. There was nothing on the papers that explained why or how the students had determined the traits for the two characters. Remember: these were tenth-grade students. The only writing was the names of the two characters plus the student's name and class period. If your child had been in one of those classes, would you have been satisfied that your child was being instructed at a tenth-grade level?

A probable factor in these totally inappropriate and significantly below-grade-level assignments were the educator's misguided sympathy for their students and their life circumstances. The vast majority of the students in these schools were living in homes greatly impacted by poverty. There was frequent expression by the staff of how unfortunate their students were and how stressful were their life circumstances.

These educators were allowing themselves to engage in deficit thinking (see chapter 3) and creating a Warm and Fuzzy school instead of a Whatever It Takes school. They did not recognize the strengths their students brought to school, including incredible resilience (Brown, 1999), and building on these strengths. Instead, they were handicapping their students by denying them an excellent education.

It is also important that educators be aware of the level of text complexity with which students are expected to interact with today's standards, especially if you have been an educator for many years. An activity to help educators get a quick understanding of the level-text complexity expected by today's standards is to gather copies of the sample titles listed in Common Core State Standards for English Language Arts & Literacy in History/Social Studies, Science, and Technical Subjects (2010, p. 32, 58).

These texts illustrate the complexity, quality, and range of materials students should be able to read and comprehend, both narrative and informational text. Make a pile or box of books that includes a copy of each title from kindergarten through twelfth grade. Do not label the books or put them in order. Make a set of index cards that have one grade level/span as used with these sample texts written on each card (K, 1, 2–3, 4–5, 6–8, 9–10, and 11–college and career ready). Spread the index cards out on a table.

Assign a mixed group of educators (from kindergarten to twelfth grade) to review the pile and sort the books by placing each book by the card that indicates the grade level/span that they believe is represented by this text. Once the texts have been sorted, provide the groups with the pages from the Common Core Standards that list these texts as illustrative of the level of text for each grade level/span. Ask each group to check their sorting with the example list, note the differences, and discuss any insights they gain from this activity. After each group has completed the exercise, ask them to share insights across the larger group.

A common insight from this exercise is that a large number of educators are unaware of the level of text complexity that students are expected to master. They are not aware of the increased expectations with the more recent standards. *Sarah Plain and Tall* by Patricia MacLachlan is a title the author regularly used with fifth-grade students when she was a reading teacher. If she used that title with fifth graders today, she would not be presenting them with the complexity of text current-day standards expect. This book is an example of text complexity for grades two and three.

A second common insight, after looking at the example text, is that educators are concerned about the selection of titles not being representative of the students in their classrooms and/or the interests of their students. Remember these titles are illustrations, *not* texts that our students are required to read. The Common Core Standards do not prescribe that all students read these texts. Once you are familiar with the complexity of texts your students should be grappling with, find texts of the appropriate complexity which interest your students and in which they can see themselves. Use those texts.

One last point about standards needs to be made. Standards are the minimum of what students should know and be able to do at each grade level. You can always teach students beyond the standards. Many students will demonstrate mastery above the standards. However, if you teach students below the standards and expect nothing more, you are enabling the gap. You are marginalizing students.

LESSON DESIGN FOR REACHING ALL STUDENTS

The ongoing debate in education of which way students learn best—through direct and/or explicit instruction or through constructivist instruction—is a false debate as it makes it appear that one method cannot be used in conjunction with the other. We will look at both of these schools of thought in instructional practices, what the evidence says regarding their effectiveness, and how they can be used together for student success.

In the strictest sense, direct instruction methods include the teacher transmitting knowledge directly to students in a clearly structured class where the objectives are defined and shared with the students, and information is presented by the teacher through explanation, modeling, or demonstrations. Students are provided guided practice while the teacher monitors and corrects their understanding as needed. This is providing "intervention" just in time. Students are then given independent practice, their learning assessed and feedback and/or grades given (Archer and Hughes, 2011; Goldenberg, 2012; Hollingsworth and Ybarra, 2009; Slavin, 2012b).

Providing intervention just in time or in the moment requires that the lesson be constructed in such a way that every student is engaged in thinking about and responding to the learning in a way that the teacher can monitor their learning in real time. A host of strategies are available to ensure all students are responding during a lesson such as thumbs up/thumbs down, use of individual white boards, Think-Pair-Share, cooperative learning, and digital individual student response systems.

Research on the efficacy of direct instruction methods range from strong support for ensuring all students learn at high levels (Adams and Engelmann,

1996; Archer and Hughes, 2011; Chall, 2000; Goldenberg, 2006) to mixed reviews with the caveat that direct instruction works well for some skills or when combined with critical thinking applications (Gorski, 2018; Schmoker, 2018; Slavin, 2012a). The mixed results may be due to the fact that, as Slavin (1986) noted, rigorous studies of direct instruction methods are difficult to conduct when teachers in both treatment and control groups already have experience with direct instruction lessons.

Constructivist learning maintains that teachers cannot give students knowledge, but rather they must construct knowledge in their own minds, often through social interaction and application of the information or knowledge. Constructivist lessons often begin with a complex problem to be solved (Slavin, 2012a; Toth and Sousa, 2019). Research on the effectiveness of constructivist learning approaches also includes a wide range of findings (Slavin, 2012a).

This range of findings could be due to the fact that there is great variety in constructivist approaches such as cooperative learning, reciprocal teaching, discovery learning, and self-regulated learning. When reviewing programs that have repeatedly shown high levels of effectiveness, cooperative learning (a constructivist approach) is frequently a characteristic of highly effective programs alongside some explicit instruction (Baye et al., 2019; Pellegrini et al., 2021; Slavin et al., 2009; Slavin, Lake, and Groff, 2009).

Since cooperative learning is a frequent component of programs found to have significant effect on improving learning outcomes for all students, let's take a moment to discuss cooperative learning. It is not uncommon to find classrooms where students are arranged in small groups as they work. Educators in these classrooms often believe that they are using cooperative learning strategies with their students.

Many of these student groups are not cooperative learning groups, but rather student work groups. Some students may be doing the work while others are involved in little, if any, of the learning. This is what often causes parents to be so adamant that they do not want their child participating in "cooperative learning." Their fear is that their child will do the work and another student will get the grade by just riding on the coattails of their child.

However, cooperative learning, when properly crafted, is a powerful tool for increasing academic outcomes and especially for students who are often marginalized and most in need of support to improve outcomes (Boykin and Noguera, 2011; Rohrbeck et al., 2003). Cooperative learning is structured to require both team interdependence and individual accountability. If these components are missing, it is not cooperative learning even if the students are working in a group.

Students work together in a small group to help each other learn. This allows the students in the group to demonstrate and model for each other and engage in discussion with peers about their insights and learning. The success of each group is dependent on all members learning rather than a single group project. Student groups are recognized and celebrated for working together to ensure *all* members of the group learn.

At the conclusion of the learning, students are individually assessed on their learning, and this assessment becomes a part of the student's individual grade, not the work they did in the group (Slavin, 1995, 2012a; Toth and Sousa, 2019). When planning cooperative learning, determine how each group will be monitored to ensure each student is learning. How will the groups be recognized for ensuring each of their members are learning? How will individual students be assessed on their learning? How will this individual assessment be a part of the student's feedback on their learning and/or a part of their grade?

Cooperative learning also requires that students are taught how to work effectively in groups including ensuring all their teammates are listening, sharing their thinking, and reflecting and providing constructive feedback to their peers. Learning to use cooperative learning masterfully takes a good deal of practice, planning, and reflection. Just reading about it is not enough. Master cooperative learning teachers can help their fellow educators to construct lessons that include all the necessary components. Then they can provide another set of eyes for feedback on how it is working in the classroom.

It takes work and plenty of practice to use cooperative learning effectively. However, it will significantly change how you interact with your students in the classroom and greatly improve your ability to ensure every student has immediate feedback and intervention, if needed, to master the day's lesson. It can be a critical support structure contributing to doing away with leveled reading and math groups in a classroom. It is not surprising that in reviews of effective programs so many of them use a type of cooperative learning and require extensive professional learning and practice by educators to master this instructional strategy.

Researchers and thought leaders frequently point out that one of the major differences in the education of our children at schools with high levels of achievement and those without is the types of learning that students are engaged in. Are the students engaged in rote, low-level knowledge and comprehension types of learning, or are they engaged in application of knowledge, critical thinking, and solving of real-life problems? Is the learning meaningful to the students (Boykin and Noguera, 2011; Ferguson, 2007; Gorski, 2018; Schmoker, 2018; TNTP, 2018)?

The commonalities from a review of the programs that repeatedly have been proven to work to ensure all students are highly educated are:

- rigorous grade level content;

- components of explicit instruction: target, demonstrations and modeling, scaffolding, and guided practice;
- social interactions to support and solidify learning (cooperative learning); and
- opportunities for problem solving, critical thinking, and real-life application.

As educators focus on doing whatever it takes to ensure all students are educated to the highest levels, we must ensure that every student masters the grade-level standards, at a minimum, each and every year. Years of research and study show us what works as well as provides a list of programs that have strong evidence of effectiveness with all students. It is time to embrace this knowledge and continuously improve our professional practice so that we are using what we know to harness the strength and power of proven instructional practices.

There are proven programs (see chapters 4 and 5), especially in literacy and mathematics, that can be adopted to provide the support needed to use proven instructional methods. These proven programs include extensive and ongoing professional learning to ensure that what is happening in the classroom is highly effective. This strong effective teaching could eliminate the achievement gap within the near future (Schmoker, 2018; Slavin, 2020). The question is, do we have the will to do whatever it takes?

SUMMING IT UP

This chapter has covered the heart of what happens in schools: instruction. We can summarize what we know is critical to success in the daily instruction as follows. These are the components to provide instruction on rigorous, high-level content to a diverse group of students.

- Know each student individually. What are their strengths, likes, dislikes, and fears?
- Set the expectation for each student to do grade-level work. Provide every student with advanced learning opportunities. Avoid remedial classes or leveled groups.
- Use the standards to guide instruction and the level of thinking expected of students.

Actual lesson design should include the following components:

a. Explicit learning targets connected to students' lives. Students know how they will demonstrate their learning.
b. Activate prior knowledge to link the new learning to what is already known.
c. Explicit instruction on concepts and skills. Chunk the learning if needed.
d. Provide in the moment feedback, correction, and/or clarification when needed.
e. Provide guided practice with close monitoring.

After the basic instruction has occurred, the learning continues with these components:

a. Apply learning to real-life problems requiring transfer of knowledge and critical thinking.
b. Summarize the learning.
c. Independent application that requires critical thinking and problem solving.
d. Independent assessment/performance.
e. Celebration of learning.

Cooperative learning strategies work well at multiple points in the lesson including guided practice, application of the learning, and summarizing the learning. Another way to summarize steps that should be included in developing instruction that is based on research is well illustrated in a graphic developed by the Southeast Regional Educational Laboratory (n.d.), located at Florida State University, and can be found at https://ies.ed.gov/ncee/edlabs/infographics/pdf/REL_SE_Evidence-based_teaching_practices.pdf.

Once again, the division between direct/explicit instruction, often deemed rote and lower-level thinking, and constructivist approaches, often deemed higher-level thinking, is more an argument of academia than practice. Let's look at one example of how explicit instruction and higher-level critical thinking can go hand in hand while teaching reading. It is not too difficult for a teacher to provide explicit instruction in the fundamentals of reading such as decoding long "a" pattern words.

However, when providing instruction in comprehension it often gets more difficult to "show" students what is happening inside the brain of a good reader as they interact with the text to make meaning. Think-Alouds are a strategy that many educators use to help make thinking become visible to the learner. So, for example, if you want to help students learn how to analyze an author's argument and then evaluate the validity of the argument, you provide explicit instruction on how you, as a proficient reader, analyze the text by reading aloud a short text with the students and frequently stopping to tell them what you are thinking while reading.

While reading, you share the questions that are raised in your mind, the connections you make to other things you know, notes that you make in the margins of the text, etc. Once you have completed reading the text, you continue to share your thinking with the students as you review the text and check your understanding/thinking to ensure you found all the author's points in support of their argument. Then you check the points in the argument against previous knowledge and determine if there are points that don't fit the argument and why you think that, or if there are points where you don't know enough to judge their validity.

After providing this explicit instruction, students can work in cooperative groups to read another short text and analyze and evaluate the author's argument or position. Students are expected to share their thinking with their teammates as well as the various groups sharing their thinking with the entire class. During this guided practice, the teacher is circling the room and listening in on all the groups to ensure all students are making progress or providing immediate intervention if not.

After adequate guided practice in small groups, students can then engage in independent practice with feedback and individual assessment of performance. There are many high-level thinking skills educators expect students to master. However, we cannot assume all of them have observed such conversations or debates in their lives outside of school. Students are perfectly capable of doing this thinking work once they know what they are being asked to do. Modeling it for them through Think-Alouds is a great way to make the thinking visible for them so they can also engage in this type of critical thinking.

If you are just starting to use Think-Alouds, you might find it very helpful to practice reading the text and sharing your thinking out loud in an empty room before teaching the lesson. That will give you the space to think about your thinking and the opportunity to practice making it visible before you are in front of students. You can even use sticky notes placed at specific paragraphs in the text to remind yourself to share how your brain was processing a specific point.

As experienced and proficient readers, all the thinking that happens as we interact with a text is often so automatic and fast that it takes some deliberate analysis of our own thinking to slow down and unpack what we are doing. A good resource for learning to use Think-Alouds is Wilhelm's (2012) *Improving Comprehension with Think-Aloud Strategies: Modeling What Good Readers Do*.

REFLECTION

There is a reflection section at the end of each of the remaining chapters of the book. It is intended to help you reflect on your school and district practices as well as your own individual practices. There is also a "Reflections and Next Steps" section at the end of the book that you may wish to use. It will allow you to make notes in one location regarding each of the chapters. This is to help you easily review your thoughts over all the issues raised throughout the book and then identify next steps to take in your own professional practice.

Reflections for chapter 6:

- Individually name your students' strengths, interests, and concerns.

- Who are the students you still need to develop individual relationships with?

- What state standard(s) are you teaching in your current lessons? What higher-level thinking is involved? Is the complexity of the text used appropriate?

- If a visitor asks your students what the target for learning is in the current lesson, what would they say? Do they know how they will demonstrate their learning?

Deeper reflections for chapter 6:

- How do you ensure that you are providing interventions immediately when needed in class and not the next day after grading papers the night before?

- When you have students work in cooperative groups, how do you structure the learning so that teams are held accountable for each student learning? How do you hold students accountable for their individual learning?

Chapter 7

Student Supports

All students must be educated to a high level, mastering the standards and college and/or career ready. That is our goal. We know from our experience as educators that some students will need more supports to reach this goal than others. We also know that some students will demonstrate proficiency in some standards from the minute they walk in our door and will need to be provided opportunities to extend their learning if school is to be a learning place for them as well. How can we ensure all students receive the supports they need? After all, that is how we have been defining equity—whatever it takes for each student to at least master the standards.

In the introduction to this book, we recognized our progress as a country toward ensuring that all students receive a free public education and are educated to the highest level. This progress has been primarily through expanding the definition of students from mainly being white males to including females, students of color, students with disabilities, and students learning English as a second language. The quest to include all students has often required federal legislation and/or judicial rulings after parents, educators, community stakeholders, and advocates have rigorously debated and pushed for such changes.

However, not all students are educated to a high level, as seen in the National Assessment of Educational Progress (NAEP) data. Traditionally marginalized students continue to perform below white and more affluent students. We recognize that while many more students are now inside our schoolhouses than when we began public education in this country, not all students are being educated to the highest levels. We still have students that are marginalized by our system, receiving a lesser education than other students.

We have attempted to provide additional supports for students through developing a host of special programs such as a variety of special education classes, reading labs, math labs, remedial classes, advanced classes, classes for speakers of other languages, classes for gifted and talented students, and so on. Obviously, when looking at student outcomes, these additional supports have not provided the success needed for many of our students. We still have too many students who are marginalized and receive a lesser education than other students. What have we learned about these special programs?

Additional supports for many students began as what we often called "pull-out" programs. Students would leave the regular classroom and receive services in another location such as a special education classroom or an English language development classroom or a special reading classroom. This practice of putting students in special classrooms for additional support services ended up with students being tracked at different academic levels with lesser expectations for learning and lower-level content than in the general classroom (Cunningham and Allington, 1994; Gorski, 2018; Hill 2017; National Council of Teachers of Mathematics, 2018; Schmoker, 2018).

Without access to grade-level standards, expectations, and instruction, it is no wonder that these students did not demonstrate proficiency on grade-level standards and eventually dropped out of school or graduated with a much lesser education than many of their peers. This chapter will review the most common supports or special programs used by schools to provide extra support to students who need it with a focus on how we can provide that support without relegating them to lesser expectations and curriculum. How do we provide students with additional support, when needed, that ensures that they at least master grade-level standards?

TIERED INTERVENTIONS

The enactment of the Individuals with Disabilities Act (20 U.S.C., chapter 33) in April of 1970 guaranteed the right of students with disabilities to a free public education. However, being admitted to the schoolhouse did not ensure that students with disabilities were provided with an education to the highest level as many of their peers without disabilities were provided. The same patterns of lower expectations, a less rigorous curriculum, as well as little or no additional supports provided to master the grade-level curriculum often characterized the education provided to these students (National Association of State Directors of Special Education [NASDSE], 2006).

In an effort to ensure all students were provided the supports needed to succeed in a rigorous curriculum, rather than pulled out to a separate program with different expectations, Response to Intervention (RTI) was endorsed by the NASDSE in 2001. The 2004 reauthorization of the Individuals with Disabilities Education Act (IDEA) allowed school districts to use up to 15 percent of their funds from IDEA for early intervention services for students "who need additional academic and behavioral support to succeed in a general education environment" (20 U.S.C., chapter 33 §1413 (f)(1)).

In addition, this reauthorization focused on providing students with disabilities the supports they need to be educated in the regular classroom to the greatest extent possible, thus giving them access to the grade-level curriculum. Specifically, it is written in code as follows:

> To the maximum extent appropriate, children with disabilities, including children in public or private institutions or other care facilities, are educated with children who are not disabled, and special classes, separate schooling, or other removal of children with disabilities from the regular educational environment occurs only when the nature or severity of the disability of a child is such that education in regular classes with the use of supplementary aids and services cannot be achieved satisfactorily. (20 U.S.C., chapter 33 § 1412 (a) (5) (A))

When students are experiencing difficulties in learning in the regular classroom with the rigorous curriculum and expectations provided to their peers, a "whatever it takes" effort was to be launched to ensure that these students were educated in this core content to a high level as well. When a student is struggling, the first response is not to place them in special education services somewhere away from their peers. The first and follow-up responses are to be the help needed for the student to succeed at the same level as their peers in a regular classroom setting; in other words, tiered interventions need to be provided.

RTI is a process or a framework (not a program) that calls for excellent and research-proven instruction being provided to all students. Then, if needed, additional proven interventions are provided. Student progress is frequently monitored, and the student data guides the decision making regarding instruction and interventions. The NASDSE (2006) defines RTI as "the practice of providing high-quality instruction/intervention matched to student needs and using learning rated over time and level of performance to make important education decisions" (p. 5).

RTI is a Three-Tier Model of School Supports for both academic and behavioral supports (p. 22). Only if excellent and proven instruction and intensive, long-term interventions have been tried and failed should a child be evaluated for special education services (NASDSE, 2006; Slavin, 2012a). In recent years a tiered framework for intervention called a multi-tiered system of support (MTSS) has gained favor in many states over RTI. An analysis of state guidance (Bailey, 2019) found more than thirty state departments of education used the term MTSS to refer to a tiered support system, while eight used RTI with the remaining states using a state-specific name.

The reasons given for the change in name of a tiered support system from RTI to MTSS are several, including MTSS includes a focus on supports for both academics and behavior, RTI had erroneously become synonymous with special education and needed to be rebranded, and a shift by the U.S. Department of Education to the use of MTSS. However, it should be noted that the RTI guidance provided by the NASDSE early on included behavior support as a part of their model (NASDSE, 2006, p. 22). The name is less important than ensuring the supports needed are provided so that all students are mastering the standards.

According to the guidance provided by the NASDSE (2006), 80 percent of our students should be able to perform at the highest levels, mastering standards in the general education program: the regular classroom. This is Tier 1 and is described as core instruction that is both preventive and proactive. Think about this for a minute. Do our NAEP reading and mathematics scores (as discussed in chapters 4 and 5) reflect that 80 percent of our students are proficient in basic reading and mathematics?

Unfortunately, and at the great detriment to our children, these outcomes tell us that we are not achieving this goal with 80 percent of our students in classrooms across this country. Tier 1 is the first place we need to redesign our system in order to ensure our students achieve the education they deserve (see chapters 4, 5, and 6). Tier 1 instruction must use proven programs and strategies that are proactive in ensuring the vast majority of students are able to demonstrate proficiency at or above grade level (Calderon, 2012).

Fien, Chard, and Baker (2021) assert that it is the institutional racism in our education system that results in the inequities seen in literacy outcomes for students. They maintain that if evidence-based practices were used at scale and efficacy of teaching was provided to all students, not just the privileged, we would achieve the goal of all students being educated to a high level.

Slavin et al. (1991) have long advocated that the goal could be reached with prevention and early intensive intervention to ensure students perform at grade level and are kept in grade-level classes rather than being placed in special education classrooms with a lower-level curriculum. They call it "never-streaming" as opposed to the special education term of mainstreaming (today, we call it inclusion), referring to the effort to move students with disabilities from special education classrooms into regular education classrooms.

Schmoker (2018) also makes the argument that with excellent, proven instruction the vast majority of students will master grade-level standards with no additional support. The number of students needing additional support on top of the regular classroom instruction should be very small. In a typical class of twenty-five students, a least twenty of the students should be mastering grade-level standards without additional support beyond Tier 1.

Using the same NASDSE (2006) guidance document, "Response to Intervention: Policy Considerations and Implementation," another 15 percent of our students should be able to reach this goal with *additional* targeted, proven, small-group intervention. This is Tier 2 of the model. In our example of twenty-five students in a classroom, this means that approximately four of the students will need both Tier 1 and Tier 2 support to master the standards.

Bear in mind that Tier 2 is additional support on top of excellent classroom instruction, not in lieu of. If a student is removed from class during literacy instruction to receive their Tier 2 or 3 literacy instruction, this student is not receiving the excellent classroom instruction that they must receive before receiving highly targeted small-group interventions. Also, note that the NASDSE calls for *targeted* instruction: support that is specific to ensuring the child can succeed in the regular classroom's instruction.

Too many times students are pulled out by reading teachers for their small-group intervention only to be presented with instruction that has nothing to do with what the child is being presented with during literacy instruction in the classroom. Erroneously, it is prevalent for Tier 2 interventions to replace or reduce access to core instruction for struggling readers (Fien, Chard, and Baker, 2021). There has been no coordination between the classroom teacher and the reading teacher, and the student is at a deficit because of this. Tier 2 is meant to supplement, not replace Tier 1 instruction.

The final 5 percent of our students, according to NASDSE (2006) guidance, will often need intensive and individual intervention. In our example of twenty-five students in a classroom, this equates to one student. This is Tier 3 of the model of school supports. If you question the reality of only 5 percent or less of our students needing Tier 3 interventions which are individual and intense, then consider these data.

In the 42nd Annual Report to Congress on the implementation of IDEA (Office of Special Education and Rehabilitative Services, 2020), the most recent data from 2018 indicates that of our 65,540,598 children ages six to twenty-one, only 9.5 percent of them had been determined to qualify for special education services. These services include all disabilities under IDEA: autism, deaf-blindness, emotional disturbance, hearing impairment, intellectual disability, multiple disabilities, orthopedic impairment, other health impairment, specific learning disability, speech or language impairment, traumatic brain injury, and visual impairment.

As educators are aware, each of these various disabilities manifests on a continuum. Some students with disabilities need only minimal support, while others need extensive supports. The vast majority of students, when provided with excellent and proven instruction, can master grade-level standards without Tier 3 supports. The point is, if schools were doing the job they should be doing at Tier 1, only a small group of students will need additional support at Tier 2 and even fewer at Tier 3.

If your Tier 1 instructional program has significant numbers of students not succeeding (often disproportionately students of color, from poverty, learning English as a second language, or with a disability as seen in the NAEP

Disability[a]	2009	2010	2011	2012	2013	2014	2015	2016	2017	2018
All disabilities below	8.4	8.3	8.2	8.2	8.3	8.5	8.7	8.8	9.2	9.2
Autism	0.5	0.5	0.6	0.7	0.7	0.8	0.8	0.9	0.9	1.0
Deaf-blindness	#	#	#	#	#	#	#	#	#	#
Emotional disturbance	0.6	0.6	0.5	0.5	0.5	0.5	0.5	0.5	0.5	0.5
Hearing impairment	0.1	0.1	0.1	0.1	0.1	0.1	0.1	0.1	0.1	0.1
Intellectual disability	0.7	0.6	0.6	0.6	0.6	0.6	0.6	0.6	0.6	0.6
Multiple disabilities	0.2	0.2	0.2	0.2	0.2	0.2	0.2	0.2	0.2	0.2
Orthopedic impairment	0.1	0.1	0.1	0.1	0.1	0.1	0.1	0.1	0.1	0.1
Other health impairment	1.0	1.0	1.1	1.1	1.2	1.3	1.3	1.4	1.5	1.5
Specific learning disability	3.6	3.5	3.4	3.4	3.4	3.4	3.4	3.5	3.5	3.6
Speech or language impairment	1.6	1.6	1.5	1.5	1.5	1.5	1.5	1.5	1.5	1.6
Traumatic brain injury	#	#	#	#	#	#	#	#	#	#
Visual impairment	#	#	#	#	#	#	#	#	#	#

Percentage was non-zero but less than 0.05 or 5/100 of 1 percent.

Figure 7.1
Source: Office of Special Education and Rehabilitative Services, 2020, p. 43.

scores), then you have an equity problem. Your school or district has a culture and/or systems that are not allowing whatever it takes to ensure that all students are achieving at the highest levels.

ACADEMIC SUPPORTS

Entire books could be and have been written on academic and behavioral supports that can be used to ensure student success at Tiers 1, 2, and 3. This book will discuss some of the most successful instructional supports that help ensure that students are mastering a rigorous grade-level curriculum. We have discussed the need to use research-proven programs for instruction in the regular classroom, especially for literacy and mathematics, and that excellent instruction at Tier 1 is critical to all students' success.

When an instructional method that is proven to meet the needs of the vast majority of students is used in the classroom, students with mild disabilities are able to learn much more (Calhoun and Elliott, 1977; Roach and Elliott 2006; Schmoker, 2018). Neitzel et al. (2021) found that whole-class instruction that serves all students, including struggling readers, can solve the difficulties that many students encounter. These whole-class programs most often included the use of cooperative learning. They noted that excellent literacy instruction throughout grades kindergarten to twelve can ensure ongoing success for struggling students.

Remember the discussion in chapter 5 about the need for academic literacy instruction throughout the content areas in order to ensure equity for all students? If academic literacy is not a part of your regular instruction across the content areas, you are not serving all students. Swanson and Hoskyn (1998) presented this same idea, but from a flipped viewpoint. They argued that the use of effective instructional strategies for students with disabilities in the regular classroom resulted in improved outcomes for all students.

Multiple researchers (Gersten et al., 2020; Vaugh et al., 2019; Neitzel et al., 2021) have all found that Tier 2 and 3 interventions can produce positive effects for struggling students, especially in literacy. Fien, Chard, and Baker (2021) argue that schools using comprehensive tiered systems of support are well suited to the use of research-proven reading practices. This is what schools should be doing.

What instructional methods and programs are you using in your school and/or district? Are the vast majority of your students succeeding with Tier 1 instruction? Is Tier 2 *additional* support and *aligned* with the core curriculum for a small number of students that need it in your district or school? What improvements need to be made to ensure you are doing whatever it takes to ensure all students master grade-level standards?

Inclusion

Inclusion is a type of academic support for students that in the past have traditionally been pulled out of the regular education classroom for special services (special education, English language development, special reading, etc.). Not being included in the regular classroom denied these students access to the grade-level curriculum and instruction and subjected them to lower expectations. These pull-out classes often provided no credit toward graduation and frequently made students feel like lesser scholars than most of their peers (Honigsfeld and Dove, 2015; Slavin, 2012a).

However, making the change to include these children in the regular classroom is not to say they will not need additional support. First and foremost, the classroom instruction must be excellent instruction and research proven so that the vast majority of the students are successful in mastering the content. For the few students who need additional support, this may be provided by the general education teacher in the regular classroom, by additional staff in the regular classroom, or in a short tutoring session outside the regular classroom *at a time when the student is not missing core instruction.*

When additional support is provided by a second staff member in the regular classroom, it may be a specialist teacher (special education, English language development, or reading specialist) or a paraprofessional working collaboratively with the general education teacher (Hanline and Daley, 2002; McLesky and Waldron 2002; Vaughn et al., 2007). In addition, more regular classroom teachers are expanding their skills to include expertise in English language development or special education to ensure that their classroom instruction is structured to support their students with these needs.

Two teachers working together in the same classroom is often called co-teaching or team teaching. Each teacher brings expertise to the instructional process so they must be equal partners in the planning, instruction, and assessment (Honingsfeld and Dove, 2015). Teachers collaborating together can be very beneficial to students needing support as it increases expectations, ensures instruction in grade-level curriculum with a content expert, provides instructional expertise in intervention supports, connects them with their peers, and improves student beliefs in their own abilities (Honingsfeld and Dove, 2015; Murawski and Dieker, 2004).

Murawski and Lochner (2011) and Murawski and Swanson (2001) found that co-teaching in secondary schools was an effective method of reaching the needs of a diverse classroom. Two teachers in a regular classroom can be beneficial to all the students in that they have access to stronger lessons developed by a team of experts, have the opportunity for specialized instruction when needed (regardless of identification), have increased opportunity to interact with a teacher, and benefit from the increased diversity in the classroom (Ferguson, Desjarlais, and Meyer, 2000; Mulholland and O'Conner, 2016; Murawski and Dieker, 2004).

There are multiple conceptualizations in the educational literature concerning the different structures that can be used when co-teaching. Honingsfeld and Dove's (2015) list of models is excellent as each iteration includes both teachers working as equals and contributing their professional expertise to the learning. Their models respect the expertise of the content teacher and the expertise of the instructional specialist (special education, English language development, reading, etc.).

Their list includes seven different models with the first two being the most sophisticated, highlighting the expertise of the two different educators (Honingsfeld and Dove, 2015):

- One group: One lead teacher and one teacher "teaching on purpose" (i.e., providing a mini-lesson in the larger lesson, pre-teaching a concept, or skill)
- One group: two teachers teach the same content (i.e., ping-ponging back and forth between the two teachers as a content teacher presents content while a language development teacher presents the literacy skills involved in the content)

The remaining models include:

- One group of students: one teaches, one assesses

- Two groups of students: two teachers teach the same content
- Two groups of students: one teacher pre-teaches; the second teaches alternative information
- Two groups of students: one teacher re-teaches; one teacher teaches alternative information
- Multiple groups of students: two teachers monitor and teach

A co-teaching team will not necessarily use the same model each day, but rather the model that best suits the needs of the students for that day's instruction. The important component when co-teaching is that both teachers are equals in the classroom (Pratt, 2014). Teachers may believe they are co-teaching as one teacher acts as an assistant to the other teacher. This is not co-teaching. The expertise of both teachers is not being accessed. This is a terrible loss of expertise and waste of resources. Remember, we are doing whatever it takes to ensure each student is successful. It takes all of our expertise to make this happen.

Co-teaching colleagues need to have shared educational beliefs such as a commitment to equity, inclusive behaviors, a strong focus on student outcomes, and the valuing of diversity (Jortveit and Kovac, 2021). Even with well-matched professionals, successful co-teaching doesn't just happen. It takes collaborative planning and preparation by the teachers. These teachers must have time built into their schedule to do this critical planning work. Building leaders must ensure that this time is provided to ensure the effectiveness of this practice (Fuchs, Fuchs, and Fernstrom, 1993; Hosingsfeld and Dove, 2015; Murawski and Dieker, 2004).

Before beginning to plan, the co-teachers need to make sure they have a shared understanding of how they will handle discipline, homework, grading and assessing, parent contacts, cooperative learning, and other classroom management issues (Murawski and Dieker, 2004). When planning, the content teacher uses their expertise to identify the content standards to be addressed. The specialist teacher uses their expertise to identify Individualized Education Programs or language goals to be addressed and modifications and/or supports that will help the students master the content. Then the planning involves melding what is to be taught with how it will be taught and assessed.

Another critical factor to make co-teaching successful is scheduling students and teachers (Murawski and Dieker, 2004). At the elementary level, if every teacher is teaching mathematics during the same time period it makes it difficult to have a co-teacher in each classroom during math instruction unless you have a co-teacher for every regular classroom, a budgetary impossibility. These schools may develop their schedules so that English language development teachers can work with fourth-grade math classes in the morning and fifth-grade math classes in the afternoon.

Schools may also cluster their English learners into several classrooms, with no more than one-third of the class population being English learners to ensure diversity in the classroom and native English-speaking peers to provide strong role models. In addition, they may often pair two students in a classroom that are native speakers of the same language if one student is a recent arrival with little to no English and the other student has a greater command of English. This allows the new arrival to have a peer that helps them acclimate to the classroom and begin developing English skills.

In the same way, students in need of special education services may be clustered into several classrooms to reduce the number of classrooms in which a special education teacher is co-teaching while also ensuring the number of students needing additional services does not exceed one-third of the class size to ensure diversity, provide strong peer role models, and avoid the subconscious lowering of expectations and/or standards.

Scheduling classes at the secondary level is always a huge puzzle. Scheduling students into classes when a co-teacher will be there makes it more difficult. The improved outcomes in mastering standards and obtaining graduation credits make it worth the effort. Try to keep the number of students in need of co-teaching support to one-third of the class and keep the number of teachers a specialist is co-teaching with small to ensure thorough planning. An example is a school with four Algebra I teachers: two may co-teach with an English language development teacher and two with a special education teacher, distributing the students as such.

There are schools where the number of students in need of English language development support comprise the majority of the population, making impossible the rule of thumb of no more than one-third of the class such students. These schools are wonderful, exciting places to work. However, it does require that all teachers have skills for working with language learners. Professional learning opportunities and hiring practices need to reflect the expectation for all teachers to have skills for working with English learners.

It is beneficial to the school and/or district if they pay for their teachers to take the additional courses needed to become dual-endorsed in English language development. One such school had 80 percent of its population identified as English language learners. Years of tradition had all of these students leaving their regular classroom each day for thirty minutes of instruction in a language lab. Not only were many of the students missing critical literacy and mathematics instruction, but a large number of students were on the move every thirty minutes.

After taking a close look at what was happening, leadership suggested the school move to a model where support for English learners was provided in every classroom so that students were receiving grade-level appropriate instruction in literacy and mathematics with language supports. They adopted this new model. The school provided extensive professional learning for staff as well as paying for teachers to earn the extra credits needed to obtain a second endorsement as an English language development teacher. They gained the highly skilled professionals needed and teachers received pay increases by moving up on the salary schedule.

Resources for Co-Teaching:

- *Collaborative Teaching in Secondary Schools: Making the Co-Teaching Marriage Work* (2009), by Wendy W. Murawski
- *Elevating Co-Teaching through UDL* (2016), by Elizabeth Stein
- *Collaboration and Co-Teaching: Strategies for English Learners* (2010), by Andrea Honingsfeld and Maria G. Dove

Scaffolding

Scaffolding is a term introduced in the discussion of instruction by Wood, Bruner, and Ross (1976) as a metaphor to illustrate the support provided by a teacher to help students master a concept that they are unable to master on their own. It is additional support provided only when the student needs it to master the rigorous content and is *connected* to knowledge or skills the student already possesses (Honingsfeld and Dove, 2015; Lipscomb, Swanson, and West, 2010).

Scaffolding is a critical component of excellent instruction that allows for students' individual needs to be met (Larkin, 2001). Scaffolding is not intended to "water down" the curriculum, but rather allow all students to master rigorous content (Nordmeyer et al., 2021). Scaffolding includes actions taken by the teacher that are very intentional: focused on helping the student master the learning objective or standard identified for that unit of instruction. The final learning outcome is not simplified.

Support or scaffolding is provided immediately when learning breaks down. Scaffolding is also a very collaborative effort between the teacher and the student as the teacher responds to the student's efforts, either reframing their learning or expanding upon their learning. Initially the support or scaffolding is often very structured and then is gradually withdrawn or "faded" when the student is able to perform on their own (Applebee and Langer, 1983; Lipscomb, Swanson, and West, 2010; Slavin, 2012a). Some of the teaching moves that could be used as a part of scaffolding are listed subsequently.

Scaffold Instruction Examples

Pre-teaching or front loading is the process of teaching knowledge and skills to select students before a lesson with the larger class. This allows these students to begin the learning process earlier to enable success with the lesson in the larger classroom setting. For example, a student who is reading below grade level may be presented with key vocabulary, concepts, and background knowledge prior to the class lesson. The student can practice reading parts of the text that will be used in the instruction. This enables the student to participate more fully and successfully in the class lesson.

Teaching prerequisites is the process of teaching skills or knowledge that a student does not have before the class lesson in order for the student to succeed in the class lesson. This could be a part of pre-teaching or front loading, or it could be entirely separate if a child needs support in learning what was intended to be mastered at an earlier level. For example, a student is taught to find common denominators before a lesson on dividing fractions. This pre-teaching must be done before the regular class lesson begins so that the student is able to fully participate in classroom instruction with their peers.

Chunking is the process of breaking concepts into smaller or individual parts. For example, when teaching students to count change to one dollar, you first need to ensure they can count from one to one hundred, count by five, count by ten, and count by twenty-five. Then students must recognize and know the values of a penny, nickel, dime, and quarter. Once they have these skills, you can then begin working on counting change to one dollar. Chunking the learning requires the teacher to conduct a task analysis regarding the individual skills and knowledge required for the student to master the objective or standard for the unit of learning.

Connecting to prior knowledge is the process of starting with what the students already know and can do. Students are reminded of what they already know and then are guided with transferring the knowledge to the new learning. Making these connections in an overt way is especially important for students with limited background knowledge in the content and for language learners.

For example, if students were going to be reading a text about a camping trip but had little to no experience camping, the teacher might ask students to recall what it was like when the class walked down to the neighborhood park to eat lunch. After talking about the wind blowing, the trees, eating outdoors, the bugs, etc., the teacher might ask the students what they would have needed if they were going to spend the night sleeping in the park. This launches a conversation that then can help students transition to understanding camping.

Visual aids, video, and other media could include a short media clip, a recording of sounds or people talking about an experience, actual objects that can be experienced or realia, and pictures. They help students build background knowledge in preparation for new learning. For example, continuing with the camping story, the teacher erects a small tent in the classroom for students to experience what a tent might look like and feel like when you crawl inside. Ever-increasing media resources make it easier to help students virtually experience things and places they might not be able to otherwise, such as observing elephants in the wild.

Modeling and/or Think-Alouds is the process of the teacher demonstrating how something is done or a skill is used or saying out loud what they are thinking about and the connections they are making as they read a passage aloud. Modeling can be as simple as skipping to help a language learner understand the word skip or working through an algebraic equation one step at a time. Think-Alouds help students understand the processes that a proficient learner goes through in their mind when taking in new information and developing new learning. (See chapter 5 for more information on Think-Alouds.)

Additional practice with gradual release of responsibility is the process of providing the student with more practice opportunities, often with the educator prompting the students on the steps to take in order to solve the problem, decode long "a" pattern words, write a paragraph, notate the chemical formula, etc. As the student practices, the educator reduces the frequency of prompts to the multi-step process until the student is able to complete the problem or process on their own.

Facilitating meta-cognitive strategies includes Think-Alouds where educators share their mental processing of information as they read text or take in information. Many of these processes are meta-cognitive strategies that we use as mature learners. Students often need to be reminded to use them. Educators can facilitate this by pausing the instruction and asking students to think about what questions they have after reading a paragraph or tell how they would paraphrase a paragraph, etc. Taking a pause during instruction and reminding students to think meta-cognitively is another way to support students when the learning gets difficult.

Graphic organizers use simple diagrams and limited text to visualize ideas. There are endless graphic organizers used by educators and students. Venn diagrams, T-charts, KWL charts, concept maps, sequence/flow charts, cause and effect, and spider graphs are all commonly used. Graphic organizers are helpful to organize a large amount of information into a simple format. They are especially good for brainstorming, summarizing, or using with students struggling with the written or spoken language.

Sentence frames/starters provide students with a partially constructed sentence that they can then complete to show they understand the content while receiving support in their language development. For example, _____ is a type of _____ because it has _____. Or, I agree with _____ because _____ confirms it.

Memory aids provide students with aids to help them with recall of basic information, especially if they have not yet had time to memorize the information or memorization is difficult for them. Such aids assist with reducing the cognitive load or freeing up more working memory so that the student can better focus on the problem. For example, provide students with a hundreds chart that they can use to help them count by two, five, or ten, or an alphabet chart as they are looking up words in the dictionary, or multiplication tables that can help them remember what nine times nine is while working on a much more complicated problem.

It is important to ensure that students understand the *concepts* of counting by different numbers, alphabetizing, or multiplying as they use these skills. However, understanding can come well before the memorization of these facts becomes part of the student's body of knowledge. These aids can help them engage in real-life problem-solving activities without getting too bogged down.

Writing supports. For some students, the physical act of writing can impede the thinking and/or drafting process. Allowing students to record their thoughts as they speak them or even using a voice-to-text application can help them communicate their thinking without getting sidetracked by the physical process of writing. After capturing their thinking, the student can then go back and work on putting their thinking into a written format. The teacher can even serve as the recorder, writing down the main points that student tells them they want to communicate and then letting the student use that outline to construct their text.

Adaptive technologies help students with more severe physical disabilities participate more fully in the learning. Students with limited motor control, visual impairments, hearing impairments, and speech impairments can particularly find these technologies useful for inclusive participation in the learning process. The support these technologies provide students, as well as their availability, is rapidly growing.

While these are some of the teaching moves that can be used as scaffolding, it is by no means an exhaustive list. Techniques that educators can use to scaffold learning for students are also techniques used in excellent instruction. They can be a part of the whole class lesson or provided to just a few students as additional support. As educators, if we are constantly checking our students' understanding as they progress through a lesson, we know when they are not understanding and are able to in the moment provide additional support or scaffolding so that students master the learning during the unit and do not have to catch up after the fact.

Tutoring

Tutoring can provide additional support to struggling learners through the use of peer tutors, small-group tutoring with a teacher or a paraprofessional, or one-to-one tutoring with a teacher or a paraprofessional. There are also some schools that use adult volunteers to "tutor" students or serve as a reading buddy to a student. Tutoring can be a Tier 2 or Tier 3 support *if* it is provided in addition to an excellent Tier 1 instruction program and the tutoring is tightly aligned with and supports the Tier 1 instruction.

Tutoring sessions in school are usually thirty to sixty minutes long and serve a small group of students (two to five) that have very similar needs. Tutoring as a Tier 2 or Tier 3 support can also be a method of providing additional time for mastering core literacy or mathematics content. The positive effects of expert tutoring have been noted by Allington (2012). The vast majority of programs with strong evidence of effectiveness for struggling readers on the Evidence for ESSA website (https://www.evidenceforessa.org/programs/reading) are or have tutoring programs.

Neitzel et al.'s (2021) most recent review of quantitative research on programs for struggling readers found strong positive effects of one-to-one and small-group tutoring, with one-to-one being only slightly more effective. Even more significantly, they found that teachers were no more effective at tutoring than paraprofessionals when the tutoring program was tightly structured and provided extensive training for the tutor. They did not find a positive effect for tutoring in the form of technology adaptive instruction. Tutoring has been found to have a significant impact for students struggling with mathematics as well (Pellegrini et al., 2021).

Note that these effective tutoring programs are structured programs that are replicable and have demonstrated their effectiveness in rigorous research. There was no evidence of unstructured, random tutoring proving to be reliably effective for students struggling with reading. This reinforces Fien, Chard, and Baker's (2021) caution that the majority of interventions do not work, so it is essential that schools use intervention programs that are proven.

The implications of these findings are significant for schools. First, the use of research-proven programs greatly increases the success of tutoring programs. Secondly, small-group tutoring is nearly as effective as one-to-one tutoring. If small-group tutoring is used for students needing Tier 2 supports in addition to Tier 1, many more students can be served by a single staff member, stretching limited resources.

In addition, if the school is using a proven program that is well structured and provides in-depth training to the staff members executing the program, the success rate with paraprofessionals is as significant as with a licensed teacher. This can be very impactful on a school's budget because often two paraprofessionals can be secured for the price of one teacher, once again increasing the number of students that can be served. Paraprofessionals with good training and the support and supervision of a reading specialist can expand the reach and impact of the school's tutoring program.

The evidence is mixed and very limited on the long-term impact of tutoring for students with reading difficulties (Neitzel et al., 2021). These reviewers recommend schools ensure their core reading program includes appropriate interventions throughout a child's education as needed. This aligns with the argument that instruction in literacy from kindergarten to grade twelve is imperative. Literacy instruction, and especially academic literacy at the secondary level, must be an integral part of education to ensure that all students are being educated to the highest level.

Additional Time

Providing additional learning time can be one way of doing whatever it takes to ensure all students at least master the standards and graduate college and/or career ready. Additional time for mastering core content such as literacy and mathematics can be provided within the school day with an additional period for tutoring or support in the core curriculum. However, this additional time comes at the loss of something else, so educators need to be extremely thoughtful about what is eliminated in order to create this additional time and ensure that students are still able to participate in curriculum areas or classes that are most interesting and engaging to the individual students. Additional time may also be provided before school, after school, and during school vacations such as during the summer.

Allington (2012) cautions that additional time should not be added to the day or year until it is ensured that the normally allocated time is being used to the maximum, including:

- programming consists of proven programs and practices delivered by expert educators,
- appropriate grade-level content is provided, and
- time on task is maximized and interruptions to the learning have been eliminated or greatly reduced.

Slavin (2012a) reviews ways to avoid losing instructional time. He recommends starting instruction promptly at the start of class and teaching until the very end; preventing interruptions and avoiding administrative duties during learning time, including stopping for late students (address them after class); having well-established class routines for procedures such as using the restroom or sharpening pencils; maintaining a rapid pace of instruction; and reducing the amount of time spent on discipline during instruction (again, address this after class). Well-planned, well-prepared, and well-presented lessons are also essential for reducing the loss of instructional time.

Additional learning opportunities after school were greatly expanded with the renewal of the Elementary and Secondary Education Act under the title of No Child Left Behind. Schools that failed to meet adequate yearly progress for three consecutive years were required to offer supplemental education to students eligible for free or reduced-price meals. This resulted in a huge increase in afterschool tutoring services provided by both public and private groups. These programs were to be supportive of the state's academic standards and improve student achievement (U.S. Department of Education, 2009).

A meta-analysis conducted by Chappell et al. (2011) found that the overall effect on student achievement by these programs was very small. They did find that programs that used well-trained tutors with four-year degrees, a prescribed curriculum, and one-to-one tutoring had a greater impact on student achievement. In addition, a quasi-experimental study was done by Munoz, Chang, and Ross (2012) about students receiving afterschool tutoring in reading and/or mathematics. This study found small positive effects but not to the degree of being statistically significant.

They determined that at best the afterschool tutoring added an additional thirty to forty hours to the school year, or less than two weeks. Slavin (2012a) also found that to improve student outcomes, afterschool programs needed to be treated more as an extension of the academic day and include well-organized coursework, rather than an add on with an unrelated curriculum.

Summer school or programs are another way to add learning time. Reviews of summer school generally find that it benefits student achievement, especially for those students living in poverty (Allington and McGill-Franzen, 2018; Borman and Boulay 2004). Allington and McGill-Franzen (2018) concluded that the achievement gap between students grows substantially over the course of elementary school, despite the fact that students in both high-poverty and low-poverty schools make similar gains during the school year. They argue that the accumulating achievement gap is the result of summer vacation with students in schools with little poverty having access during the summer to enrichment programs, camps, and literacy opportunities at home that students in high-poverty schools do not usually have.

Their review also found that the number of books in a student's home was almost as good a predictor of student reading achievement as the student's socioeconomic status. Therefore, in order to do whatever it takes to ensure all students are reading on or above grade level, Allington and McGill-Franzen (2018) assert that schools must do more to ensure students living in poverty have a year-round supply of interesting books to read both at school and at home.

In a series of studies, McGill-Franzen and Allington (2018) found that students living in poverty that were given free books over the summer made as much growth as those that attended summer school, especially when the children were allowed to select the free books that they were given. In a matched control study, they found that there was a statistically significant difference in reading growth over the summer by the group that was provided free books than by the group that did not receive summer books.

They warn that summer reading should not be seen as more school or homework, but rather appeal to the student's interests. Allington and McGill-Franzen's *Summer Reading: Closing the Reading Achievement Gap*, second edition, contains the evidence for their arguments as well as ideas on how to implement summer reading programs that provide books for students living in poverty that the students find interesting and engaging.

One summer reading program that worked with elementary students living in poverty in the inner city met twice a week. They gathered at a community center for fun activities around reading. For example, the stories shared by the facilitators on one day might have been multiple versions of "Cinderella" from various cultures. Then students would head to a park for lunch and a walk through the woods to find a castle (an old Victorian house). They were welcomed inside to a large display of books on tables. They selected a book to keep. There was a large variety so students could select more "Cinderella" stories or something completely different.

The second day of the week might be focused around folktales that involved drums with a local drummer giving a demonstration for the students. Then students engaged in some drumming exercises using construction buckets and their hands. The day again ended with students selecting a book to keep. A local group of retirees made each of the students a small bookshelf that they were given so that they had a place to keep their growing book collection. Each week throughout the summer, the sessions focused on building excitement and connections around reading while providing students with free books that they selected.

Another summer reading program of note was constructed around the summer food program for those students qualifying for free or reduced-price meals. There were multiple serving locations throughout the county. However, at least one day a week each site also included a visit from a special truck and trailer that had been outfitted as a book mobile. The students had lunch while enjoying a special presentation from a librarian, local geologist, musician, etc. Then the students selected a couple of books from the truck to keep and read for the week.

The following week the truck returned, and students again participated in a special program, returned the books from the previous week, and selected new books to read for that week. Students started coming for the food and soon found themselves engaged in fun reading activities. This arrangement also eliminated the need for parents or older siblings to take the elementary students to a local library on a regular basis to select books for reading, which seldom happened due to their long work hours. The library and lunch came to them.

An additional way to add time for learning is to lengthen the school day and/or year. This is a less frequently used method. However, research shows that adding significant instructional time to the school year results in improved student outcomes (Fraizer and Morrison, 1998; Patall, Cooper, and Allen, 2010). Adding time to the school day often takes negotiations with teacher associations, rearranging of transportation and other support services, and reallocating fiscal resources to pay for it. It is not easy, but it is worth the effort for students who need the time to master the rigorous standards.

Staff at a struggling school proposed to administration that an additional hour be added to their day since most of the students were reading below level and were home alone after school. This request was denied due to scheduling difficulties. The buses in that district each ran two routes a day. If the school day was extended for an hour, the school would need bus service in the morning on the early route and service in the afternoon on the late route, eliminating the ability to use that bus for two routes. This was before the current bus driver shortage. The district declined to take on the expense of an additional route to give students more time for learning.

Years later, in that same district, the board reconstituted a different school due to more than twenty years of poor performance. As a part of this change, the staff asked to extend the school year and day. This school served a very densely populated and high-poverty area with no buses needed to get students to school. The teachers' association was on board with extending the time with additional pay for the staff, so permission was granted. They calculated the additional hour each day plus four weeks added to the year to provide the equivalent of six more weeks of instruction. In five years, the school moved from being one of the worst to one of the best.

Another school in a different city had an extended school year due to the number of language learners it served. The different calendar caused the district to deal with two different bus schedules and a lot of other juggling of schedules for staffing, student lunches, professional learning, etc. They did it as a point of pride that they were providing whatever it took for those students. The only problem was that this was not their only school with a high number of English language learners. They did not provide the opportunity to the other schools, who had students who could have greatly benefited from additional learning time as well.

SPECIAL PROGRAMS BY GROUP

This chapter on special supports starts with the idea of a tiered system of support in schools for any and all learners. The first tier, which should completely meet the needs of at least 80 percent of the students, is an excellent and rigorous curriculum delivered through a proven instructional program. This first tier also provides significant support to those students that need additional support at Tier 2 and/or Tier 3. Without a solid Tier 1 instructional system, Tiers 2 and 3 are bound to fail. Tier 1 is the foundation for all students' learning. It must be rigorous and proven effective for all students.

Equity for all students, or doing whatever it takes to ensure all students graduate high school college and career ready, requires educators to ensure that daily instruction is rigorous and proven to meet the needs of the vast majority of their students. If only 40, 50, 60, or even 70 percent of students are demonstrating proficiency in literacy and mathematics, they are not being provided instruction that meets the needs of the vast majority of students.

After it has been ensured that there is a rigorous and proven program for Tier 1 instruction, there will need to be proven programs and practices for Tiers 2 and 3, as a small number of students will need these additional supports on top of Tier 1. We have reviewed how supports at Tiers 2 and 3 can be provided through inclusive practices, scaffolding of instruction, tutoring, and additional time. All of these supports can be used for any student needing them, regardless of how they are identified.

However, since our education system is focused on identifying students in some specific groups for the purposes of legal mandates, accountability, and funding, we will take some time to review what we know from the body of educational research about how to best serve students in some frequently identified groups including students with disabilities, students learning English as a second language, students identified as gifted, and students engaged in advanced opportunity classes.

Special Education Programs

Special education includes services provided to students with disabilities in addition to the provision of the general education program. Public Law 94–142, Education for the Handicapped Act, passed by Congress in 1975, provided legal rights to and ensured educational services appropriate to students' disabilities be funded by public dollars to school-aged children with disabilities.

Over the years, this law has been updated to include education for children ages three to five, services for infants and toddlers who have severe disabilities, transition plans for adolescents after high school, and replaced the term "handicapped" with the term "disabilities." In addition, it increased educational expectations for children with disabilities, increased the role of parents in their children's education, implemented the use of early interventions to prevent or reduce the need for special education services, and demanded that states monitor and correct racial disparities in assignment of special education services (Slavin, 2012a).

Children receiving special education services are to be served in the least restrictive environment, leading to increased inclusion in the regular education classroom. Students receiving special education services must have an Individualized Education Program developed by a team including classroom and special education teachers, parents, school psychologist, and other specialists as needed. It specifies services the student is to receive including goals and objectives, specific special education and related services to be provided, the amount of time and the dates of service, and a process for evaluating progress toward the goals.

Students with disabilities are a diverse group coming from all races and ethnicities, cultures, languages, and backgrounds. The range of disabilities is vast including varying degrees of severity under each of the recognized disabilities of autism, deaf-blindness, developmental delay, emotional disturbance, hearing impairment, intellectual disability, multiple disabilities, orthopedic impairment, other health impairment, specific learning disability, speech or language impairment, traumatic brain injury, and visual impairment.

The Office of Special Education Programs (2019–2020) noted the following trends when examining the data on all children with disabilities disaggregated by race and ethnicity.

Asian students with disabilities are:

- more likely to be identified with autism or hearing impairment than other students with disabilities,
- less likely to drop out, and
- more likely to graduate with a regular high school diploma than other students with disabilities.

Black or African American students with disabilities are:

- more likely to be identified with an intellectual disability or emotional disturbance than other students with disabilities, and

- more likely to receive a disciplinary removal than other students with disabilities.

Hispanic students with disabilities are:

- more likely to be identified with hearing impairment or specific learning disability than other students with disabilities.

American Indian or Alaska Native students with disabilities are:

- more likely to drop out than other students with disabilities, and
- less likely to be inside regular class more than 40 percent of the day than other students with disabilities.

White students with disabilities are:

- more likely to be served inside a regular class 80 percent or more of the day than other students with disabilities, and
- less likely to be identified with a specific learning disability or intellectual disability than other students with disabilities.

These data once again illustrate the marginalization of some groups of students compared to other groups. Race and/or ethnicity is not a determinate of a specific disability. It is a system that marginalizes some groups of students based on the assumptions or biases made about the students' race/ethnicity and learning difficulties.

The great diversity of disabilities and their varied intensity has made it difficult to conduct research on effective programs. This great diversity of needs and services with small numbers of students with similar needs makes research that relies on equivalent groups and larger numbers of students for solid analysis almost impossible (Odom et al., 2005; Ohio Special Education Research Project, 2013). Despite these difficulties in researching to find proven programs and practices, what we do know guides us as we adopt a stance of equity: doing whatever it takes to ensure all students graduate high school ready for college and/or career.

We do have a large and growing body of evidence of programs and practices that enable the vast majority of students to succeed in the core curriculum, especially in literacy and mathematics. Schools must first use proven programs in every classroom so that 80 percent of students are finding success in Tier 1. The fact that traditionally marginalized students, such as Black, Hispanic, and Native American, are overrepresented among students identified for special education services reveals that schools are continuing and compounding their marginalization. A solid Tier 1 program is the first step in breaking this pattern.

Next, ensure that students with disabilities are included in the core instruction and the regular classroom to the greatest extent possible. This means doing whatever it takes as some students with disabilities will need additional supports to succeed in the regular classroom. It is educators' responsibility to see that these supports are provided for inclusion, scaffolding of instruction, and tutoring (with proven programs) as needed. The strategies discussed in the Inclusion, Scaffolding, and Tutoring subsections inform educators on what works to help students that are in need of additional support to master the core curriculum.

Researchers have reviewed high-performing schools where students with disabilities are achieving at high levels and found common traits. These schools have high expectations for all students, ensure that students with disabilities have access to the core curriculum, frequently use co-teaching for inclusion, and engage in frequent collaboration between classroom and special education teachers. In addition, they have student management programs that focus on rewards for good behavior rather than punishment for negative behaviors, and create nurturing, inclusive environments that value all individuals (Ohio Special Education Research Project, 2013).

The Council for Exceptional Children and the Collaboration for Effective Educator Development, Accountability, and Reform Center joined forces to review the literature and identify high-leverage practices that improve instructional outcomes for children with disabilities. They identified twenty-two practices that they deemed to be high-leverage practices. They identified them as high leverage because they are foundational to effective instruction and to managing student behaviors (Brownell, Cuillo, and Kennedy, 2020–2021; McLeskey et al., 2017).

These practices are strikingly similar to those already identified as ways to provide scaffolding to students needing it. Excellent teaching is critical for all students regardless of how they are identified. These practices include providing positive and constructive feedback, teaching social behaviors, teaching cognitive and meta-cognitive strategies, providing scaffolded supports, and using explicit instruction. Also included is the use of intensive instruction. This is providing instruction on a small number of high-priority skills and/or concepts with multiple opportunities to practice with feedback and clarification when needed (McLeskey et al., 2017).

English Language Learners

Students who are English learners with limited English proficiency have been and continue to be one of the fastest-growing populations in our schools

(Grantmakers for Education, 2013; Irwin, et al., 2021). Within this group of students there is great diversity of cultures and languages and also great diversity in their academic needs (Izquierdo, 2012). The languages they speak are diverse with many urban districts serving students from over a hundred different first languages. The presence of students learning English is rapidly growing in our rural areas as well.

There is also diversity among English learners in their educational backgrounds. Some come with a solid education experience, although in a different language, and others arrive with very little to no previous formal schooling. A district in the mid-Atlantic had a large number of recent immigrant students from Africa, many of them arriving just in time to enter high school in hopes of earning a U.S. high school diploma. Some of the students were from a country with a well-established system of education and the students were highly educated in literacy, mathematics, and science—just not in the English language.

Other students were from a country that had provided them with little to no formal education even though they were of the age to be enrolled in their first year of high school. The needs of these students were extremely different, and it was important that teachers supporting them knew their students well so that they could provide the support and scaffolding that each student needed for their particular situation. Knowing their students allowed the teachers to build on the students' strengths as they helped students connect their learning to prior knowledge.

The recent heightened focus on immigration to our country often leads to a false perception about our students learning English. Most of our English learners are first-, second-, or even third-generation born in the United States and have always gone to school in our country. However, their families speak a first language at home other than English so while they might speak enough English for navigating simple social situations, they are not proficient in English and especially not in academic English (Izquierdo, 2012). Academic literacy instruction as a part of content instruction is critical to their success.

Students learning English as a second language, like all students, need rigorous content as well as language development in order to be educated to the highest level. The rigorous and highly effective instruction that works with English-proficient students also works well with English learners (Goldenberg, 2012; Slavin, 2012b). When additional supports are needed, their effectiveness is built on the use of proven programs at Tier 1. Scholars focused on supporting English learners in our educational system have repeatedly noted that English learners are often not given the rigor needed to graduate high school college and/or career ready.

Every teacher that supports these students needs to have knowledge of and the ability to use instructional strategies that support learners acquiring language. Every teacher, regardless of their content area, needs to be a literacy teacher engaged in teaching vocabulary, discourse, reading, and writing in their academic discipline (Calderon, 2012). English learners need plenty of opportunities to develop proficiency in English, so English language development instruction must go hand-in-hand with content instruction (Goldenberg, 2012).

Separating English language development from content has demonstrated only a very modest effect on student outcomes. Sheltered programs for English learners should be used very sparingly, if at all. There is not a great deal of evidence that these programs help English learners learn advanced content (Goldenberg, 2012). Schools that expect students to develop a good command of English before providing English learners with content are not teaching to rigorous standards, but rather widening the gap.

Gifted and Talented Programs

Federal law acknowledges the existence of gifted students, although it does not provide any mandates or yearly resources for providing for the needs of these students. It does provide funds for competitive grants for research regarding the identification and education of gifted students in subsection 4644 of the Every Student Succeeds Act (Elementary and Secondary Education Act reauthorized December 2015) known as the Jacob K. Javits Gifted and Talented Education Program.

In 1993, the U.S. Department of Education issued its report, "National Excellence: A Case for Developing America's Talent." On page twenty-six of this report, it contains the following definition of giftedness:

> Children and youth with outstanding talent perform or show the potential for performing at remarkably high levels of accomplishment when compared with others of their age, experience, or environment.
>
> These children and youth exhibit high performance capability in intellectual, creative, and/or artistic areas, possess an unusual leadership capacity, or excel in specific academic fields. They require services or activities not ordinarily provided by the schools.
>
> Outstanding talents are present in children and youth from all cultural groups, across all economic strata, and in all areas of human endeavor.

Despite this recognition that giftedness exists across all groups of students, our data on students who have been identified and receive gifted and talented education services would indicate otherwise. Yaluma and Tyner (2018) in their research on gifted education across the country found significant differences in the students supported by these programs. They found that approximately two-thirds of elementary and middle schools had gifted programs and schools with large numbers of students living in poverty were generally just as often to have a gifted program as schools with small numbers of students living in poverty.

Nationwide, 9 percent of the students in elementary and middle school participated in gifted and talented education programs. However, when separated by percentage of students served in schools with few students living in poverty, 12.4 percent of the students were identified as gifted compared to schools with large numbers of students living in poverty, in which only 6.1 percent were identified. Once again, some groups of students are being marginalized.

They found that white and Asian students were overrepresented, while Black and Hispanic students were underrepresented in gifted education. While Asian students comprised 4.8 percent of the total elementary and middle school population, 8.6 percent of the Asian students were identified as gifted. White students were 47.9 percent of the overall population, and 55.2 percent of those identified as gifted were white. On the other hand, Hispanic students comprised 27.6 percent of the overall population and 20.8 percent of the gifted students, while Black students were 15 percent of the total population and 10 percent of the gifted students.

So what can be done to identify more of our gifted and talented marginalized students? Yaluma and Tyner (2018) provide three recommendations: (1) universal screening, (2) use of local norms, and (3) counter bias with teacher training in recognizing giftedness among diverse students. Olszewski-Kubiliu and Clarenbach (2012) argued that educators should expect more than proficiency from their students, expand access to a rigorous curriculum, and provide education for teachers on how to identify and serve gifted students that are low-income and/or culturally and linguistically diverse.

They also recommended that governmental leaders reduce zip code and socioeconomic status that factor into which schools are selected to provide a rigorous education. Davis (2010) advocates that educators and parents understand the unique challenges that diverse gifted students, in particular Black students, experience. She states that these students often feel the burden of representing their race while still facing discrimination, lack of understanding of their culture, low expectations, and peer pressure to not act "white."

More and more schools are recognizing that, once again, our educational system is designed to serve some children better than others. More districts are implementing universal screeners with components that do not rely on English literacy. Teams of educators can then dig through the data from these universal screeners to identify students for further observation and documentation of giftedness.

Some districts have conducted data analysis on the results from already required assessments to identify those students that are making gains outside normal bounds and then observed and looked for further documentation that these students might be gifted. An example might be students who are showing incredible gains across all domains in their English language acquisition. These students are often difficult to screen with measures dependent on English literacy; however, a student's rapid growth in acquiring English, while still not proficient, could be an indicator of giftedness.

Looking at growth on such a measure is also a great way to move from deficit thinking to recognizing student assets. A diverse district developed an assessment procedure that involved a team of teachers reviewing a student's portfolio. This eliminated the single score or rating to determine giftedness and relied on the expertise of a diverse group of educators. The expanded understanding of what comprises giftedness has also helped to capture and include students who previously were marginalized.

Giftedness is, as in the definition previously discussed, now being looked for in more than just traditional intellectual abilities but also in the areas of creativity, the arts, and leadership. Educators are working together to better understand what giftedness looks like in the arts or in leadership. Schools are facilitating professional learning for all their staff to better equip them for identifying and supporting giftedness, especially with diverse learners.

One district witnessed exponential growth in identification of gifted students when educators developed a more inclusive and holistic understanding of giftedness. In this district, gifted education programs were not provided in all schools initially, only at the schools with more economically advantaged families. This essentially resulted in students being identified and served by their zip code. Those schools without programs had no advocate on staff that was supporting their colleagues in identifying and serving gifted students and no students identified as gifted.

Additional gifted and talented teachers were hired, and programs were started at all the district's schools. The teachers supporting these programs across the district began meeting regularly to support their professional growth in identifying and serving these students. They worked together to develop a portfolio system to identify students and workshops for their general education colleagues so that they too could assist in identifying and supporting gifted students.

Some of the gifted and talented teachers included students not yet identified as gifted in some of their instructional units based on individual student interests and observed them for possible giftedness. This allowed for enrichment to benefit students who were not currently identified as well. Schools that had originally had no students identified as gifted now had a growing number of diverse students identified and receiving these services.

Advanced Opportunity Classes

Advanced opportunity classes include Advanced Placement (AP) classes, dual credit classes (earning both high school and college credit in one class), International Baccalaureate courses, and/or early college high school models (Chatterji, Campbell, and Quirk, 2021; National Forum on Education Statistics, 2015). Successful participation in these classes is often an indication that a student is college and/or career ready.

In addition, the rigor of high school Career and Technical Education classes has increased to prepare students for the post-secondary education they will need to earn a credential if they so choose. The Forum College and Career Working Group (National Forum on Education Statistics) defined college and/or career ready as when a student has "attained the knowledge, skills, and disposition needed to succeed in credit-bearing (non-remedial) postsecondary course work or a workforce training program in order to earn credentials necessary to qualify for a meaningful career aligned to his or her goals and offering a competitive salary" (p. 1).

While in the past these courses might not have been the expectation for all students, it is critical that students be able to succeed in college and/or career coursework in order to have a good job. Carnevale et al. (2019) defined a good job as "one that pays family-sustaining earnings. Good jobs pay a minimum of $35,000 for workers between the ages of 25 and 44 and at least $45,000 for workers between the ages of 45 and 64" (p. 3). With current inflation, the salary amounts have most certainly increased.

Per the National Forum on Education Statistics (2015), individuals with only a high school education or less comprised 72 percent of the country's workforce in 1973. By 2007, that number had fallen to 41 percent of the workforce with predictions that the percentage would continue to decrease. While many states have identified data that can be tracked to help determine how well their students are prepared for post-secondary education (college or technical programs), the measures used are not consistent from state to state (National Forum on Education Statistics, 2015; Chatterji, Campbell, and Quirk, 2021).

The U.S. Department of Education (2019a) analyzed the data they had on high school graduates for 2013 to determine what percentage of students had any high school credits from an AP, International Baccalaureate, or dual credit course. This data could be analyzed only for 79 percent of the high school graduates that year who had complete transcript data. Of those 79 percent with complete transcript data, only 46.3 percent had at least one credit for an AP, International Baccalaureate, or dual credit course.

When further examined by race and ethnicity, the data show that 76.8 percent of the Asian students, 34.2 percent of the Black students, 42 percent of the Hispanic students, and 49 percent of the white students had earned such credits. An examination by socioeconomic status indicates that 69.3 percent of the students from families in the top one-fifth, 41.9 percent of the students from the middle three-fifths, and 30.9 percent of students from the bottom fifth had earned such a credit.

Chatterji, Campbell, and Quirk (2021) further examined the data on students who had participated in AP classes based on the U.S. Department of Education Civil Rights Data Collection from 2015–2016. They looked at the data by the number enrolled, the number who took the AP exam at the end of the course, and the number who passed the AP exam. They translated their findings into an estimate of how many students per one thousand per each category. Their findings are in table 7.1.

The benefits of advanced coursework include improved student self-esteem, greater engagement in school, and increased probability of graduating and going on to college and earning a degree (Chatterji, Campbell, and Quirk, 2021). They identified multiple barriers or inequities to advanced coursework for some students including access, underrepresentation in coursework, and systemic gaps in which populations were more likely to achieve a passing score on AP exams. Also, they found the gap in AP class enrollment widened for Black, Latinx, and Indigenous students as the level of access grew. Access alone did not close the gap.

From these findings, Chatterji, Campbell, and Quirk (2021) looked at various actions that schools could take to increase the number of students, especially traditionally marginalized students, that participate and succeed in advanced classes. These actions included increasing access to advanced coursework, improving student identification and enrollment in advanced

Table 7.1 Advanced Placement Class Achievements for Every One Thousand Students

	All Students	White Students	Black Students	Hispanic Students	Asian Students	American Indian/Native Students
Enroll in an AP Course	174	185	105	156	375	93
Take an AP Exam	130	139	73	111	313	59
Pass an AP Exam	75	90	21	51	215	7

Source: Data from Chatterji, Campbell, and Quirk, 2021, p. 3.
Note: AP = Advanced Placement.

courses, improving ability to participate successfully in exams, and supports for teachers on how to teach these classes and include marginalized students.

Efforts of these types are being undertaken in high schools across the country. One high school began with a small effort of having the teaching staff come together and review the lists of students rising to grades eleven and twelve for the following year. They identified students that were not taking at least one advanced opportunity class, but whom they believed had the literacy and mathematics skills to do so if encouraged and supported.

Then each teacher took the name of one or two students and committed to personally invite the students to take a specific advanced opportunity class with their support the coming school year. These courses were often classes that the teacher inviting the student taught. Students were amazed that teachers had noted their interests and abilities and asked them personally to enroll in a specific advanced class with the promise to support them through it.

In addition, Latinx parents were invited to a special meeting, conducted all in Spanish, about how to ensure their child would graduate high school college and/or career ready. Young Latinx staff members who were first-generation college graduates themselves conducted the meeting. Parents were informed that their children had to take rigorous high school classes and that they should not sign off on their child's classes unless they knew that the course selection included advanced math or science, etc. The parent liaison got quite a few calls from parents who wanted to check with someone other than their child that their course selections were rigorous.

One of the school's teachers proposed a class that would support first-generation students for both high school graduation and post-secondary education. Students received an elective credit for the class, learned how to advocate for themselves with their teachers, read and analyzed Carol Dweck's 2006 *Mindset: The New Psychology of Success*, learned how to prepare for AP or college exams, improved their academic writing skills, and formed a small community that supported and encouraged each other.

After one year, the number of first-generation students wanting to take advanced classes exploded. The number of support classes quadrupled as well due to the number of students participating. Shortly thereafter, the high school ended its Algebra I course that was paced over two years. This class had been created for students who staff believed needed more support in math. The only problem was these classes were comprised of primarily marginalized students and after spending two of four years of high school on Algebra I, there wasn't enough time left to matriculate to advanced math classes before it was time to leave high school.

The U.S. Department of Education's Office of Civil Rights (2014) has noted that early mastery of Algebra I is crucial to students being prepared for advanced classes and graduating high school college and/or career ready.

The school moved to a single Algebra I format with the same curriculum for all students. Students needing additional support had a second period of math during the day for that support. Soon the number of students needing a second period of math decreased as expectations for all students to complete Algebra I by the end of the ninth grade became the norm, changing the way teachers taught and what students did in class.

The school's district set a goal to close the gap between the percentage of white students that participated in at least one advanced opportunity class and Latinx students that participated in an advanced opportunity class. They achieved over 90 percent of students in both student groups participating in at least one advanced opportunity class. Now it was time for them to focus on monitoring the data for average number of advanced opportunity classes students in both groups took and erasing any gaps in that data.

Schools and districts that want to ensure that the vast majority of their students are participating in advanced opportunity classes can use some of these same strategies to make it happen. Many schools use the AVID education program (Advancement via Individual Determination), instead of creating their own support classes, to support first-generation students. AVID is a proven program that provides supports for both teachers and students at the secondary level with a focus on closing the opportunity gap.

Also, schools and districts that desire to have all their students participating in advanced classes in high school need to ensure that all students are reading on or above grade level, are mathematical thinkers, and are developing literacy in the content areas. The expectations and instruction for students from kindergarten to grade twelve needs to be focused on mastering rigorous grade-level standards. This creates the pipeline of students that will then be the students in advanced opportunity classes.

SUMMING IT UP

Special programs were designed to provide the additional support that some students need for success in school. However, despite these good intentions, they often have the opposite impact and provide barriers to all students being educated to a high level with at least mastery of grade-level standards. The data show that our traditionally marginalized students are most often the students that are impacted by the barriers of special programs rather than helped by them. This is once again a system issue; despite the good intentions at its creation, this system often hinders the provision of equity or whatever it takes to ensure all students succeed.

The system needs to be recreated to ensure that all students are provided high expectations, a rigorous core curriculum, and excellent instruction in each and every class. All students need to be provided with the skills to be on track to take advanced courses in high school and then take these classes once they reach their junior and senior years of high school. The system can be recreated if we work together as a team, rather than in silos by our individual specialties.

Educators that are experts in how to support the instructional needs of students need to combine their power with educators who are experts in the content areas and know the literacies of the various content areas. We must continuously monitor our data. Are the students in special programs being included in classrooms with high expectations, rigorous curriculum, and excellent instruction? Are there student groups that are over- or underrepresented? Are the vast majority of our students succeeding in Tier 1 instruction? Are appropriate scaffolds being provided in Tier 1 instruction? Why or why not? What will we do about it?

REFLECTION

There is a reflection section at the end of each of the remaining chapters of the book. It is intended to help you reflect on your school and district practices as well as your own individual practices. There is also a "Reflections and Next Steps" section at the end of the book that you may wish to use. It will allow you to make notes in one location regarding each of the chapters. This is to help you easily review your thoughts over all the issues raised throughout the book and then identify next steps to take in your own professional practice.

Reflections for chapter 7:

- Who are the students not mastering grade-level standards in your classroom? Are they included in appropriate Tier 1 instruction? What scaffolds do they receive?

- What do you need to do to ensure at least 80 percent of your students are successful in Tier 1 grade-level instruction? (Be careful of deficit thinking.)

- What percent of your students take at least one advanced level course in high school? Are some of your student groups underrepresented? Why? What can you do about it?

- Do your special programs provide equity, or do they continue the marginalization of students? If students are still being marginalized, what will you do about it?

Chapter 8

Social Services

Why We Need Them

Schools were created to educate our children. Initially, this included primarily reading, writing, and arithmetic for those students fortunate or privileged enough to have access to this education. Over the years, the students in our schools have become much more diverse as we have expanded who has the right to a public education to include not just white male citizens, but also females, students of color, students with disabilities, students who do not yet speak English, and undocumented students. In addition, what we expect our children to learn in school as well as be provided by the school has greatly expanded (Vollmer, 2010).

    Today, we expect and need schools that educate all students to the highest levels, ensuring they have mastered grade-level standards and graduate high school college and career ready. The pressure on educators has greatly increased along with these expectations for educating all students rather than select students. While the expectations for what schools must accomplish has greatly increased, the time provided to schools and often the relative resources to achieve these expectations has not changed much over the years.

    So, with these increasing and voluminous expectations, why should educators be worried about or take on the challenge of providing social services to our students as well? Educators are not generally trained in these areas. Academics and how students learn is their area of expertise. Social services should not push in on the limited time that schools have to accomplish their goals just because, as schools, they happen to have our children gathered together into one convenient place. Or at least this was the thinking of a young, new principal.

    She viewed an important part of her job as protecting the learning time of students in school. That included keeping outsiders from imposing on classrooms to accomplish their goals of teaching their non-profit's version of tolerance and mindfulness or ensuring all students received fluoride treatments on their teeth or sharing their latest art exhibit, or any number of worthy but time-encroaching activities.

However, she came to realize, educators are often struggling to accomplish their goals of ensuring every single child was mastering the standards because some students were frequently not in school, or were so traumatized by the fight at home last night they couldn't focus on reading, or dealing with mental health issues so they couldn't engage in critical thinking. These and many more barriers were getting in the way of accomplishing their goal. She was learning that social services and supports were critical to accomplishing the goal of educating every child to the highest level. The blindness that her privilege had caused was now fading.

Many of these social services and supports make it possible for educators to focus on teaching and learning rather than distracting from it (Boykin and Noguera, 2011). Her focus changed to finding the social services her students needed in order to learn and building collaborations with other agencies that could provide the expertise to ensure her students had the supports they needed to learn to the highest level. This realization changed her approach to leading and providing for her school and helped a multitude of her future students find success in school and in life.

Many years later, as a district administrator, she was checking in on a high school student that was receiving support from the school's mental health therapist in order to continue learning (rather than be suspended) and moving toward graduation while also battling his addiction issues. The student asked her why she cared if he used drugs. It wasn't her business. She responded by telling him that it was her responsibility to ensure all students in the district, including him, graduated high school college and/or career ready. That was her charge from the state, the community, and his parents.

Therefore, if his drug use was getting in the way of accomplishing that, then it was her concern as well. She told him that until he graduated college and career ready, his brain cells were a part of her purview. The school was supporting him so that he could stay in school and that included requiring him to participate in sessions with the mental health therapist to grapple with his dependency. He didn't have much to say after that other than admitting he liked coming to school to see his friends.

She continued to check in on him every few weeks. Over time, his view of himself improved, he found he actually liked learning, his grades improved, and he did get back on track to graduate. They also became friends, and he would frequently report to her, when he found her walking down the halls of his high school, how his brain cells were doing! He was not the only student with substance abuse issues that was helped by that school. The school staff and the community became quite proud of the fact that they were supporting students to graduation rather than expelling them from school for substance abuse issues.

Food and housing insecurity, trauma, drugs and alcohol, lack of mental health supports, and so forth can often become distractions to students in their quest to learn at school. It is estimated that one in five children in our country experiences a mental, emotional, or behavioral problem while only one-fifth of these children receive the care they need (Bruns et al., 2016; Weir, 2020). However, the good news is that there is strong evidence that mental health interventions can greatly improve academic outcomes for students.

Kase et al. (2017) reviewed thirty-six primary research articles and meta-analysis articles spanning seventeen years and found significant benefits of mental health interventions on the academic outcomes for students. If educators aspire to create Whatever It Takes schools, so all students graduate college and career ready, they will continue to provide or collaborate to provide those social services when needed. It is a matter of equity. The Carnegie Council Task Force on Education of Adolescents (1989) noted that schools are not responsible for meeting every need of students, "But when the need directly affects learning, the school must meet the challenge."

Schools are stepping up to meet the challenge of providing social service supports for students so that they are able to focus on their learning. Some of these supports are provided directly by the school such as nutrition, social emotional learning instruction, counseling, and health screenings. Additional services are provided by other governmental agencies and non-profits in close collaboration with the schools. These supports often include nutrition and housing, mental health supports and other health supports, as well as wraparound services.

SOCIAL EMOTIONAL LEARNING

Social emotional learning (SEL), while not new to schools, has gained more prominence recently. In 2016 the Collaborative for Academic, Social, and Emotional Learning launched the Collaborating States Initiative to help states support educators in developing students' social and emotional learning. The Collaborative for Academic, Social, and Emotional Learning reports that it is working with over forty states and that more than twenty states have adopted SEL standards and/or competencies.

SEL can provide a foundation for learning as well as help to develop and strengthen a positive school culture (Weir, 2020). A meta-analysis of eighty-two school-based SEL programs found that students in such programs had better emotional skills, attitudes, and indicators of well-being (Taylor

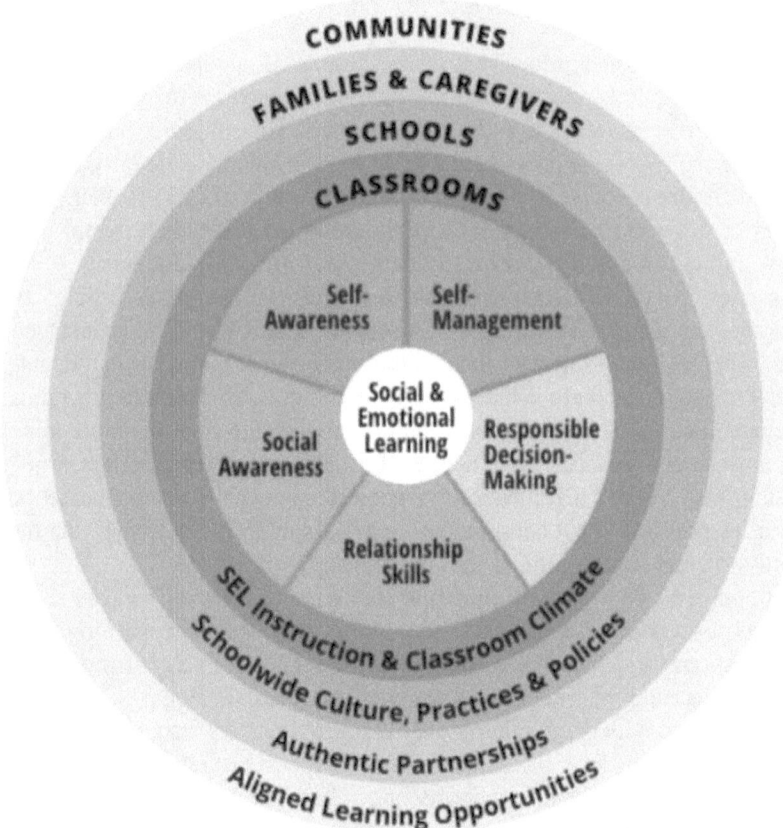

Figure 8.1 CASEL Framework
Source: ©2021 CASEL. All Rights Reserved [Source: Retrieved June 17, 2022 at https://casel.org/fundamentals-of-sel/what-is-the-casel-framework/.]

et al., 2017). Weir (2020) found similar results, as well as improved academic outcomes, in a meta-analysis of 213 school-based SEL programs.

Social emotional development also serves as prevention against mental health problems as students learn to manage emotion, care for others, develop positive relationships, make good choices, resolve conflicts, handle challenges, and calm themselves. In addition, such development helps shape school cultures that address systemic issues such as bullying, alienation, and lack of student engagement (Adelman and Taylor, n.d.).

Educators are often hesitant to embrace the role of facilitating SEL. It may be that they have little training and/or experience in this area as their teacher preparation was focused on their academic content area. It could be that the expectations to teach SEL adds another lesson for which they must prepare.

Asking teachers to ensure students are meeting SEL standards adds to expectations for educators. The payoff is more students being successful in school, moving toward the goal of all students educated to high levels. SEL is the support that many students need to achieve. It is a part of equity.

However, educators do not have to go it alone and create their own content. There are multiple, research-proven SEL programs that can be adopted by schools and districts to provide consistency across grade levels and reduce some of the lesson preparation burden on educators. These programs and their evidence of effectiveness can be found on several different websites listed in this chapter.

When teaching for SEL, as in all of our instruction, we must be careful to acknowledge and value the assets our students bring with them: respecting the culture and values of their home and community while teaching social emotional skills (Anderson, 2013; Boykin and Noguera, 2011). Schools can play a huge role in a student's development of a sense of identity, value, and ability (Hill, 2017). Reinforcing the values in a student's home and community culture is important to their positive development of identity.

Contrary to some misinformation in parts of our current society, SEL is not a cover for teaching critical race theory or teaching students values that are in opposition to their parents' teachings. Teaching students to be kind, persevere, respect others, and make good decisions has always been a part of what we expect our children to learn. These skills are the basis of a civil society. Some of the recent focus on these skills has been in response to an increase of violence in some schools. SEL creates an intentional effort to teach these skills rather than a random and by chance teaching of these skills.

Our most marginalized students often bring incredible grit to the schoolhouse. However, many well-intended community members and even some educators advise that we just need to teach our students to have grit so that they will work harder in school and achieve better outcomes. A new public schools superintendent was invited to meet with the headmaster of a local, prestigious private school. The superintendent was new to the community and the headmaster was graciously reaching out and offering to partner with the district regarding the work that their private school was engaged in to help their students develop grit.

The superintendent heard the familiar refrain that establishing grit in students would help them not give up so easily and perform better in school. While he wanted to engage with the headmaster and find ways for them to partner, this focus on teaching all students about grit was not going to be very helpful. Many of the superintendent's students could teach this private school's students (from very wealthy and privileged families) a great deal about grit. His students demonstrated grit each day. Living their lives required daily grit. They did find other ways to partner.

Gorski's (2018) view of grit is that it is a cousin of deficit ideology. Be careful before jumping on the grit bandwagon, dragging your colleagues with you. Know your students' life circumstances. How do they already exhibit grit in life? Educators are not about blaming our students for not achieving at grade level or above. Rather, they are about identifying their students' strengths and building on them so they are achieving at grade level. They are about making it happen.

Evidence of Effectiveness for Social Emotional Learning Programs

- The What Works Clearinghouse under the topic Behavior at https://casel.org/about-us/our-mission-work/collaborating-states-initiative/ from the U.S. Department of Education.
- Evidence for ESSA under the topic of Social Emotional Learning Programs at https://casel.org/about-us/our-mission-work/collaborating-states-initiative/ from Johns Hopkins University.
- Blueprints for Healthy Youth Development at https://www.blueprintsprograms.org/ from the University of Colorado at Boulder.

Mental Health Supports

Adelman and Taylor (n.d.) state that for many large urban districts over 50 percent of their students have symptoms of behavior and/or emotional problems. They attribute many of these issues to limited opportunities, racial injustices, and the living conditions of poverty that many of these students face daily. These are often marginalized students who are further marginalized by not having the emotional and mental health supports needed and to which more privileged students have access.

Adelman and Taylor argue that schools have a role in supporting good mental health, intervening when needed, and ensuring students with chronic problems receive the service and supports they need so that they can succeed in school. The National Association of School Psychologists (2021) reminds us that mental health services in schools are critical to ensuring safe schools as well as supporting the mission of all students learning.

Weir (2020) notes that suicide rates for ages ten to twenty-four have increased from 6.8 per one hundred thousand youth in 2007 to 10.6 per one hundred thousand in 2017. In addition, the percentage of youth with major depression disorder increased from 8.7 percent in 2005 to 11.3 percent in 2014. Both of these increases were before the COVID-19 pandemic caused an even greater increase in these areas of concern. These and similar mental health issues greatly impact a student's ability to succeed in school. If we are focused on equity, doing whatever it takes for each student to be highly educated, then we will have to grapple with these mental health issues for many of our students.

Bruns et al. (2016) as well as the National Association of School Psychologists (2021) note that the education sector provides an opportunity to address the shortcomings of a more traditional mental health system, especially for underserved students. They further note that the educational setting promotes quick identification and the beginning of services when needed compared to other settings. Adelman and Taylor (n.d.) assert that three-fourths of children receiving mental health services do so in the educational arena, which would reinforce the idea that the education sector is a conducive setting for delivering such services.

Public schools often have some type of minimal support services provided by social workers, school counselors, and/or school psychologists. However, in the vast majority of the cases these services are very limited as every dollar spent by schools on social services competes with the dollars spent in classrooms. Counselors, especially at the secondary level, are primarily tasked with the guidance responsibilities of helping students navigate what courses to take as they strive for graduation, while school psychologists have their schedules filled with assessing students for special education services and other programs.

However, due to the critical role these professionals can play in providing equity, or whatever it takes for every single student to graduate high school college and career ready, educators must rethink how these professionals are used in their schools and districts. They must recreate systems so that they can provide their services in expanded or different ways. The recent impact of the pandemic on students makes it even more imperative that schools provide or partner with providers to ensure students are receiving the mental health supports needed.

A school serving a high-poverty neighborhood asked district leadership if rather than having the traditional allocation from the district of a part-time school psychologist, a part-time social worker, and a part-time counselor, could they use the dollars from these traditional allocations to have a full-time school psychologist and a full-time social worker and no counselor. (This is not to say that counselors are not valuable contributors to students' success.) This school of one thousand students wanted to have staff that were fully dedicated to establishing relationships with their students, rather than serving multiple buildings and being stretched even thinner.

In exchange, the staff asked that the school psychologist not only perform student evaluations as typical, but also dedicate a portion of time every week to conducting small-group therapy or support sessions and to observing individual students in the classroom. The names of individual students to be observed were submitted by teachers to the school psychologist for their assistance in learning more about how the student learned and how instruction and/or interventions could be adapted to better support the student.

The social worker was tasked with the typical work of connecting students and families to social services in the community for food, housing, etc., as well as being expected to dedicate time every week to small-group and individual student therapy or support. This example makes the point that the school collectively decided what supports their students needed and changed the traditional system to one that better supported their students within the boundaries of the larger system of the district. These social services personnel became extremely valuable and integral members of the staff.

Many schools also partner with community social service agencies to increase support for students. According to Weir (2020), mental health providers are increasingly based in the schools through some type of partnership. Some of the most successful are schools that partner with an agency to provide their services and expertise within the school. One school was able to offer space to a non-profit to provide mental health services that were either billed to the state's health insurance for children or covered by donations made to the non-profit. Student and family therapy was easy to access as the issue of needing transportation across town was eliminated.

The school also partnered with the local health department so that a mini-health station was available to the community at the school. The school provided the space and utilities, and the health department provided the staff and medical supplies. Students and families had easy access to health services, and the school's vaccination rate for its students soared to 95 percent. When the school nurse's screenings indicated a need for more comprehensive services, they were easily scheduled at the health clinic right in the building. When it was time for the medical exam, it was easy to get the student to their appointment.

In addition to these services, this same school also partnered with the city library so that the school's library was expanded to become a community branch library. The school also partnered with the local parks and recreation department to provide afterschool and evening programming, with the police department to have a substation in the building providing more security for the late evening hours, and with senior services to provide space for a daily senior meal and activity.

The senior citizens served as foster grandparents in classrooms in the mornings, then gathered together at noon for their meal, followed by an afternoon of their own activities such as board games, ceramics, a guest speaker, etc. Many of the children in this school were immigrants and had no grandparents living near them. Having these senior citizens serving as foster grandparents was very special to the students and provided another caring adult in their lives. In turn, the senior citizens learned to value the newly arrived families in the community.

In each of these cases, partnering with these agencies involved the school providing space, keeping the lights on, and holding regular partnership meetings to ensure good communication and problem solving to facilitate working together across all the agencies. For the agencies it provided easier access to the people they were tasked with serving and reduced costs as they had no rent to pay. Most importantly, for the students it provided the whatever it took to ensure they could be successful in school.

In some places it can be impossible to find agencies to partner with for the social services students need. One school found itself in a location where there was an incredible lack of mental health services in the community. While the local clinic was very willing to partner with the school regarding getting mental health services to students who desperately needed them, this partnership never began in reality as the clinic was constantly struggling to staff the clinic and serve its current clients. Even referring a student or family to the clinic was difficult due to the long waiting list.

However, the district realized that a major barrier to improving its graduation rate was related to substance abuse. Students were put out of school for such infractions and then were never able to secure the supports needed to get back to school. So the district set out to hire its own mental health therapist to oversee this work in the district along with support from the school's social workers. This allowed the district to keep many of its students in school that it had previously put out of school. Only those students who were distributing substances were subject to suspension or expulsion.

Creating this position (reallocating dollars) was not easy and involved difficult board meetings as views on this idea of keeping students in school while coping with substance abuse were highly varied and passionate. However, it was a part of doing whatever it took to ensure students graduated college and career ready. Previously, students of privilege were able to wrestle with their substance abuse and stay in school due to access to the resources to make it happen. Marginalized students did not have access to resources for these supports. The district was able to ensure its students with fewer means were also able to stay in school and graduate on time.

Another piece of the puzzle to ensure students have the mental health supports they need to be successful includes all staff being able to recognize a need and get support to students when needed. This does not mean all staff are able to provide interventions or therapy, but rather they are able to recognize a possible need and connect the resources to the student. They do not need to be experts in mental health; they just need to recognize signs or symptoms of a possible need.

The vast majority of schools have some type of psychological first aid team for students in crisis. These teams jump into action when there is an incident at school or outside the school that greatly impacts the students in the school. They manage the incident, mobilize support, and provide follow-up. They are most often responsive to an incident such as a student death, threat against the school, etc. They are not, however, as proactive in preventing incidents and ensuring students have strong mental health supports before a crisis occurs.

More and more schools are providing training for all staff on how to detect possible mental health needs and how to connect a student to support. Educators should not be expected to be experts in providing mental health supports. The vast majority of educators have an expertise in teaching and learning, not mental health. However, they can provide support in an emergency and get the right support in place for the long term. Think of it as CPR support for a mental health crisis.

Most educators have had CPR training and refresher courses over their years in education. They are ready to assist an individual having a cardiopulmonary emergency. They can step in and provide the support while also calling for the emergency medical technicians, the trained experts, to come and provide the assistance needed and get the individual to a hospital with even more specialized support.

There are multiple trainings staff can use in learning how to recognize and provide emergency mental health supports. One that is frequently used is Youth Mental Health First Aid. This is an eight-hour training that teaches adults working with youth how to recognize and help a student who is experiencing mental health crises. School staff from principals to teachers to bus drivers learn how to help the students in the immediate and connect them to mental health experts that can provide more intensive support. You can learn more about this program at their website: https://www.mentalhealthfirstaid.org/population-focused-modules/youth/.

Discipline

The way we deal with disruptive behaviors in our classrooms and schools reveals a great deal about us and our stance regarding providing equity: whatever it takes to ensure all students graduate college and career ready. It has repeatedly been found, including by the U.S. Department of Education's Office of Civil Rights, that students living in poverty conditions, students of color, and students with disabilities receive a disproportionate number of disciplinary actions including being removed from classrooms, suspended, or expelled (Hill, 2017; Morgan et al., 2014; Youth.gov, n.d.).

We have already discussed creating positive school cultures and establishing positive relationships with our students (see chapters 3 and 6). However, a quick review of how school cultures and student-teacher relationships impact school discipline is appropriate at this time. When reflecting on your school's culture, what evidence do you see that it is a caring and nurturing place for all students? Caring about students is manifested in our relationships with our students (Nelson, Lott, and Glenn, 2000).

Do we check in with them to find out what is going on when they are absent from school, have missing assignments, or act rudely toward another person, or do we assume we know and immediately make a judgment and issue a "consequence"? Do we listen deeply to our students, provide them encouragement, frequently celebrate their accomplishments, and provide them choice and voice in our classrooms and schools? Do we teach and model expected behaviors for our students including how to politely disagree and how to advocate for yourself (Hill, 2017)?

Shalaby (2021), an advocate for more caring student discipline, recently called for teaching students the kind of compassion needed so that students can hold themselves accountable when they cause harm to others by their behaviors. In addition, she insightfully offered that "when kids are giving us trouble, we have an opportunity to model for all the other kids how to respond to behaviors that are challenging, how to respond to people who are struggling in our community" (p. 15).

Morgan et al. (2014) examined schools that are most successful in reducing discipline disparities among student groups as well as reducing suspensions and expulsions and found that these schools have a positive school culture where students feel safe, connected, and supported; use tiered behavioral support systems; and focus on preventing youth arrest or referral to the justice system for minor school-based offenses.

These are schools that view mistakes as learning opportunities and focus on solving problems rather than punishment (Nelsen, Lott, and Glenn, 2000). They proactively teach and model behavior expectations, use natural consequences rather than punishments, provide a way back to good standing in the classroom for students who have engaged in inappropriate behavior, and focus on teacher relationships with students and families (Hill, 2017).

The U.S. Department of Education (Youth.gov, n.d.) recommends creating a school culture that includes support to prevent and change inappropriate behavior through clear and consistent expectations and consequences. Practices that focus on learning and problem solving rather than punishment include daily class meetings as detailed in *Positive Discipline in the Classroom* (Nelson, Lott, and Glenn, 2000).

Positive Behavioral Interventions and Supports (PBIS; https://www.pbis.org/) and Restorative Justice (https://www.restorativejustice.com/) are two programs that help schools focus on positive behaviors. PBIS focuses on "improving behavior by teaching prosocial skills and redesigning school environment to discourage problem behaviors" (McIntosh, Goin, and Bastable, 2018, p. 1). Restorative Justice is a "social movement to institutionalize non-punitive, relationship-centered approaches for avoiding and addressing harm, responding to violations of legal and human rights, and collaboratively solving problems" (Fronius et al., 2019).

The research of effectiveness on these programs is very limited and in the early stages. A review conducted by McIntosh, Goin, and Bastable (2018) found a decrease in disciplinary actions that put students out of school, including a reduction in rates for students of color, in schools that implemented PBIS schoolwide. A recent review of the Center for PBIS website reveals that a majority of states have support staff for PBIS implementation in their departments of education.

A review of the literature regarding Restorative Justice in schools found that research on the program or method is in the early stages, but there is promise of positive effects in regard to discipline, attendance, graduation, and school culture (Fronius et al., 2019). Goodwin (2021) also acknowledges that there is not the rigorous research needed on the use of Restorative Justice practices, but he does note the promising findings that these practices can reduce serious incidents, suspensions, and expulsions.

However, we do have a huge amount of data from decades of using punitive programs in schools and society (i.e., prison) that punishments are not significantly impactful on changing behaviors, as Goodwin (2021) also notes. Schools have had great success with Restorative Justice programs, PBIS programs, and even cooperative learning programs to increase positive behaviors, reduce harmful behaviors, and improve success in keeping students in school.

A large inner city high school in the mid-Atlantic region taught their students how to use cooperative learning for both problem solving and learning. The high school had been designated a failing school by the state. A consultant worked with the leadership team to collect data, including through classroom observations, in preparation for a root cause analysis to identify how to improve student outcomes at their school. She was struck by how often she heard staff telling her that the problem with their school was their classes were so large that teachers couldn't provide students the supports they needed.

However, when she was visiting classrooms, she consistently found only four to ten students per class. She asked the leadership team about the fact that many staff believed a root cause of their problem was too large a class size yet she kept observing very small classes. The team helped her understand that the class rosters indicated that there were thirty to forty students enrolled in almost every course section. However, in reality only four to ten students were showing up for each class each day. Long story short, the school began learning to use cooperative learning to teach students appropriate collaboration skills and to engage students in learning.

As word got around that the classrooms in the high school were no longer chaotic and/or endless lectures and that the students attending school were actually enjoying classes, more and more students began attending school. Those students listed on the rosters but not in school were now starting to show up. The school then really did develop a class size problem. The problem was they had more students than desks or chairs! However, despite the crowded classrooms, the school was buzzing with students engaged in learning.

Schools need to have student management programs that focus on:

- teaching and reinforcing positive behaviors,
- teaching students to problem solve,
- making amends when harm is created, and
- keeping students in school.

Schools must constantly monitor and correct when their data indicates that some groups of students are being denied an excellent education due to disciplinary practices.

In addition, rigorous research is needed on the effectiveness of programs that are designed to help schools move from punitive disciplinary actions to programs that teach positive, caring behavior. Schools need evidence of what works for the vast majority of their students so that they do not waste time, energy, and money on programs that do not help them ensure all students achieve at high levels.

Attendance

Poor attendance by some students is another issue that schools must address when doing whatever it takes to ensure all students graduate. Reasons for missing school are many. Students miss school or leave school due to financial obligations that require them to work to support themselves or their families, the need to provide childcare for siblings or their own children, and the lack of transportation. Some students disengage from school due to substance abuse, lack of academic supports, poor instruction, discipline policies, and/or poor relationships with teachers and staff (Baker, Sigmon, and Nugent, 2001; Ecker-Lyster and Niileksela, 2016).

According to Ecker-Lyster and Niileksela (2016), school-level characteristics account for almost half of the variance in dropout rates. Attendance issues for younger children can be impacted by school variables as well as by realities at home. However, good attendance from early on sets the stage for success in school. Despite the fact that many of the reasons for poor attendance appear to be non-school factors, if schools are equity schools—doing whatever it takes to ensure all students graduate high school college and career ready—they will do whatever it takes to help students attend school.

There was a first-grade student who was absent multiple days each week. To make matters worse, she was repeating first grade. The school set up a plan that if the child was not in school at the five-minute until school started mark, her teacher would notify the office. The principal, an assistant principal, or even the school secretary would jump in their car and go and get her. This child's parent worked nights and by the time she was to go to school the parent was usually fast asleep.

They learned from this situation that many of their other students were also struggling to get themselves to school, especially on time as their parents had already gone to work. They extended morning care hours (no charge) and provided alarm clocks (along with lessons on how to use them) so that students would know when it was time for them to leave for school. The school was in a very dense neighborhood, so it was a reasonable walk to school; students just needed to know when to head out.

There is a growing body of research on indicators that can help target students at risk of dropping out long before they reach that point (Baker, Sigmon, and Nugent, 2001; Balfanz, Herzog, and MacIver, 2007; Center for Equity and Excellence in Education, 2012). Two critical junctures in detecting early warning signs and preventing students from dropping out are sixth grade (often the transition for students from elementary to middle school) and the freshman year of high school. Ecker-Lyster and Niileksela (2016) found that students who end their freshman year on track to graduate are four times more likely to actually graduate.

Early warning signs of increased risk for dropping out include poor attendance, academic failure, suspension and other disciplinary issues, and a lack of good relationships with teachers and peers. Schools that learn to attend to these warning signs early on and intervene when found are much more successful in keeping students in school, ensuring students are mastering rigorous content, and improving their graduation rate.

A large high school and a small high school in the same district were both struggling with graduation rates. One school had graduation rate issues across all student groups while the other school had great graduation rates for white and more affluent students and poor rates for their Latinx students that often lived with economic hardships. They began tackling their graduation issues by focusing on students who were seniors and at risk for not graduating at the end of the year.

That tactic was helpful, even though for many of these seniors it took a fifth year of high school to graduate, but the exponential gains came when they started focusing on students as they entered their doors as freshman. They began using an early warning system and providing interventions as needed from the first day of high school. They continued to work with these students all the way through high school. This work led to significant increases in graduation rates.

It is never too late to intervene when a student is at risk for not graduating, even if it takes them an additional year of schooling. Educators need to celebrate the work schools do to get their fifth-year students across the line. Five years to graduate might be a demerit in the state's accountability system; however, getting a student to graduation is a life-long game changer for that student and their family. Celebrate it, whether it takes four years or five years.

Educators that stick with struggling students to keep them in school and help them graduate, even if it takes five years, are evidence of a Whatever It Takes school, especially when many of these struggling students often come to these schools in their junior and senior years of high school behind on the graduation pathway. However, if you teach in a Whatever It Takes school, when a student has multiple early warning signs going off much earlier in their school career, intervene right then and stick with them to the end.

This same district came to embrace intervening with attendance problems from kindergarten on. Each year, schools started the school year by identifying students that had unexcused absences of more than ten and more than thirty in the previous year. Before school began, they reached out to families to see what assistance was needed and established relationships with the families. When attendance issues did crop up, parents were much more willing to work with the school to improve their child's attendance. Previously, schools had just reported poor attendance to the court system, which then alienated parents and resulted in little improvement.

Models that have shown promise for increasing the graduation rate include Project Transition, Talent Development High School, High Schools that Work, Project GRAD, and First Things First (Center for Equity and Excellence in Education, 2012; Ecker-Lyster and Niileksela, 2016) More information on improving attendance and increasing graduation rates can be found at the websites listed here.

Evidence of Effectiveness for Attendance and/or Graduation Programs

- The What Works Clearinghouse under the topic Path to Graduation https://ies.ed.gov/ncee/wwc/FWW/Results?filters=,Path-to-Graduation from the U.S. Department of Education.

- Evidence for ESSA under the topic of Attendance at https://www.evidenceforessa.org/programs/attendance from Johns Hopkins University.
- Blueprints for Healthy Youth Development at https://www.blueprintsprograms.org/ from the University of Colorado at Boulder.

Basic Needs

Maslow's Hierarchy of Needs (1943) begins with the theory of human physiological needs as being most basic to human motivation. Educators are acutely aware that some students do not have their most basic physical needs met. Schools have and continue to be major players in providing for these needs to their students, especially students living with the impacts of poverty. Schools play a role in helping students access adequate nutrition, clothing, personal hygiene products, transportation, and health screenings.

The National School Lunch Act became law in 1946 (USDA Food and Nutrition Service, 2019). It is estimated that this act served 7.1 million children in its first year and more than thirty million children in 2016. The onset of the COVID-19 pandemic and the upheaval it caused in our society resulted in the federal government waiving the requirements regarding qualifications for the program and making meals available to any and every school-aged child during that time. Over the years, the program has also expanded to include school breakfast for millions of students. This program has been a foundation for meeting the nutrition needs of children.

In addition to this federal program, many schools and districts also partner with local food banks and other charities to provide nutritious food to students. These partners often provide backpacks of food to students and their families each weekend so that students are not without food when school is not in session. Some schools have bowls of nutritious snacks, provided by food banks, in classrooms and school offices that students can access, no questions asked, at any time during the day when they are hungry. Schools also often serve as weekly distribution sites for food banks, making it easier for families to access these services.

In one district, the non-profit providing food to families in need taught a cooking class once a week in a high school that served some of the district's most food-insecure students. Students learned to prepare nutritious, low-cost meals. At the end of each class, students were provided with a bag of groceries that included all the ingredients needed so that they could cook the meal they had just learned to prepare for their family that evening.

Clothing is another common need for which schools and their partners provide assistance. Many schools have clothing closets in order to easily access clothing, including winter coats and boots, to give to students when needed.

Schools frequently partner with organizations to ensure that students have winter clothing, school uniforms, etc., as needed. Schools have gone as far as having washers and dryers on their campus so that students can have clean clothes to wear. Students impacted by poverty often wear and sleep in the same clothes for days at a time, resulting in unpleasant smells that embarrass students and can result in shunning by their peers.

Some schools also engage families in using the washers and dryers not only for laundering their clothes, but also for bedding, linens, etc., to help remove head lice from the home. Schools often provide personal hygiene products and shower facilities to help students as well. Elementary schools that do not have locker rooms often have shower facilities installed on their campus for the sole purpose of supporting their students' personal hygiene.

In addition to laundry facilities, some schools offer vacuum cleaners for check out to help families improve hygiene at home as well as remove head lice from the home. Many years ago, an elementary school began checking out vacuum cleaners to families to help them eradicate head lice and get their children back in school. It took a little while, but the school eventually realized that it did not do any good to check out a vacuum to the family if they did not first provide a mini-lesson in how to use the vacuum cleaner! Don't assume that every family has had experience with how to use a vacuum cleaner.

Most schools have some type of limited health services. Some school districts provide adequate staff for a good school-nurse-to-student ratio and the nurses are able to provide a great first line of care and connect families with medical services that they need. Unfortunately, many school districts have a ratio of nurse to students that makes this almost impossible. These nurses are stretched very thin, making even minimal vision and hearing screening difficult. Some schools also provide dental screenings, especially in collaboration with their local dentist association, and scoliosis screenings.

Vision problems are often an issue that schools grapple with as they strive to educate students. When the school vision screening detects a possible need, getting the student an appointment with the eye doctor and then a pair of glasses is often a huge barrier. Parents lose wages if they have to take off from work to take their child to an eye exam, money to pay for the exam is a concern, and then if glasses are prescribed even more money is needed. In rural locations, getting to the eye doctor or glasses dispensary can be a ninety minute or more drive.

In one rural district there was an eye doctor available a couple of days a week. However, the local eyeglasses store did not provide glasses to students who were reliant on Medicaid. A shop that would accept Medicaid was an hour and a half away, a trip that hourly wage parents could not easily undertake. When the superintendent was getting her new glasses, she stumbled into a situation where the father was being told his daughter needed glasses. He would need to take a day off to drive her to and from another town for glasses. The superintendent discreetly paid for the child's glasses. She was one of her students and struggling to learn to read!

A recent study of the effects of school-based vision interventions on academic performance showed significant improvement for the most struggling students when they received glasses (Neitzel et al., 2021). In this study, students needing glasses were provided glasses at their school. In five years, this program tested the vision of more than sixty-four thousand students and distributed over eight thousand pairs of glasses through a partnership established between Johns Hopkins Schools of Education and Medicine, Baltimore City Public Schools, the Baltimore City Health Department, Warby Parker (an eyewear retailer), and Vision to Learn.

These researchers and schools are now grappling with how to ensure students are wearing their glasses each day, as well as how to quickly get them replaced when needed. This work and the results found in the study show strong promise for school and community partnership opportunities that are critical in closing another gap in the effort to ensure all of our students are reading on or above grade level.

SUMMING IT UP

The primary task of schools is to educate all our children so that they graduate high school college and/or career ready. The reality of many students is that circumstances in their lives such as poverty, mental health issues, substance abuse, and family needs become hurdles to achieving the education they need and deserve. If educators are committed to providing equity to students so that they do in fact all graduate college and/or career ready, they must address these issues. They cannot blame these circumstances for not reaching the goal.

Blaming the circumstances in which some students live is to fall into the trap of deficit thinking. All students bring incredible and widely varied assets to the table. Educators must approach these issues with an equity mindset and provide what is needed for each child to succeed. What is provided will not be the same for every child; it should be what each child needs so that they all are highly educated. Equity educators engage with their colleagues and partner with other organizations so that they can attend to students' mental, social, and physical health for the benefit of ensuring all children are well educated and ready to become the citizens our country needs for a bright future.

REFLECTION

There is a reflection section at the end of each of the remaining chapters of the book. It is intended to help you reflect on your school and district practices as well as your own individual practices. There is also a "Reflections and Next Steps" section at the end of the book that you may wish to use. It will allow you to make notes in one location regarding each of the chapters. This is to help you easily review your thoughts over all the issues raised throughout the book and then identify next steps to take in your own professional practice.

Reflections for chapter 8:

- How does your school support SEL for your students?

- How do you access resources for students that are struggling with mental health issues?

- What are your students' most critical social service needs? What agencies or non-profits could be helpful partners with these concerns?

- When a student's living situation is blamed for the lack of success in school, what do you do?

Chapter 9

Allocating Resources for Equity

If we define equity as providing each student whatever it takes to ensure they are mastering rigorous grade-level standards and graduating high school college and career ready, then we are saying that some students will need more than others to achieve this goal. That means we must allocate our resources, (time, people, and money) in ways that support equity. This means that some students will get more of a resource than others based on their needs. Gorski (2018) states, "There is no path to educational equity that does not involve a redistribution of access and opportunity" (p. 34).

Travers (2018) defines resource equity as "the allocation and use of resources to create student experiences that enable all children to reach empowering rigorous learning outcomes, no matter their race or income" (p. 1). Students living in adverse conditions must have schools that are able to provide more services in order to overcome these hurdles to learning (Darling-Hammond, 2019; Martin et al., 2018), as discussed in chapter 8. Darling-Hammond's research shows that when more money is expended on education for students living in poverty, achievement, graduation rates, and life outcomes improve.

TIME RESOURCES

Time is a resource that there is never enough of in education. Adding more time to the school year or day impacts budgets and competes with other interests of families. When resources are reallocated to add time to the school day or the school year, it is much easier to accomplish if the vast majority of the students in the school are living below or close to the poverty line. Extending times for school is helpful to these families.

However, if your student population is mixed to include both students living in poverty and more privileged students, you awaken the debate about students needing time for other activities, family time, and vacations. There are numerous schools where adding time was a successful intervention for ensuring all students achieved at high levels (see chapter 7). However, for most schools adding time requires not only reallocating the fiscal resources to pay for it, but also ensuring the community is in agreement.

Before adding time to the school day or year, educators should audit how the time they currently have is being used. What the leaders spend their time on sends a powerful message to stakeholders about district priorities. Some things to investigate as you audit how time is spent include the following:

- What percentage of time does the superintendent spend on teaching and learning?
- How often does the superintendent visit classrooms? Meet with teachers?
- What does a review of cabinet or other leadership meeting agendas indicate are priority issues?

What the principal and school leadership teams spend the most time on also communicates to the students and staff what are the most important issues:

- What percentage of time does the principal spend on teaching and learning?
- How often does the principal visit classrooms or attend collaboration meetings?
- What does a review of staff meeting agendas indicate are the priority issues?
- How much time is spent *implementing* a plan to improve student outcomes?

Analyzing student data is an important task for educators. However, analyzing the data without taking action is a waste of time. Some schools are excellent at gathering quarterly data and then spending the entire quarter analyzing the data without taking any action. Next thing they know, they are at the end of the quarter and have new data to start analyzing. All they are doing is analyzing data. They are not taking any action in regard to the data. Don't fall victim to data analysis paralysis!

Lastly, look at how time is being used in the classroom when auditing:

- How much instructional time is spent on teaching and learning versus housekeeping tasks, busy work, transitions, or down time?
- How much time is spent each day on developing literacy (in all content areas)?
- How much time is spent on learning that does not address grade-level standards?

- How often are there schoolwide special programs that do not directly relate to the standards being taught?

Learning time is a precious commodity in schools. It needs to be treated as such. This is not to say that school is about cracking the whip and holding the nose to the grindstone. School can be and should be incredibly fun and engaging. Educators' professional abilities come into play when they ensure that fun and engaging learning is moving students toward mastering the rigorous grade-level standards.

The first place that schools should start when looking for more time is to look honestly and carefully at how they use the time they currently have. They need to find the opportunities for recapturing some time from the daily and weekly routines. They need to ensure the stated priorities are really the priorities. If you teach in an elementary school and literacy and mathematics are the priority, they need to be a part of each day no matter what.

If you teach in a secondary school, do you adjust the schedule so that every class meets every day regardless of other events and put spirit assemblies at the end of the day, or is every event always scheduled for second period, greatly impacting instructional time for that period? Pep assemblies, celebrations, and other such activities can be scheduled at the end of the day so that students dismiss directly from the auditorium or gymnasium rather than needing to use precious time to get students back to class and settled down into the routine again.

Human Resources

The human resources in a school or district are the most valuable asset. We discussed in chapter 3 the importance of having the right people on staff for the development of a positive culture. Hill (2017) noted that "[t]eachers who are *willing* to serve a school's population of students are very different than teachers who *want* to serve that population" (p. 12, italics added). It is crucial that Whatever It Takes schools have staff that *want* to be there and see it as their purpose in life to be there.

Hiring staff that want to live near the school district, who just need a way to support themselves and see teaching as a possibility, or who believe that working in a school with large numbers of students living in poverty will result in fewer demanding or difficult parents (McKenzie and Scheurich, 2004) results in hiring staff that are willing, but do not *want* to serve the population of students in the school.

In addition to hiring the right people, schools and districts must also continue to develop and nurture their human resources. Educators are learners. Supporting the professional learning of staff keeps them engaged and energized. It is also an excellent opportunity to recognize that they are professionals and like all professionals are constantly refining and updating their skills. It is a time to let them know how much you value them.

Hiring Staff

Martin Haberman made a career of studying what makes some educators successful with marginalized youth while others fail. He used what he learned to help schools find ways to better determine which applicants had what it takes to be successful with their students and which ones were more likely to fail with more marginalized students and/or even leave the profession. The Haberman Educational Foundation continues this work today.

Haberman (1995) found these successful educators have the following characteristics:

- Have persistence and/or commitment.
- Protect learners and learning. Learning is primary; do not allow distractions.
- Engage students in active classrooms. Students can explain what they're learning.
- Are aware of *why* they are doing something and what will be accomplished.
- Do not blame the victim. Take responsibility for teaching and learning.
- Deeply respect and care for students.
- Manage the bureaucracy. Know what must be done and what can be ignored.
- Are fallible. Acknowledge mistakes and learn from them.
- Are emotionally and physically strong.
- Are organized.
- Elicit student effort. Convince students that they are needed in school.
- Do not threaten students.
- Are self-aware. Know prejudices.

Schools and districts committed to establishing equity seek out these types of educators to join their team. Carter (2000) noted that high-performing, high-poverty schools scour the earth to find such educators and keep on looking until they find the right match. The right match includes staff who want to work at your school and who are collaborative, learners, and willing to follow the evidence.

Unfortunately, as previously noted in chapters 4 and 5, not all teacher preparation programs prepare new teachers to follow the science of reading and use research-proven programs. Not all preparation programs prepare secondary content teachers for teaching the literacy of their discipline. So ensure, when hiring, that the person you are offering the position to is a continuous learner, collaborative, and willing to follow the research.

There are times when it is best not to hire for a position immediately despite having a pool of applicants. If the right person is not in that pool, keep looking. It will take juggling while staff help cover for the vacancy, but the juggling is worth it to get the right person in the position. Hiring the wrong person can result in incredible harm to students, their learning, and the school or district culture, not to mention the time, effort, and stress that will have to be endured to remove a wrong hire.

Developing Staff

We discussed professional learning in chapter 3 as it is a critical component of developing a strong, positive school or district culture. However, professional learning is also a resource. It is a way of investing in and keeping valuable personnel as well as a cost to be included in the district or school budget. We will review it briefly again, this time from the resource lens.

Costs involved in professional learning include time such as full days, half days, and time during the regular school day when staff can work and collaborate together. Also included are the costs of trainers and/or consultants, instructional coaches, administrative time for organizing professional learning, and any supplies or materials needed (Odden and Archibald, 2009). The investment in professional learning is worth it when it changes what happens in classrooms for improved student learning.

Professional learning that improves student learning is embedded, ongoing, and focused on instruction. It involves the collective participation of educators focusing on problems students are having in mastering the content and developing effective strategies for supporting students. Developing staff is a cost. It is an area that often is suggested for cuts when developing budgets, especially in leaner years. However, developing staff reaps rewards both in student outcomes and in staff retention.

Odden and Archibald (2009) found that schools that doubled student performance added many days of professional learning and used instructional coaches with a very specific focus that they worked on school or district wide. New York City District 2 eliminated most categorical program and instruction support staff at the district office in order to free up funds for professional development. Districtwide, they used those funds to relentlessly develop teacher expertise in teaching reading (Elmore and Burney, 1999).

Schools or districts have also found funds for professional learning by using categorical funding (such as Title I, Title III, etc.), combining district and school funds, and redeploying staff from resource rooms and the district offices to serve as instructional coaches. When operating from an equity perspective, some schools within a district will receive more professional resources based on the needs of their students and staff. Schools where the majority of their students are not mastering the standards may receive intensive support to strengthen their Tier 1 instruction while the other schools are not involved in these efforts.

Staff development funds have often been assaulted when budgets are tight, and there is always competition to use the funds for additional staff or increased compensation. In addition, the general public often does not realize the importance and power of professional learning, but rather see it as time when students are not in school causing childcare concerns for working parents.

Schools and districts need to actively articulate a comprehensive and coherent professional learning plan including the why and the expected gains. Darling-Hammond (2019) found that investments in developing teacher quality provided the largest gains in student performance. There will always be naysayers to professional learning who immediately brand it as a waste of time and money, including from staff who are threatened by the need to improve instruction. It is important to clearly articulate what the district or school goals are and why and how professional development is critical to achieving those goals.

Money Resources

The primary funding model for schools is each state provides money to school districts to cover expenses involved in providing education to students including such things as teacher salaries, support staff, materials, transportation, and facilities maintenance. Some states allocate money based on student or district characteristics, some based on school staffing positions, some based on property tax rates and equalization, and others use a hybrid of these methods.

Education Commission of the States (Fischer, Duncombe, and Syverson, 2021) data indicates that more than thirty states provide a minimum dollar amount for each student, or a base amount per student. States often provide additional funding for specific groups of students such as students receiving special education services (forty-nine states and DC), English language learners (forty-seven states and DC), students living in poverty (forty-three states and DC), gifted and talented (thirty-four states), and districts that are very small or isolated geographically (thirty-three states).

Money spent on education matters in regard to student outcomes, particularly for schools and districts that serve large numbers of marginalized students (Darling-Hammond, 2019; Knoff, 2019; Martin et al., 2018; Necochea and Cline, 1996; The Century Foundation, 2020). Necochea and Cline (1996) state that inequities in funding are compounded for students living in poverty as they are the most in need and whose families have the least capacity to meet these needs.

Whether looking at school and district funding across states, within individual states, or across districts, it is frequent that schools serving students with the greatest needs receive the fewest resources from their state and/or district (Baker and Corcoran, 2012; Darling-Hammond, 2019; Knoff, 2019; Martin et al., 2018). A review of state funding for education (Darling-Hammond, 2019) based on 2015 funding found that only twelve states provide additional funding of at least 5 percent for schools in which large numbers (30 percent or more) of students live in poverty.

Even more shocking, in the same review Darling-Hammond (2019) found that seventeen states actually provided fewer funds to districts with large numbers of students living in poverty. Her report, "Investing for Student Success: Lessons from State School Finance Reforms," includes a table (p. 3) that compares each state's spending per average student and for students in districts with 30 percent or greater of their students living in poverty. (See the report at https://learningpolicyinstitute.org/sites/default/files/product-files/Investing_Student_Success_REPORT.pdf.)

The number of states spending less for students living in poverty is disgraceful and certainly not equitable. Compounding the problem, wealthy states spend approximately three times what poor states spend. The wealthiest districts spend two to three times more per student than the poor districts. Darling-Hammond (2019) notes that there twenty-four states still not back to pre-2008 funding levels, when funding was greatly cut. Since 2008 the average student achievement based on National Assessment of Educational Progress has declined and gaps between white and Black students have increased. Both funding and student outcomes declined together after 2008.

Most federal funds for education are sent to states for them to distribute to districts. The funds are to supplement the state funds at schools serving large numbers of students living in poverty, students with disabilities, and/or English language learners. Federal funds are not intended to address funding inequities within states or across state lines (Martin et al., 2018).

Even within a state's border, the impact of Title I revenues to bolster resources for a poverty district is often minimal (Baker and Corcoran, 2012). When a district with large numbers of students in poverty gets a lesser state allocation per student than a district within the same state and with fewer students in poverty, you wonder if federal funds are supplementing state funds or are they supplanting: a clear violation of federal code.

Federal funds are often spread so thin within a state that their impact is minimal. Title I funds are intended to go to schools with large numbers or percentages of students living in poverty. The distribution of funds from the federal level to the states in basic grants per formula-eligible child (children living in poverty) varies widely. A 2019 report (Snyder et al.), on the formulas used to distribute these funds found the average allocation per formula-eligible child nationwide was $1,227. However, the average per formula-eligible child by state varied greatly from $984 in Idaho to $2,590 in Vermont.

The Office of Elementary and Secondary Education (2018) says that states are to provide Title I funds to districts "in which the number of children from low-income families is at least 10 and at least 5% of the [local education agency's] school aged population." This low bar (5 percent) allows states to distribute funds to the vast majority of districts in their state. Giving every district at least a little something from these funds is easier than taking a stand that the funds are going to be used to support only schools where there are students with the greatest needs.

So, against this background, what can educators in districts and schools do to more equitably distribute the resources needed by our most marginalized students? Of the funds received by districts, the vast majority of these funds, approximately 80 percent, are spent at the school site (Odden and Archibald, 2009). Districts and schools can use an equity lens for allocating resources even if the state does not.

The vast majority of district and school funds (85 percent or more) are spent on personnel costs. In order to reallocate resources equitably, personnel must be factored into this reallocation. This is often difficult for staff that work in districts or schools where specific staff positions are seen as a given or staff are asked to change schools because another school has a greater need. Staff often see themselves as employees of a particular school, rather than an employee of the district.

For example, a school that has always had four sections of first grade might assume that they will continue to have four sections of first grade despite their declining enrollment. Or at the secondary level because Latin has always been taught it is assumed it will always continue to be taught even when enrollment has dropped so low as to not even provide a full class load to one teacher. In other districts, all-day preschool programs might be provided in schools that have students significantly impacted by poverty, where schools in more affluent neighborhoods might not offer all-day preschool programs. Not every school gets the same thing.

Staff may take offense when the leadership proposes reallocating these positions to another school with greater need or to another position in the school that better serves students needing additional support. Usually, larger districts are more accustomed to staff transfers based on where the student needs are located. However, districts that have not been using an equity lens to assign staff often have developed the mentality that staff resources must be allocated equally rather than equitably. The concept that staff and resources follow students' needs takes some time for everyone to understand.

When budgeting resources for personnel, the starting point for a district or school is usually the number of students assigned to each teacher during the day or class period (Odden and Archibald, 2009). Many districts have guidelines in regard to ideal staffing ratios in classrooms. Once staff are allocated to meet these guidelines, the district or school can then analyze student needs and make decisions on where additional resources may be needed.

Student outcomes must remain the bottom line and be the determinant of how additional resources are allocated. If they are spread evenly across schools, grade levels, and/or student groups, there is a failure to recognize the need for equity to ensure that all students are mastering the rigorous grade-level standards. Martin et al. (2018) in their report "A Quality Approach to School Funding," state that schools serving large numbers of at-risk students must have additional, not just the same, resources in order to ensure all students master high standards.

Depending on the needs of their students, schools and/or districts may decide to reallocate more resources to grades kindergarten through third in order to improve student reading outcomes, or add more specials teachers (i.e., physical education, art, music, computer science, etc.) in an elementary school to provide time for all the teachers at a grade level to collaborate, analyze student data, and plan together during the school day.

Secondary schools might decide to decrease class sizes in Algebra classes while keeping other classes larger or rework the schedule so that teachers teach three classes per day per quarter instead of having six or seven classes a day per semester. This reduces the number of students that a single teacher is working to support at any one time. As discussed in chapter 8, schools may also redistribute personnel resources to better serve student mental health needs or other much needed social service supports.

Districts should allocate funds to schools based on the needs of the students in that school rather than ensuring that every school gets the same thing. This means that some schools will get additional state and/or district funds than others based on student needs, not just based on a total number of students. Schools should then follow suit and allocate their resources within the school once again based on student needs.

Carter's (2000) study of high-performing, high-poverty schools found that in high-performing schools the money is spent intentionally and targeted to improve student performance rather than spent by tradition or evenly dividing the funds. More and more districts are using formulas based on equity needs to distribute funds to schools. These formulas are not perfect any more than those used for Title I Basic Grants at the federal level. However, more and more districts use some types of equity formulas in an attempt to identify variables in student needs and get the money where it can best support students.

These schools and districts also review their formulas each year in an effort to continuously improve them. The use of formulas helps staff across the district understand how funds are distributed so that while they may not agree with the formula, at least they can determine that their school was allocated the correct number of personnel. If you are in a district that has not used equity formulas to distribute funds before, the first year or two of using them can be trying as much time is needed to help everyone understand the process.

In one district where a new superintendent was creating her first budget for the district, all of the elementary schools were given the same number of reading specialists as additional support. There was no consideration of enrollment or number of students needing additional reading support. She created a formula based on student assessment data that allocated reading specialists to schools based on the number of students in grades kindergarten through third that were reading below grade level.

She did not increase the pool of reading specialists (the district was already having to cut its budget), but rather redistributed them in a more equitable way. Some reading specialists had worked many years in a particular building and were now being asked to support students at another building. This was a new experience for them and their colleagues, and it was difficult at first. However, she was proud to report that staff rose to the challenge!

Schools must also look at the needs of their students when allocating their individual building resources. It is becoming less common for schools to be allocated a specific number of staff by position (i.e., three fourth-grade teachers, two fifth-grade teachers, etc.) and instead they are allocated a number of teaching positions that the school then distributes as needed. For example, an elementary school might be given thirty-six teaching positions and the school determines how to best use these positions.

An elementary principal and his leadership team were very concerned about their rising fourth-grade class. This class was performing much lower than their other classes. Despite efforts to provide more tutoring to these students in third grade, this class was still significantly below grade level. They decided to put more teachers at the fourth grade to have very small classes (with larger classes at grades three and five) and provide intensive instruction to these students.

The fourth-grade teachers had classes of twelve and focused intently on literacy and math. Their students made great progress that year, and the majority moved to fifth grade now on level. It was hard, intense work, but they seized the opportunity of having smaller classes to change their instruction so that every student was mastering the standards. Other schools have traded in some paraprofessional positions so that they could add another teaching position to create smaller classes for more intense instruction.

Creating and using equity formulas does not happen overnight. Schools and districts need to give themselves plenty of lead time when budgeting to create the formulas, try them out for unintended consequences, and ensure that all staff understand how they work. School leadership also needs to know what positions can be swapped out with each other without putting the district or school in a position of non-compliance with state or federal regulations.

For example, teaching and paraprofessional positions in the general fund can be swapped out with each other, but not swapped out by mixing in special education funds for general fund needs. However, a special education teacher and paraprofessional positions can be swapped with each other in the same budget to serve students with disabilities. The following are some sample equity budgeting formulas to provide some ideas on the types of concerns that schools and districts might want to consider in developing their own formulas.

There is evidence (Baker and Corcoran 2012; Darling-Hammond 2019; Martin et al., 2018) that indicates for many schools the fiscal resources spent to employ teachers is considerably greater in high-performing schools than in struggling schools. This is usually attributed to more experienced teachers teaching in these high-performing schools, especially since they are more likely to be suburban schools or schools in more privileged neighborhoods.

If struggling schools are staffed primarily by newer teachers, their salaries will be less and the overall expenditure for teachers at these schools will be less. This has led to the requirement that districts report the amount of dollars expended at each school on the ESEA state report cards (U.S. Department of Education, 2019b). This is something you will want to consider as you allocate resources. You might consider allocating an actual dollar amount per school for general education teachers and then allowing the school to determine how many teachers it can hire with those funds.

However, the author has also seen it work the other way. The experience of a teacher does not necessarily translate to effectiveness with students living in poverty or from other cultures. Schools have shown great improvement while employing a number of fairly new and therefore less expensive teachers. These new teachers were not set in their ways and were more open to embracing teaching methods that ensured all students were mastering the standards. They embraced the mindset of whatever it takes.

Sample Equity Staffing/Budgeting Formulas

Student numbers are based on estimated enrollments for the coming year. Rounding is used to create final allocation to feasible numbers (i.e., 0.2 = one work day) while also staying within the fixed number of full-time equivalency (FTE) available.

General Education Classrooms: Elementary Schools

(number of kindergarten students/twenty per class) + (number of first-grade students/twenty per class) + (number of second-grade students/twenty per class) + (number of third-grade students/twenty-five per class) + (number of fourth-grade students/twenty-five per class) + (number of fifth-grade students/twenty-five per class) = general education teacher FTE allocation. Each school can use the allocation as calculated or may put more teachers at one grade level and fewer at another as long as the total number of teachers does not exceed the total allocation. Each school can also use other general education positions or funds to increase the number of classroom teachers.

General Education Classrooms: Secondary Schools

[(number of students (in grades six, seven, and eight) x seven class periods a day) divided by twenty-five students per class] divided by five classes taught per day per teacher = number of general education teacher FTE allocation. Each school can use the allocation as calculated or may put more teachers at one grade or content level and fewer at another as long as the total number of teachers does not exceed the total allocation. Each school can also use other general education positions or funds to increase the number of classroom teachers.

English Language Development: Co-Teaching Model

Up to eight English learners per grade level/class equals a section. English language development teachers at the elementary level can support six sections per FTE; at the secondary level they can support five sections per FTE. Schools must be careful to schedule English learners into co-taught classes in a cluster of students, with no more than eight English learner students per class so that there are ample English-speaking peers in each section as well.

Elementary schools: (number of first-grade sections + number of second-grade sections + number of third-grade sections + number of fourth-grade sections + number of fifth-grade sections) divided by six sections/teacher = number of teacher FTE.

Secondary schools: (# of ninth-grade sections + number of tenth-grade sections + number of eleventh-grade sections + number of twelfth-grade sections) divided by five sections/teacher = number of teacher FTE.

Elementary Reading Specialists

This formula is based on the assumption that the district has a limited number of reading specialist positions that can be allocated. In this example, there are a total of twenty reading specialists to be allocated among the elementary schools.

Table 9.1. Reading Specialists Allocations

Reading Specialists Allocations				
Weighted Measure	School A	School B	....	Districtwide Total
(number of students scoring at the 20th percentile or below in reading in grades one to three) x 1.0	60 X 1.0 = 60	20 x 1.0 = 20	....	
(number of students scoring between the 40th and 21st percentile in reading in grades one to three) x 0.5	20 x 0.5 = 10	60 x 0.5 = 30	....	
Total weighted measure	70	50	....	500
Proportion of districtwide weighted total	14%	10%	....	
Calculated full-time equivalent reading specialists	2.8	2	....	20

Social Workers

Six components were included in this formula for social workers based on their primary responsibilities in the example district. Each component is weighted by the number of students in this category and the estimated number of hours/year/student that category requires on average. Social workers in the district were the developers of this formula. A social worker's primary tasks and number of estimated hours per year per student for each task was determined to be:

- All students: classroom lessons, response to intervention, support group meetings = one hour/student
- Free/reduced meal student: parent paperwork, nutrition support = two hours/student
- 504 plan student: planning meeting, follow-up, documentation = five hours/student
- Homeless student: identification, plan, follow-up, resources = twelve hours/student
- Behavioral support student: weekly sessions = thirty-six hours/student

- High absenteeism student: Family check-ins, resources, monitor = six hours/student

Table 9.2 Social Worker Allocations

Social Worker Allocations				
Weighted Measure	School A	School B	....	Districtwide Total
Total school enrollment x 1 hour	200 x 1 = 200	400 x 1 = 400	....	
Total number of free/reduced price meal students x two hours	60 X 2 = 120	80 x 2 = 160	....	
Total number of students with a 504 plan x five hours	10 x 5 = 50	30 x 5 = 150	....	
Total number of homeless students x twelve hours	10 x 12 = 120	0 x 12 = 0	....	
Total number of behavioral support students	0 x 36 = 0	5 x 36 = 180	....	
Total students with more than ten absences	5 x 6 = 30	10 x 6 = 60	....	
Total weighted measure	556	950	....	5000
Proportion of districtwide weighted total	11%	19%	....	
Calculated social worker full-time equivalent allocation	1 (1.1 rounded)	2 (1.9 rounded)		10

Special Education

Special education allocations can be some of the most difficult formulas to devise. Districts have created them by calculating the total number of special education minutes on Individualized Education Programs (IEPs) districtwide and then distributing the resources based on the school's proportion of the total minutes of special education services needed district wide (per student IEPs). This can lead to padding of IEPs with minutes to justify the need for a higher allocation at a school. Minutes on IEPs should reflect a student's needs, not the school's desire to have additional staff.

More successful formulas provide a weighting based on disability category. Then for students that are in the top quartile or are an outlier as far as the number of minutes per week, compared to other students with the same disability, there is an additional weighting added. Each school is assigned a minimum of one special education teacher and additional allocation of resources is based on the weighting calculations.

Weighting components could include:

- Speech services = 0.5 weight; speech/language development = 1.0 weight
- Other health impaired, learning disabled, deaf/hard of hearing = 1.0 weight
- Multiple disabilities, developmental delay, traumatic brain injury = 2.0 weight
- Autism spectrum disorder, emotional disability, intellectual disability = 3.0 weight
- Excess minutes: top quartile = 0.5 weight
- Excess minutes: outlier = 0.75 weight

Facilities and Equipment

In addition to time and personnel, school and/or district funding pays for instructional materials and facilities. The case that schools with large numbers of marginalized students are most often under-resourced has already been made. This under-resourcing of schools and districts does not just apply to staffing concerns, but also to overall resources available. This under-resourcing results in great disparity in the instructional materials and facilities that students experience as well.

Inequities in funding that result in inadequate equipment and unsafe conditions for learning are also a part of the inequities that many of our students experience. Learning-Ready Facilities is one of the dimensions of resource equity called for by Travers (2018) in his dimensions of resource equity that support student achievement. This does not mean that every school has to be a brand new facility. Rather, students should have a safe and supportive place to learn.

Safe and supportive schools have good air quality including heating, cooling, and fresh air exchange and purification so that students are able to focus on their learning and reduce the risk of spreading germs or breathing highly polluted air. Every year there continues to be school closures due to lack of adequate heat or cooling. The COVID-19 pandemic has reinforced the need for ensuring students have purified air to breath.

A school in middle America was located directly across the highway from a major aircraft manufacturing plant. Not far from that were other plants that created asphalt and concrete as well as a landfill and incinerator. It is not surprising that this school was listed as one of the top ten schools in the country for students breathing polluted air in the early 2000s. The number of students with asthma that the school nurse was constantly assisting with inhalers and breathing treatments suggested that something was impacting the neighborhood.

Other schools, especially in August and September, release early for the day when temperatures soar. Many of the schools are old brick buildings with no air conditioning and by noon on a hot day the classrooms are ovens with only wide-open windows and a few fans to try to reduce the temperatures. It is common for classroom temperatures to be above a hundred degrees Fahrenheit. Warming temperatures will continue to create schools without adequate air conditioning as unsafe learning environments.

Adequate drinking water and restroom facilities can also be big hurdles for schools. There was a great deal of news coverage of the Flint, Michigan, water crisis and its impact on its children and their schools. There are schools where all the drinking fountains are shut off due to the old plumbing in the building contaminating the water. Students get a carton of milk and a carton of water at lunch. In addition, many of the restroom facilities are no longer working and the district does not have funds to repair them. This means that some restrooms have no working toilets while others might have only one working toilet.

Our marginalized students, students living in poverty, students of color, and students learning English are our most likely students to be attending school in old buildings without adequate heating, cooling, and fresh air ventilation, and in buildings with inadequate and unsafe plumbing. They are the ones most impacted by development that puts incinerators and potentially harmful manufacturing in close proximity to schools.

Instructional equipment is another big variable between the schools with adequate resources and those without. Graphing calculators, high-powered microscopes, well-stocked chemistry labs, kilns in the art class, a plethora of musical instruments, resource-rich media centers, learning devices or computers for every student, etc., are standard issue in well-resourced schools. However, such resources are often very thin if even available in schools where our most marginalized students attend. These are the families that are least able to provide their children with laptops and graphing calculators.

The onset of remote learning on a grand scale with the COVID-19 pandemic enabled more schools to obtain learning devices for each child thanks to an infusion of federal funds. However, internet connectivity for children living in poverty or very remote areas is not a given. Some districts had previously developed after-hour study spaces where students could connect at school. They created partnerships with local fast-food places, libraries, and recreation centers to provide space for students to connect and work on their devices outside school.

However, when the pandemic started, even these places were closed. How were these children able to access what was needed for their learning if they had no connectivity? When the pandemic started, a district had adequate devices for each student to have one at home. However, there were many homes without connectivity due to the remoteness of their house or lack of financial resources. The district's technology office, curriculum and instruction office, superintendent, and school leaders jumped into action to get these families connected one way or another.

Funds had to be found to pay for these connections and monthly costs of subscriptions. The above noted people worked to secure a great deal of funding from several local foundations so that they had funds to connect every family that needed it and to pay their bill for the next eighteen months. (At that time, they had no idea how long distance learning would be their reality.) They were extremely proud of pulling this all together in one month's time. They had worked with multiple internet providers to make it happen and had gone to numerous homes to help families connect.

They were proud to have secured the resources to make it happen. However, not everyone felt the same way about it. A board of education member's conversation with the superintendent shortly after revealed a different point of view. The member was irritated that it took a month to get every last child connected and secondly upset that the district was paying for some students' connectivity, although grant funded. He felt like this was a parent responsibility and they should just make it happen if they wanted their child to learn. Doing whatever it takes to ensure all students are highly educated was not a part of his mindset.

As a country we developed a greater understanding of the disadvantages many of our students have when they do not have devices and internet connections for learning at home. Let's hope that with the recently passed federal infrastructure bill connectivity for learning will be something every child has, regardless of their circumstances, in the near future. It is an essential utility. The same as power and water.

It should also be noted that distance learning during the pandemic failed miserably as measured by student outcomes. While some students continued learning or even thrived under these conditions, overall student achievement across our country in literacy and mathematics declined as illustrated by state assessment data. Our most vulnerable students once again got the short end of the stick.

This book is not advocating for devices and connectivity for every student in order to increase distance learning. Rather, it is advocating for devices and connectivity for every student to support their learning, both in the classroom and at home. Just as pencil and paper have been critical tools for student learning (previously slates and chalk), computers and/or similar devices and connectivity is a critical tool for student learning in this era. Those students without these tools are immediately at a disadvantage.

SUMMING IT UP

Some of the most telling facts that highlight the inequality of our schools are the differences in student outcomes between schools with a large number of marginalized students and those with few marginalized students as well as the difference in resources available to these two types of schools. If we want to seize the American dream that education is the great equalizer for all children, then we must invest the resources needed to make it so. We must acknowledge that some schools will need more time, people, and money than other schools to ensure all students graduate high school college and/or career ready.

The Century Foundation (2020) in their report on closing the funding gaps, states:

> One of the starkest examples of this inequality, as well as a leading cause of it, is our nation's highly unequal and highly segregated K-12 public education system. By underinvesting in our public schools, we rob millions of American children—particularly Black, brown, and low-income children—of the opportunity to succeed. Inequality in effect begins at birth.

Our choices as a nation and as citizens of our states and territories have created this funding gap inequity and corresponding gap in student outcomes as a result.

REFLECTION

There is a reflection section at the end of each of the remaining chapters of the book. It is intended to help you reflect on your school and district practices as well as your own individual practices. There is also a "Reflections and Next Steps" section at the end of the book that you may wish to use. It will allow you to make notes in one location regarding each of the chapters. This is to help you easily review your thoughts over all the issues raised throughout the book and then identify next steps to take in your own professional practice.

Reflections for chapter 9:

- What would be the result of a time audit on your classroom, school, or district? What would it indicate are the priorities? How could you improve your use of time?

Allocating Resources for Equity 183

- When hiring personnel for your school or district, how do you ensure new hires *want* to serve your students?

- How does your classroom, school, or district allocate resources through an equity lens rather than an equal lens? What more could it do?

Epilogue

Our children are our most precious resource. They are the joy of our lives and our hope for the future. The idea that our children are our most precious resource includes all our children, not just our biological or adopted children: all children in our country. While this book was being written, the news media continued to point out the current struggles with which our country was grappling: a pandemic, an increasing number of violent deaths, hunger and homelessness, refugees fleeing violence and persecution, civil discord and hostility, climate change happening at an alarming rate, and economic uncertainty for millions of people.

Humankind has faced multiple threats before and prevailed. Our country has faced threats before and led the way with ingenuity and passion in addressing and overcoming these threats. We can prevail again, if we put our minds and hearts to the tasks. However, it will take us working together to implement solutions. Every day, educators can make it happen in their classrooms, schools, and districts. They can ensure that all of their children are learning to the highest levels.

If each educator, across the country, ensures that our children, the children for whom we have been given the responsibility to educate, are educated to the highest level, then together all our children are learning at high levels. All of our children must be educated to the highest levels so that they can prevail in solving the problems of our country and our world. They must master rigorous standards and graduate high school college and career ready. This is our American ideal—a thorough education for all. When this gift is given to all our children, our future will be bright.

Currently not all of our children graduate mastering the standards and college and/or career ready. Our ideal has not yet been achieved. Some of our most precious resources, our children, are not having their potential maximized. We currently have an education system that allows many of our children to be educated to a lesser standard. As everyday educators, we can change this. We can reach our goal of all students graduating college and/or career ready by providing every child whatever it takes to help them master rigorous standards. This book details some of the things that educators can do to make this happen in their schools and districts.

It will take courage and relentlessness, but it is possible. We can continuously, relentlessly, and simultaneously assess our cultures and our systems within our schools and districts for barriers that impede many of our students. We can relentlessly and step by step address and remove these barriers. Remember, education in our country started out for the few and the privileged. Look how far we have come. Our schools include all children. Now we must ensure *all* students achieve at high levels. The goal is in sight. Let's go get it.

We can address our cultural issues in our schools and districts by:

- searching our hearts and minds to root out bias, deficit thinking, and racial erasure (McKenzie and Scheurich, 2004),
- identifying and addressing bias and deficit thinking in our school cultures,
- celebrating and encouraging inclusiveness and doing whatever it takes,
- seeking out and onboarding like-minded educators to work alongside us,
- sharing our passion to educate all students and inviting our community to join, and
- modeling learning as we improve our craft for the success of all children.

We can address our systemic issues in our schools and districts by:

- ensuring that every student is reading on or above grade level by third grade;
- ensuring that every student is literate in the content areas;
- expecting all students to learn and providing appropriate grade-level instruction;
- providing rigorous, *research-proven*, and scaffold instruction;
- supporting all students in completing advanced opportunity classes;
- ensuring all students have preventative mental health supports and interventions;
- providing discipline that is caring, instructive, and fair for all students;
- ensuring students' basic needs are met to enable them to engage in learning; and
- allocating our resources with equity so that all students have what they need.

Accomplishing this list will not be easy and is not for the faint of heart. However, schools throughout our country do this every day. They have the will and the courage to constantly assess and improve their culture and their systems to ensure that all of their students graduate high school college and career ready. If you are just starting, tackle one cultural and one systemic issue at a time. Work on the culture and the system together.

For example, you might start culturally by tackling deficit thinking by learning more about what it is, identifying the strengths your students bring to school, and gently calling out deficit thinking when you hear or observe it in your school. One school had a quarter jar in the teacher's lounge. Expressing deficit thinking required that you put a quarter in the jar. It was a gentle way of keeping the staff on their toes and creating a fund for hosting a staff and family celebration at the end of the year.

While working on your culture, you also need to tackle at least one of the systemic issues in your school that is creating barriers. If you work in an elementary school, you might rework your system for teaching reading so that every child is reading on or above grade level by third grade. There are research-proven programs that can help you do this. If you work in a secondary school, you might ensure that students are developing literacy in their content classes so that they can read, reason, and write like budding scientists, mathematicians, etc. Provide the professional learning teachers need to teach the literacy of their content.

This work is not without its hardships. When you engage in this work you will face opposition from some parents of more privileged high achievers who believe such actions will threaten the quality of education for their own children. Opposition may also come from staff who often resent that they are being asked to teach students working below level (rather than believing that all students can achieve at high levels) and community members who feel threatened by the concept and establishment of equity (Boykin and Noguera, 2011).

The author was once told by a school board member to quit using the word equity. This opposition will take aim at you in your school and/or district, on social media, through the traditional news media, and in community gathering places. They may say they can't trust you or you are not being transparent or teachers are working in fear and intimidation or teachers aren't working hard enough or you are part of the liberal left or the radical right. These are common experiences for those who strive for equity. Superintendents, principals, district leaders, and equity task forces get accused of the same things over and over.

School board members will also be under attack. School boards are the governing bodies of school districts. As McGhee (2021) noted, racial resentment is often aimed at the government with accusations that the government is racist. Either the government is racist by tolerating Jim Crow laws, and separate but equal facilities, etc., or the government is racist because of civil rights laws, social spending, and affirmative action. Either view sees the government as untrustworthy. School boards and district leaders are experiencing the phenomenon of no matter what they do, some groups don't approve and therefore do not trust them.

Remember how far we have come. Education in the United States started out primarily for white males with privilege. Over the years, we have invited more groups to the education table. The educators before us did the hard work to do this. We have increased our standards for what we expect all children to know and be able to do. We now expect all students to graduate high school college and/or career ready. As the educators that came before us did this hard work, it is now our turn to continue the forward progress until we reach the ideal of a rigorous education for all students. We can do this. Our most vulnerable children are depending on us.

Bibliography

Adams, G. L., and Engelmann, S. (1996). *Research in direct instruction: 25 years beyond DISTAR*. Seattle, WA: Educational Achievement Systems.

Adams, M., and Bell, L. A. (Eds). (2016). *Teaching for diversity and social justice*, third edition. New York, NY: Routledge.

Adams, M., and Zuniga, X. (2007). Getting started: core concepts for social justice education. In M. Adams, L. A. Bell, and P. Griffin (Eds.). *Teaching for diversity and social justice*, third edition, 27–53. New York, NY: Routledge.

Adelman, H., and Taylor, L. (n.d.). *Embedding mental health as schools change*. Los Angeles, CA: Center for Mental Health in Schools and Student/Learning Supports.

Allington, R. L. (2012). *What really matters for struggling readers: Designing research-based programs*. Boston, MA: Pearson Education, Inc.

Allington, R. L., and McGill-Franzen, A. (Eds.) (2018). *Summer reading: Closing the rich/poor reading achievement gap*, second edition. New York, NY: Teachers College Press.

Anderson, M. (2013). Connecting working-class and ethnic-minority students and families to school. In J. S. Brooks and N. W. Arnold (Eds.). (2013). *Antiracist school leadership: Toward equity in education for America's students*, 113–51. Charlotte, NC: Information Age Publishing, Inc.

Applebee, A. N., and Langer, J. (1983). Instructional scaffolding: reading and writing as natural language activities. *Language Arts, 60*(2), 168–75.

Archer, A. L., and Hughes, C. A. (2011). *Explicit instruction: Effective and efficient teaching*. New York, NY: Guilford Press.

Aukerman, M. and Schuldt, L. C. (2021). What matters most? Towards a robust and socially just science of reading. *Reading Research Quarterly, 56*(S1), S85–S103.

Australian Society for Evidence Based Teaching. (n.d.). *Evidence-based teaching*. Retrieved on November 27, 2021, at https://www.evidencebasedteaching.org.au/.

Bailey, T. R. (2019). *Is MTSS the new RTI? Depends on where you live*. Center on Multi-Tiered Supports at the American Institutes for Research. Retrieved September 17, 2021, at https://mtss4success.org/blog/mtss-new-rti-depends-where-you-live.

Baker, B. D., and Corcoran, S. P. (2012). *The stealth inequalities of school funding: How state and local school finance systems perpetuate inequitable student spending*. Center for American Progress. Retrieved November 5, 2021, https://www.americanprogress.org/article/the-stealth-inequities-of-school-funding/.

Baker, M. L., Sigmon, J. N., and Nugent, M. E. (2001, September). Truancy reduction: Keeping students in school. *OJJDP Juvenile Justice Bulletin*. Washington, DC: U.S. Department of Justice, Office of Justice Programs.

Balfanz, R., Herzog, L., and MacIver, D. J. (2007). Preventing student disengagement and keeping students on the graduation path in urban middle-grades schools: Early identification and effective interventions. *Educational Psychologist, 42*, 223–35.

Barth, R. S. (1990). *Improving schools from within: Teachers, parents, and principals can make the difference*. San Francisco, CA: Jossey-Bass.

Barth, R. S. (2001). *Learning by heart*. San Francisco, CA: Jossey-Bass.

Baye, A., Lake, C., Inns, A., and Slavin, R. E. (2019). Effective reading programs for secondary students. *Reading Research Quarterly, 54*(2), 133–66.

Borman, G. D., and Boulay, M. (Eds.). (2004). *Summer learning: Research, policies, and programs*. Mahwah, NJ: Lawrence Erlbaum Associates Publishers.

Boykin, A. W., and Noguera, P. (2011). *Creating the opportunity to learn: Moving from research to practice to close the achievement gap*. Alexandria, VA: ASCD.

Brendefur, J. L., and Carney, M. B. (2016). The relationship between high-school mathematics teachers' beliefs and their practices in regards to intellectual quality. *Journal of Mathematics Education, 9*(1), 88–111.

Brendefur, J., Strother, S., Carney, M., and Hughes, G. (2013). *Mathematical thinking for instruction workbook: MIT workbook K-3*. Boise, ID: Developing Mathematical Thinking Institute, Inc.

Brooks, J. S., and Arnold, N. W. (Eds). (2013). *Antiracist school leadership: Toward equity in education for America's students*. Charlotte, NC: Information Age Publishing.

Brown, T. J. (1999). *Teaching the poor and children of color*. Columbia, MD: Brown and Associates Educational Consultants.

Brownell, M. T., Ciullo, S., and Kennedy, M. J. (2020–21). High Leverage Practices: Teaching students with disabilities—and all students who need a learning boost. *American Educator, 44*(4).

Bruns, E. J., Duong, M. T., Lyon, A. R., Pullmann, M. D., Cook, C. R., Cheney, D., and McCauley, E. (2016). Fostering SMART partnerships to develop an effective continuum of behavioral health services and supports in schools. *American Journal of Orthopsychiatry, 86*(2), 156–70.

Buehl, D. (2011). *Developing readers in the academic disciplines*. Newark: DE: International Reading Association.

Burns, M. (2004). Writing in math. *Educational Leadership, 62*(2), 30–33.

Calderon, M. (Ed.). (2012). *Breaking through: effective instruction and assessment for reaching English learners*. Bloomington, IN: Solution Tree Press.

Calhoun, G., and Elliot, R. (1977). Self-concept and academic achievement of educable retarded and emotionally disturbed children. *Exceptional Children, 44*, 379–80.

California Department of Education. (2000). *English-language arts content standards for California public schools: Kindergarten through grade twelve*. Sacramento, CA: California Department of Education.

California Department of Education. (2013). *California common core state standards: English language arts & literacy in history/social studies, science, and technical subjects*. Sacramento, CA: California Department of Education.
Cannon, J. S., Kilburn, M. R., Karoly, L. A., Mattox, T., Muchow, A. N., and Buenaventura, M. (2017). *Investing early: Taking stock of outcomes and economic returns from early childhood programs*. Santa Monica, CA: RAND Corporation.
Carnegie Council on Adolescent Development's Task Force on Education of Young Adolescents. (1989). *Turning points: Preparing American youth for the 21st century*. Washington, DC: Carnegie Council on Adolescent Development's Task Force on Education of Young Adolescents.
Carnevale, A. P., Strohl, J., Gulish, A., Van Der Werf, M., and Campbell, K. P. (2019). *The unequal race for good jobs: How whites made outsized gains in education and good jobs compared to Blacks and Latinos*. Washington, DC: Georgetown University, Center on Education and the Workforce.
Carter, S. C. (2000). *No excuses: Lessons from 21 high-performing, high-poverty schools*. Washington, DC: The Heritage Foundation.
CASEL. (n.d.). *Collaborating states initiative*. Retrieved October 21, 2021, https://casel.org/about-us/our-mission-work/collaborating-states-initiative/.
Center for Equity and Excellence in Education. (2012). *Evidence based resources for keeping students on track to graduation*. Arlington, VA: George Washington University.
Center for Public Education. (2016). *Educational equity: What does it mean? How do we know when we reach it?* Center for Public Education. Retrieved February 11, 2021, at https://www.nsba.org/-/media/NSBA/File/cpe-educational-equity-research-brief-january-2016.pdf.
Chall, J. S. (2000). *The academic achievement challenge: What really works in the classroom?* New York, NY: Gilford Press.
Chambers, B., Cheung, A. C. K., and Slavin, R. E. (2016). Literacy and language outcomes of balanced and developmental-constructivist approaches to early childhood education: A systematic review. *Educational Research Review, 18*, 88–111.
Chappell, S., Nunnery, J., Pribesh, S., and Hager, J. (2011). A meta-analysis of supplemental educational services (SES) provider effects on student achievement. *Journal of Education for Students Placed at Risk, 16*(1), 1–23.
Chatterji, R., Campbell, N., and Quirk, A. (2021). *Closing advanced coursework equity gaps for all students*. Washington, DC: Center for American Progress.
Checkley, K. (2001). Algebra and activism: Removing the shackles of low expectations—A conversation with Robert P. Moses. *Educational Leadership, 59*(2), 6–11.
Chenoweth, K. (2007). *It's being done: Academic success in unexpected schools*. Cambridge, MA: Harvard Education Press.
Cheung, A. C. K., and Slavin, R. E. (2012). Effective reading programs for Spanish-dominate English language learners (ELLs) in elementary grades: A synthesis of research. *Review of Educational Research, 82*(4), 351–95.
Collins, J. (2001). *Good to great: Why some companies make the leap and other don't*. New York, NY: Harper Collins Publishers

Common Core State Standards Initiative. (n.d.). Retrieved on February 18, 2021, at http://www.corestandards.org/about-the-standards/development-process/.

Common Core State Standards Initiative. (2010). *Common core state standards for English language arts & literacy in history/social studies, science, and technical subjects.* Retrieved August 30, 2021, at http://www.corestandards.org/wp-content/uploads/ELA_Standards1.pdf.

Common Core State Standards Initiative. (2010). *Common core state standards for mathematics.* Retrieved September 2, 2021, at http://www.corestandards.org/wp-content/uploads/Math_Standards1.pdf.

Council of Great City Schools. (2014, September). *Implementing Common Core assessments challenges and recommendations.* Retrieved February 18, 2021, at https://www.cgcs.org/cms/lib/DC00001581/Centricity/Domain/4/Implementing%20Common%20Core%20Assessments-2014.pdf.

Cruz, L. F. (2019, August 13). *How can we collectively create school cultures that eliminate gaps* [Leadership Teams Workshop]. Hailey, ID: Blaine County School District.

Cummins, J. (1984). *Bilingual education and special education: Issues in assessment and pedagogy.* San Diego, CA: College Hill

Cunningham, P. M., and Allington, R. L. (1994). *Classrooms that work: They can all read and write.* New York, NY: HarperCollins College Publishers.

Darling-Hammond, L. (2019). *Investing for student success: Lessons from state school finance reforms.* Palo Alto, CA: Learning Policy Institute.

Darling-Hammond, L., Hyler, M. E., and Gardner, M. (2017). *Effective teacher professional development.* Palo Alto CA: Learning Policy Institute.

Darling-Hammond L., Wei, R. C., Andree, A., Richardson, N., and Orphanos, S. (2009). *Professional learning in the learning profession: A status report on teacher development in the United States and aboard.* Oxford, OH: National Staff Development Council.

Davis, J. L. (2010). *Bright, talented, and Black: A guide for families of African American gifted learners.* Scottsdale, AZ: Great Potential Press.

Deal, T. E., and Peterson, K. D. (2016). *Shaping school culture*, third edition. San Francisco, CA: Jossey-Bass.

DiAngelo, R. (2021). *Nice racism: How progressive white people perpetuate racial harm.* Boston, MA: Beacon Press.

Donohoo, J. (2017). *Collective efficacy: How educators' beliefs impact student learning.* Thousand Oaks, CA: Corwin.

DuFour, R., DuFour, R., Eaker, R., Many, T. W., and Mattos, M. (2016). *Learning by doing: A handbook for professional learning communities at work.* Bloomington, IN: Solution Tree Press.

Dweck, C. S. (2006). *Mindset: The new psychology of success.* New York, NY: Random House Publishing Group

Ecker-Lyster, M., and Niileksela, C. (2016). Keeping students on track to graduate: A synthesis of school dropout trends, prevention, and intervention initiatives. *Journal of At-Risk Issues, 19*(2), 24–31.

Elliott, S. N., and Bartlett, B. J. (2016). *Opportunity to learn*. Oxford Handbooks Online, Retrieved February 21, 2021, at https://www.oxfordhandbooks.com/view/10.1093/oxfordhb/9780199935291.001.0001/oxfordhb-9780199935291-e-70.

Elmore, R. F. (2008). *School reform from the inside out: Policy, practice, and performance*. Cambridge, MA: Harvard University Press.

Elmore, R. F., and Burney, D. (1999). Investing in teacher learning: Staff developing and instructional improvement. In L. Darling-Hammond and G. Sykes (Eds.). *Teaching as the learning profession: Handbook of policy and practice*, 263–91. San Francisco, CA: Jossey-Bass.

Every Student Succeeds Act. 20 U.S.C. § 6301 (2015). https://www.govinfo.gov/content/pkg/USCODE-2010-title20/pdf/USCODE-2010-title20-chap70-subchapI.pdf.

Ferguson, D., Desjarlais, A., and Meyer, G. (2000). *Improving education: The promise of inclusive schooling*. Newton, MA: National Institute for Urban School Improvement.

Ferguson, R. F. (2007). *Toward excellence with equity: An emerging vision for closing the achievement gap*. Cambridge, MA: Harvard Education Press.

Fiarman, S., Kyles-Smith, K., and Less, A. (2021). Is your approach to continuous improvement colorblind? *Educational Leadership*, 87(6), 16–21.

Fien, H., Chard, D. J., and Baker, S. K. (2021). Can the evidence revolution and multi-tiered systems of support improve education equity and reading achievement? *Reading Research Quarterly*, 56(S1), S105–S118.

Fiester, L. (2010). *Early warning! Why reading by the end of third grade matters*. Annie E. Casey Foundation. Retrieved February 22, 2021, at https://www.aecf.org/resources/early-warning-why-reading-by-the-end-of-third-grade-matters/.

Fiester, L. (2013). *Early warning confirmed: A research update on third grade reading*. Annie E. Casey Foundation. Retrieved on February 22, 2021, at https://gradelevelreading.net/wp-content/uploads/2013/11/EarlyWarningConfirmed.pdfv.

Fischer, A., Duncombe, C., and Syverson, E. (2021). *50-State comparison: K-12 and special education funding*. Education Commission of the States. Retrieved November 2, 2021, at https://www.ecs.org/50-state-comparison-k-12-and-special-education-funding/.

Fischer, A., Keily, T., and Weyer, M. (2020). *Exploring new research on pre-k outcomes*. Education Commission of the States. Retrieved December 15, 2021, at https://www.ecs.org/wp-content/uploads/Exploring_New_Research_on_Pre-K_Outcomes.pdf.

Flesh, R. (1955). *Why Johnny can't read: And what you can do about it*. New York: Harper and Brothers.

Frazier, J., and Morrison, F. (1998). The influence of extended-year schooling on growth of achievement and perceived competence in early elementary school. *Child Development*, 69(2), 495–517.

Fronius, T., Darling-Hammond, S., Persson, H., Guckenburg, S., Hurley, N., and Petrosino, A. (2019). *Restorative justice in U.S. schools: An updated research review*. San Francisco: CA: WestEd Justice and Prevention Research Center.

Fuchs, D., Fuchs, L. S., and Fernstrom, P. (1993). A conservative approach to special education reform: Mainstreaming through trans environmental programming and curriculum-based measurement. *American Educational Research Journal*, 30, 149–77.

Fullan, M. (2007). *The new meaning of educational change*. New York, NY: Routledge

Gay, G. (2002). Preparing for culturally responsive teaching. *Journal of Teacher Education*, 53(2), 106–16.

General Social Survey. (2016). NORC at the University of Chicago. https://gss.norc.org/About-The-GSS.

Gersten, R., Haymond, K., Newman-Gonchar, R., Dimino, J., and Jayantha, M. (2020). Meta-analysis of the impact of reading interventions for students in the primary grades. *Journal of Research on Educational Effectiveness*, 13(2), 401–27.

Goldenberg, C. (2006). Improving achievement for English-learners: What the research tells us. *Education Week*, 25(43).

Goldenberg, C. (2012). Research on English learner instruction. In Caldron, M. (Ed.), *Breaking through: Effective instruction and assessment for reaching English learners*, 39–61. Bloomington, IN: Solution Tree Press.

Goldenberg, C. (2020). Reading wars, reading science and English learners. *Reading Research Quarterly*, 55(S1), S131–144.

Goldman, S. R., Greenleaf, C., Yukhymenko-Lescroart, M., Brown, W., Ko, M.-L. M., Emig, J. M., George, M., Wallace, P., Blaum, D., and Britt, M. A. (2019). Explanatory modeling in science through text-based investigation: Testing the efficacy of the Project READI intervention approach. *American Educational Research Journal*, 56(4), 1148–216.

Goodwin, B. (2021). Does restorative justice work? *Educational Leadership*, 79(2), 82–83.

Gorski, P. C. (2018). *Reaching and teaching students in poverty: Strategies for erasing the opportunity gap*, second edition. New York, NY: Teachers College Press.

Grantmakers for Education. (2013). *Educating English language learners: Grantmaking strategies for closing America's other achievement gap*. Retrieved, October 19, 2021, at http://edfunders.org/sites/default/files/Educating%20English%20Language%20Learners_April%202013.pdf.

Great Schools Partnership. (2016). *The glossary of education reforms*. Retrieved February 11, 2021, at https://www.edglossary.org/equity/.

Guthrie, J. T. (2004). Teaching for literacy engagement. *Journal of Literacy Research*, 36(1), 1–30.

Haberman, M. (1995). *Star teachers of children in poverty*. West Lafayette, IN: Kappa Delta Pi.

Hanline, M. F., and Daley, S. (2002). Mom, will Kaelie always have possibilities? *Phi Delta Kappan*, 84(1), 73–76.

Hattie, J. (2009). *Visible learning: A synthesis of over 800 meta-analyses relating to achievement*. New York, NY: Routledge.

Hill, P. T., Campbell, C., and Harvey, J. (2000). *It takes a city: Getting serious about urban school reform*. Washington, DC: Brookings Institute Press

Hill, T. D. (2017). *Combating the achievement gap: Ending failure as a default in schools*. New York, NY: Rowman & Littlefield.
Hollingsworth, J., and Ybarra, S. (2009). *Explicit direct instruction: The power of the well-crafted, well-taught lesson*. Thousand Oaks, CA: Corwin Press.
Honingsfeld, A., and Dove, M. G. (2015). *Collaboration and co-teaching for English learners: A leader's guide*. Thousand Oaks, CA: Corwin.
Hurst, D., Tan, A., Meek, A., and Sellers, J. (2003). *Overview and inventory of state education reforms: 1990 to 2000*. Washington, DC: U.S. Department of Education, National Center for Education Statistics.
Individuals with Disabilities Act. 20 U.S.C., Chapter 33 (2004). https://uscode.house.gov/view.xhtml?path=/prelim@title20/chapter33&edition=prelim.
Institute for Effective Education. (n.d.). *Evidence 4 impact*. Education Endowment Foundation. Retrieved on August 18, 2021, at https://www.evidence4impact.org.uk/what-is-e4i#.
Irwin, V., Zhang, J., Wang, X., Hein, S., Wang, K., Roberts, A., York, C., Barmer, A., Bullock Mann, F., Dilig, R., and Parker, S. (2021). *Report on the condition of Education 2021 (NCES 2021–144)*. Washington, DC: U.S. Department of Education, National Center for Education Statistics.
Izquierdo, E. (2012). Leadership matters for learning English and learning in English. In Calderon, M. (Ed.). (2012). *Breaking through: Effective instruction and assessment for reaching English learners*, 207–22. Bloomington, IN: Solution Tree Press.
Jean-Marie, G., and Mansfield, K. C. (2013). School leaders' courageous conversations about race: Race and racial discrimination in Schools. In Brooks, J. S., and Arnold, N. W. (Eds.), *Antiracist school leadership: Toward equity in education for America's student*, 19–36. Charlotte, NC: Information Age Publishing, Inc.
Jortveit, M., and Kovac, V. B. (2021). Co-teaching that works: Special and general educators' perspectives on collaborations. *Teaching Education*. Retrieved September 15, 2021, at https://www.tandfonline.com/doi/full/10.1080/10476210.2021.1895105.
Kase, C., Hoover, S., Boyd, G., West, K. D., Dubenitz, J., Trivedi, P. A., Peterson, H. J., and Stein, B. D. (2017). Educational outcomes associated with school behavioral health interventions: A review of the literature. *Journal of School Health*, 87(7), 554–62.
Kendi, I. X. (2020, September). Is this the beginning of the end of American racism? *The Atlantic*. Retrieved from https://www.theatlantic.com/magazine/archive/2020/09/the-end-of-denial/614194/.
Knoff, H. (2019). The impact of inequitable school funding: Solutions for struggling schools without the money to fully help struggling students. *American Consortium for Equity in Education*. Retrieved November 5, 2021, at https://ace-ed.org/inequitable-school-funding/.
Krashen, S. D. (2004). *The power of reading: Insights from research*, second edition. Portsmouth, NH: Heinemann.
Lambert, R. (2021). The magic is in the margins: UDL math. *Mathematics Teacher: Learning and Teaching PK-12*, 114(09), 660–69.

Landson-Billings, G. (1994). *The dreamkeepers: Successful teachers of African American children*. San Francisco, CA: Jossey-Bass.

Larkin, M. J. (2001). Providing support for student independence through scaffolded instruction. *TEACHING Exceptional Children, 34*(1), 30–34.

Lee, O. (2012). Teaching science with English language and literacy (chapter 7). In Caldron, M. (ed.) (2012). *Breaking through: Effective instruction and assessment for reaching English learners*, 107–26. Bloomington, IN: Solution Tree Press.

Lent, R. C. (2016). *This is disciplinary literacy: Reading, writing, thinking, and . . . doing content area by content area*. Thousand Oaks, CA: Corwin Literacy.

Lezotte, L. W., and Pepperl, J. C. (1999). *The effective schools process: A proven path to learning for all*. Okemos, MI: Effective Schools Products, Ltd.

Lindsay, J. (2010). *Children's access to print material and education-related out-comes: Findings from a meta-analytic reviews*. Naperville, IL: Learning Point.

Lipscomb, L., Swanson, J., and West, A. (2010). Scaffolding (chapter 21). In Orey, M. (ed.). *Emerging perspectives on learning, teaching, and technology*. Global Text Project. Retrieved September 22, 2021, at https://textbookequity.org/Textbooks/Orey_Emergin_Perspectives_Learning.pdf.

Martin, C., Boser, U., Benner, M., and Baffour, P. (2018). *A quality approach to school funding: Lessons learned from school finance litigation*. Center for American Progress. Retrieved November 5, 2021, at https://cf.americanprogress.org/wp-content/uploads/2018/11/LessonsLearned_SchoolFunding-report-4.pdf?_ga=2.228707870.388706713.1636320160-1656654438.1633023570.

Marzano, R. J., and Waters, T. (2009). *District leadership that works: Striking the right balance*. Bloomington, IN: Solution Tree Press.

Marzano, R. J., Waters, T., and McNulty, B. A. (2005). *School leadership that works: From research to results*. Alexandria, VA: Association for Supervision and Curriculum Development.

Maslow, A. H. (1943). A theory of human motivation. *Psychological Review, 50*(4), 370–96.

McConachie, S. M., and Petrosky, A. R. (Eds.). (2010). *Content matters: A disciplinary literacy approach to improving student learning*. San Francisco, CA: Jossey-Bass.

McEwan, E. K. (2009). *10 traits of high effective schools: Raising the achievement bar for all students*. Thousand Oaks, CA: Corwin Press.

McGhee, H. (2021). *The sum of us: What racism costs everyone and how we can prosper together*. London, England: Profile Books, Ltd.

McGill-Franzen, A., and Allington, R. L. (2018). What have we learned about addressing summer reading loss? In Allington, R. L., and McGill-Franzen, A. (Eds.). *Summer reading: Closing the rich/poor reading achievement gap*, second edition. New York, NY: Teachers College Press.

McIntosh, K., Goin, C., and Bastable, E. (2018). *Do schools implementing SWPBIS have decreased racial and ethnic disproportionality in school discipline?* PBIS Positive Interventions & Supports, Office of Technical Assistance Center. Retrieved October 25, 2021, at https://assets-global.website-files.com/5d3725188825e071f1670246/5d7ac87c3af0212c7783631e_do%20schools

%20implementing%20swpbis%20have%20decreased%20racial%20and%20ethnic%20disproportionality%20in%20school%20discipline-2.pdf.

McKenzie, K. B., and Scheurich, J. J. (2004). Equity traps: A useful construct for preparing principals to lead schools that are successful with racially diverse students. *Educational Administration Quarterly*, *40*(5), 601–32.

McLeskey, J., Barringer, M.-D., Billingsley, B. Brownell, M., Jackson, D., Kennedy, M., Lewis, T., Maheady, L., Rodriguez, J. Scheeler, M. C., Winn, J., and Zieger, D. (2017). *High-leverage practices in special education*. Arlington, VA: Council for Exceptional Children and CEEDAR Center.

McLeskey, J., and Waldron, N. L. (2002). School change and inclusive schools: Lessons learned from practice. *Phi Delta Kappan*, *84*(1), 65–72.

Meloy, B., Gardner, M., and Darling-Hammond, L. (2019). *Untangling the evidence on preschool effectiveness: Insight for policy makers*. Palo Alto, CA: Learning Policy Institute.

Meloy, B., and Schachner, A. (2019). *Early childhood essentials: A framework for aligning child skills and educator competencies*. Palo Alto, CA: Learning Policy Institute.

Milner IV, H. R. (2021). Disrupting racism and whiteness in researching a science of reading. *Reading Research Quarterly*, *55*(S1), S249–S253.

Minaya-Rowe, L. (2012). Effective teaching for ELs and all students: Vocabulary, reading, and writing within all subjects. In Caldron, M. (Ed.). *Breaking through: Effective instruction and assessment for reaching English learners*, 107–26). Bloomington, IN: Solution Tree Press.

Morgan, E., Salomon, N., Plotkin, M., and Cohen, R. (2014). *The school discipline consensus report: Strategies from the field to keep students engaged in school and out of the juvenile justice system*. New York, NY: Council of State Governments Justice Center.

Mulholland, M., and O'Conner, U. (2016). Collaborative classroom practice for inclusion: Perspectives of classroom teachers and learning support/resource teachers. *International Journal of Inclusive Education*, *20*(10), 1070–83.

Munoz, M. A., Chang, F., and Ross, S. M. (2012). No child left behind and tutoring in reading and mathematics: Impact of supplemental educational services on large scale assessment. *Journal of Education for Students Placed at Risk*, *17*(3), 186–200.

Murawski, W. W. (2009). *Collaborative teaching in secondary schools: Making the co-teaching marriage work*. Thousand Oaks, CA: Corwin.

Murawski, W. W., and Dieker, L. A. (2004). Tips and strategies for coteaching at the secondary level. *Council for Exceptional Children*, *36*(5), 52–58.

Murawski, W. W., and Lochner, W. W. (2011). Observing co-teaching: What to ask for, look for, and listen for. *Intervention in School and Clinic*, *46*(3), 174–83.

Murawski, W. W., and Swanson, H. L. (2001). A meta-analysis of co-teaching research: Where are the data? *Remedial and Special Education*, *22*(5), 258–67.

National Association of School Psychologists. (2021). *Comprehensive school-based mental and behavioral health services and school psychologist*. Bethesda, MD: National Association of School Psychologists.

National Association of State Directors of Special Education. (2006). *Response to intervention: Policy considerations and implementation*. Alexandria, VA: National Association of State Directors of Special Education, Inc.

National Center for Education Statistics. (n.d.). *NAEP History and Innovation*. Institute of Education Sciences, Retrieved February 18, 2021, at https://nces.ed.gov/nationsreportcard/about/timeline.aspx#tab-4.

National Commission on Excellence in Education. (1983). *A nation at risk*. Retrieved February 21, 2021, at https://www2.ed.gov/pubs/NatAtRisk/index.html.

National Council of Teachers of Mathematics. (2018*). Catalyzing change in high school mathematics: Initiating critical conversations*. Reston, VA: National Council of Teachers of Mathematics.

National Equity Project. (n.d.). Retrieved February 11, 2021, at https://www.nationalequityproject.org/education-equity-definition.

National Forum on Education Statistics. (2015). *Forum guide to college and career ready data*. Washington, DC: U.S. Department of Education, National Center for Education Statistics. Retrieved September 26, 2021, at https://nces.ed.gov/pubs2015/2015157.pdf.

National Reading Panel. (2000). *Report of the national reading panel: Teaching children to read. Executive summary and report of the subgroups*. Washington, DC: U.S. Department of Health and Human Services, National Institutes of Health. Retrieved on August 8, 2021, at https://www.nichd.nih.gov/about/org/der/branches/cdbb/nationalreadingpanelpubs.

Necochea, J., and Cline, Z. (1996). A case study analysis of within district school funding inequities. *Equity and Excellence in Education, 29*(2), 69–77.

Neitzel, A. J., Lake, C., Pellegrini, M., and Slavin, R. E. (2021). A synthesis of quantitative research on programs for struggling readers in elementary schools. *Reading Research Quarterly, 0*(0), 1–31.

Neitzel, A. J., Wolf, B., Guo, X., Shakarchi, A. F., Madden, N. A., Repka, M. X., Friedman, D. S., and Collins, M. E. (2021). Effect of randomized interventional school-based vision program on academic performance of students in grades 3 to 7: A cluster randomized clinical trial. *JAMA Opththalmology, 139*(10), 1104–14.

Nelson, J., Lott, L., and Glenn, H. S. (2000). *Positive discipline in the classroom: Developing mutual respect, cooperation, and responsibility in your classroom*, third edition. Roseville, CA: Prima Publishing.

NextGenScience. (2013). *Next Generation Science Standards*. NextGenScience, WestEd. Retrieved on August 16, 2021, at https://www.nextgenscience.org/staff/staff.

No Child Left Behind Act. 20 U.S.C. § 6301 (2001). https://files.eric.ed.gov/fulltext/ED556108.pdf.

Noguera, P. A. (2008). *The trouble with Black boys . . . and other reflections on race, equity, and the future of education*. San Francisco, CA: Jossey-Bass.

Nordmeyer, J., Boals, T., MacDonald, R., and Westerlundh, R. (2021). What does equity really mean for multilingual learners? *Educational Leadership, 78*(6), 60–65.

Odden, A. R., and Archibald, S. J. (2009). *Doubling student performance: And finding the resources to do it*. Thousands Oaks, CA: Corwin Press.
Odem, S. L., Brantlinger, E., Gersten, R., Horner, R. H., Thompson, B., and Harris, K. R. (2005). Research in special education: Scientific methods and evidence-based practices. *Council for Exceptional Children, 71*(2), 137–48.
Office of Elementary and Secondary Education. (2018). *Improving basic programs operated by local education agencies (Title I, Part A)*. Washington, DC: U.S. Department of Education. Retrieved on November 2, 2021, at https://www2.ed.gov/programs/titleiparta/index.html.
Office of Special Education and Rehabilitative Services. (2020). *42nd annual report to Congress on the implementation of the Individuals with Disabilities Education Act, 2020*. Washington, DC: U.S. Department of Education.
Office of Special Education Programs. (2019–2020). *OSEP fast facts: Race and ethnicity of children with disabilities served under IDEA Part B*. Washington, DC: Office of Special Education Programs, U.S. Department of Education. Retrieved September 27, 2021, at https://sites.ed.gov/idea/osep-fast-facts-looks-at-race-and-ethnicity-of-children-with-disabilities-served-under-idea/.
Ohio Special Education Research Project. (2013). *Identifying successful practices for students with disabilities in Ohio schools: Evidence-based practices in special education a review of the literature*. Columbus, OH: Ohio Department of Education, Office for Exceptional Children.
Olszewski-Kubilius, P., and Clarenbach, J. (2012). *Unlocking emergent talent: Supporting high achievement of low-income, high-ability students*. Washington, DC: National Association for Gifted Children.
Patall, E. A., Cooper, H., and Allen, A. B. (2010). Extending the school day or school year: A systemic review of research (1985–2009). *Review of Educational Research, 80*(3), 401–36.
Pellegrini, M., Neitzel, A., Lake, C., and Slavin, R. E. (2021). Effective programs in elementary mathematics: A best-evidence synthesis. *AERA Open, 7*(1), 1–29.
Peters, S. G. (2006). *Do you know enough about me to teach me? A student's perspective*. Orangeburg, SC: The Peters Group Foundation.
Pratt, S. (2014). Achieving symbiosis: Working through challenges found in co-teaching to achieve effective co-teaching relationships. *Teaching and Teacher Education, 41*, 1–12.
Putman, H., and Walsh, K. (2021). *State of the states 2021: Teacher preparation policy*. Washington, DC: National Council on Teacher Quality.
Rech, J. F., and Harrington, J. (2000). Algebra as a gatekeeper: A descriptive study at an urban university. *Journal of African American Men, 4*(4), 63–71.
Reisman, A. (2012). Reading like a historian: A document-based history curriculum intervention in urban high schools. *Cognition and Instruction, 30*(1), 86–112.
Roach, A., and Elliott, S. (2006). The influence of access to general education curriculum on alternate assessment performance of students with significant cognitive disabilities. *Educational Evaluation and Policy Analysis, 28*(2), 181–94.

Rohrbeck, C. A., Ginsburg-Block, M. D., Fantuzzo, J. W., and Miller, T. R. (2003). Peer-assisted learning interventions with elementary school students: A meta-analytic review. *Journal of Educational Psychology*, *95*(2), 240–57.

Saad, L. F. (2020). *Me and white supremacy: Combat racism, change the world, and become a good ancestor*. Naperville, IL: Sourcebooks.

Schmidt, W. H., Burroughs, N. A., Zoido, P., and Housang, R. T. (2015). The role of schooling in perpetuating educational inequality: An international perspective. *Educational Researcher*, *44*(7), 371–86.

Schmoker, M. (2018). *Focus: Elevating the essentials to radically improve student learning*, second edition. Alexandria, VA: ACSD.

Seidenberg, M. S., Borkenhagen, M. C., and Kearns, D. M. (2020). Lost in translation: Challenges in connecting reading science and educational practice. *Reading Research Quarterly*, *55*(S1), S119–S130.

Sergiovanni, T. J. (1990). *Value-added leadership: How to get extraordinary performance in schools*. San Diego, CA: Harcourt Brace Jovanovich, Publishers.

Shalaby, C. (2021). [Interview] Carla Shalaby on radically inclusive discipline. *Educational Leadership*, *79*(2), 14–18.

Simms, J. A., and Marzano, R. J. (2019). *The new art and science of teaching reading*. Bloomington, IN: Solution Tree Press.

Slavin, R. E. (1986). The Napa evaluation of Madeline Hunter's ITIP: Lessons learned. *Elementary School Journal*, *87*, 165–71.

Slavin, R. E. (1995). *Cooperative learning: Theory, research and practice*, second edition. Boston, MA: Allyn and Bacon.

Slavin, R. E. (2012a). *Educational psychology: Theory and practice*, tenth edition. Boston, MA: Pearson.

Slavin, R. E. (2012b). Effective whole-school teaching for English learners. In Calderon, M. (Ed.). *Breaking through*: *Effective instruction and assessment for reaching English learners*, 27–37). Bloomington, IN: Solution Tree Press.

Slavin, R. E. (2017). Evidence-based reform in education. *Journal of Education for Students Placed at Risk*, *22*(3), 178–84.

Slavin, R. E. (2020). How evidence-based reform will transform research and practice in education. *Educational Psychologist*, *55*(1), 21–31.

Slavin, R. E., Inns, A., Pellegrini, M., and Lake, C. (2019). *Response to Proven Intervention (RTPI): Enabling struggling learners*. Baltimore, MD: Center for Research and Reform in Education, Johns Hopkins University.

Slavin, R. E., Lake, C., Chambers, B., Cheung, A., and Davis, S. (2009). Effective reading programs for the elementary grades: A best-evidence synthesis. *Review of Educational Research*, *79*(4), 1391–466.

Slavin, R. E., Lake, C., and Groff, C. (2009). Effective programs in middle and high school mathematics: A best-evidence synthesis. *Review of Education Research*, *79*(2), 839–911.

Slavin, R. E., Madden, N. A., Karweit, N. L., Dolan, L., Wasik, B. A., Shaw, A., Mainzer, K. L., and Haxby, B. (1991). Neverstreaming: Prevention and early intervention as alternatives to special education. *Journal of Learning Disabilities*, *24*, 373–78.

Snow, C. E., Burns, M. S., and Griffin, P. (Eds.) (1998). *Preventing reading difficulties in young children*. Washington, DC: Committee on the Prevention of Reading Difficulties in Young Children, National Academy Press.

Southeast Regional Educational Laboratory. (n.d.). *Evidence-based teaching practices: principles of instruction*. Washington, DC: U.S. Department of Education, Institute of Education Sciences: National Center for Education Evaluation and Regional Assistance. Retrieved August 31, 2021, at https://ies.ed.gov/ncee/edlabs/infographics/pdf/REL_SE_Evidence-based_teaching_practices.pdf.

Stein, E. (2016). *Elevating co-teaching through UDL*. Wakefield, MA: CAST Professional Publishing.

Swanson H. L., and Hoskyn, M. (1998). Experimental intervention research on students with learning disabilities: A meta-analysis of treatment outcomes. *Review of Education Research, 63*(3), 277–321.

Synder, T. D., Dinkes, R., Sonnenberg, W., and Cornman, S. (2019). *Study of the Title I, Part A grant program mathematical formulas*. Washington, DC: U.S. Department of Education, National Center for Education Statistics.

Taylor, R. D., Oberle, E., Durlak, J. A., and Weissber, R. P. (2017). Promoting positive youth development through school-based social and emotional learning interventions: A meta-analysis of follow-up efforts. *Child Development, 88*(4), 1156–71.

The Century Foundation. (2020). *Closing America's education funding gaps*. Retrieved November 5, 2021, at https://tcf.org/content/report/closing-americas-education-funding/.

Thernstrom, A., and Thernstrom, S. (2003). *No excuses: Closing the racial gap in learning*. New York, NY: Simon and Schuster.

TNTP. (2018). *The opportunity myth: What students can show us about how school is letting them down—and how to fix it*. New York, NY: TNTP.

Toth, M. D., and Sousa, D. A. (2019). *The power of student teams*. West Palm Beach, FL: Learning Sciences International.

Travers, J. (2018). *What is resource equity?* Watertown, MA: Education Resource Strategies.

Tyack, D., and Cuban, L. (1995). *Tinkering toward utopia: A century of public school reform*. Cambridge, MA: Harvard University Press.

U.S. Department of Education. (1993). *National excellence: A case for developing America's talent*. Washington, DC: U.S. Department of Education, Office of Educational Research and Improvement.

U.S. Department of Education. (2009). *Supplemental educational services non-regulatory guidance*. Washington, DC: U.S. Department of Education.

U.S. Department of Education. (2014). *Civil rights data collection: Data snapshot college and career readiness*. Washington, DC: U. S. Department of Education, Office for Civil Rights.

U.S. Department of Education. (2019a). *Advanced placement, international baccalaureate, and dual-enrollment courses: Availability, participation, and related outcomes for 2009 Ninth-Graders: 2013*. Washington, DC: National Center for Education Statistics.

U.S. Department of Education. (2019b). *Opportunities and responsibilities for state and local report cards under the Elementary and Secondary Education Act of 1965, as amended by the Every Student Succeeds Act.* Retrieved November 5, 2021, at https://www2.ed.gov/policy/elsec/leg/essa/report-card-guidance-final.pdf.

U.S. Department of Education. (n.d.). *ESSA consolidated plans.* Retrieved February 18, 2021, from https://www2.ed.gov/admins/lead/account/stateplan17/index.html.

USDA Food and Nutrition Service. (2019). *National school lunch program (NSLP) fact sheet.* Washington, DC: U.S. Department of Agriculture.

Valencia, R. R. (2010). *Dismantling contemporary deficit thinking: Educational thought and practice.* New York, NY: Routledge.

Vaughn, S., Levy, S., Coleman, M., and Bos, C. S. (2002). Reading instruction for students with LD and EBD: A synthesis of observation studies. *Journal of Special Education, 36*(1), 2–13.

Vaughn, S., Roberts, G. J., Miciak, J., Taylor, P., and Fletcher, J. M. (2019). Efficacy of a word- and text-based intervention for students with significant reading difficulties. *Journal of Learning Disabilities, 52*(1), 31–44.

Vollmer, J. (2010). *Schools cannot do it alone: Building public support for American's public schools.* Fairfield, IA: Enlightenment Press.

Weir, K. (2020). Safeguarding student mental health. *Monitor on Psychology, 51*(6), 46–52.

What Works Clearinghouse. (n.d.). *What we do.* Washington, DC: Institute for Education Sciences, U.S. Department of Education.

WIDA. (2020). *WIDA English language development standards framework, 2020 edition: Kindergarten–grade 12.* Board of Regents of the University of Wisconsin System.

Wilhelm, J. D. (2012). *Improving comprehension with think-aloud strategies: Modeling what good readers do.* New York, NY: Scholastic.

Wilkerson, I. (2020). *Caste: The origins of our discontents.* New York, NY: Random House.

Williams, J. K. (2013). Upspoken realities: White, female teachers discuss race, students, and achievement in the context of teaching in a majority black elementary school. In Brooks, J. S., and Arnold, N. W. (Eds.). *Antiracist school leadership: Toward equity in education for America's students,* 153–84. Charlotte, NC: Information Age Publishing.

Wood, D. M., Bruner, J. S., and Ross, G. (1976). The role of tutoring in problem solving. *Journal of Psychology and Psychiatry, 17*(2), 89–100.

Yaluma, C. B., and Tyner, A. (2018). *Is there a gifted gap? Gifted education in high-poverty schools.* Washington, DC: Thomas B. Fordham Institute.

Youth.Gov. (n.d.). *Implications for school discipline.* Retrieved October 25, 2021, at https://youth.gov/youth-topics/school-climate/implications-for-school-discipline.

Zwiers, J. (2014). *Building academic language second edition: Meeting Common Core standards across the disciplines.* San Francisco, CA: Jossey-Bass.

Appendix A
Professional Learning Plans

EXAMPLE OF ALIGNED PROFESSIONAL LEARNING PLANS

District Plan:

The district has set the following goal: *All students will demonstrate proficiency at grade level or above in literacy*. The district identified five strategies to use in achieving this goal. They are:

1. establish high expectations for all students,
2. eliminate tracking of students for literacy instruction,
3. use the Science of Reading and a proven program to guide reading instruction,
4. develop academic literacy across all secondary content areas, and
5. develop secondary students' academic writing skills.

For each of these five basic strategies, the district develops detailed plans, timelines, and benchmarks for fully implementing the strategies and accomplishing their goal. Each of the five strategies have a series of tasks to be completed in order to implement each specific strategy. The details of the plan are put into a document that allows stakeholders to easily review the plan as well as track progress on the plan.

High Expectations

The district invites thought leaders once or twice a year over the next couple of years to work with staff-help them reflect while they realize that they have different expectations for different groups of students as evidenced by white, upper-income students enrolled in advanced classes while Latinx,

Table A.1. Sample District Improvement and Professional Learning Plan

Goal: *All students will demonstrate proficiency at grade level or above in literacy.*

Strategy 1: Establish high expectations for all students.	Strategy 2: Eliminate tracking of students for literacy instruction.	Strategy 3: Use the Science of Reading and a proven program to guide reading instruction.	Strategy 4: Develop academic literacy across all secondary content areas.	Strategy 5: Develop secondary students' academic writing skills.
Task 1 and Progress Notes:	Task 1 and Progress Notes:	Task 1 and Progress Notes:	Task 1 and Progress Notes:	Task 1 and Progress Notes:
Task 2 and Progress Notes:	Task 2 and Progress Notes:	Task 2 and Progress Notes:	Task 2 and Progress Notes:	Task 2 and Progress Notes:
Task 3 and so on				

lower-income students are enrolled in general education classes. The thought leaders are from different racial and ethnic groups, further helping staff see the variance in expectations.

After the district presentations, staff at each school come together as they examine their positionality as staff and the positionality of their students. They identify ways that they communicate their expectations for literacy to different groups of students and detail plans for changes to their systems so they have high expectations for all students. The plan details how they will eliminate the inadvertently different expectations for different groups of students.

During the summers for the next couple of years, book studies from some of the writings of these or similar thought leaders are organized across the district for those who wish to participate for more reflection and learning. Staff are asked to recommend books they have read and have impacted their expectations for students that can also be used for book studies. Participation is optional. The superintendent even hosts a culminating book study experience with dessert and sharing at her house.

Over the next three years, teams from across the district (i.e., first-grade teachers, English 9 teachers, chemistry teachers, etc.) meet to review the standards for their content area related to literacy. They unpack the standards and create ways for students to demonstrate their mastery of these standards and develop rubrics that will be needed for scoring. They examine texts and other instructional materials listed in the district's curriculum maps to ensure that they are at the appropriate level of difficulty and representative of all students. This work is facilitated by master educators who are respected by their peers and get incredible results from their students.

Undoing Tracking of Students in Literacy

Leaders from all schools meet regularly to plan for and take action to eliminate tracking of students in literacy. This work begins by schools reporting what they find as they explore ways in which students are tracked from the beginning with reading groups of advanced, grade-level, and the below-level reading groups. It continues with pull-out classes at the elementary and middle school level that remove students from the regular classroom to remediate (fix) students while they miss grade-level instruction, falling further behind. It continues with content classes of varying difficulty such as basic math versus advanced math for college credit.

After identifying harmful ways that students are tracked, the group develops recommendations for district wide expectations on how students are to be grouped for instruction so that all students experience high expectations and receive the support they need to succeed. These expectations are presented to district leadership for approval and each school works to untrack their school with the regular meetings now serving as a means of accountability and support among the schools as they engage in this work.

Science of Reading

The district wants to ensure that all elementary school teachers are using the Science of Reading with a research-proven instructional program as the basis of their reading instruction due to the overwhelming evidence, from extensive research, that all students can become proficient readers. Elementary educators (including principals) are provided instruction in the Science of Reading and proven instructional programs. This instruction may be provided by experts within the district who will nurture the work over the next three years or by an outside expert or team of both.

Elementary educators examine their own practices to identify strengths and weaknesses in using the selected proven program. What they learn from this examination provides guidance for future district work and individual building work. Grade-level teams meet periodically across the district to examine model lessons and learn more about these instructional strategies from peer experts. In the individual buildings, they identify staff needs in relation to using the Science of Reading with the proven instructional program and develop professional learning plans to address the needs.

These plans might include coaching support, online learning opportunities, guest experts modeling and co-teaching with staff, professional readings, and recording themselves teaching a lesson for further study. In each building, teacher teams examine student data, engage in lesson studies and planning, and work together to improve their practice for improved student outcomes. They may even observe each other to further their learning. These teacher teams are comprised of grade-level teachers as well as English language teachers, special education teachers, and other professionals also in the classroom to provide extra support.

Academic Language

Middle school educators (including principals) gather to learn about literacy in the content areas and academic language (more information is in chapter 5). They examine the content and literacy standards to identify much of the academic language that students will need to know. Discussions are held and rubrics developed for assessing students' ability to use academic language. Exemplars are presented and collected over time from across the district.

This work is facilitated by experts within the district who nurture the work over the years or by an outside expert or a combination of both. Similarly, content teams meet across the district to examine model lessons and learn from peers more about teaching academic literacy in their content area. Each school identifies staff needs for teaching academic literacy and develops professional learning plans to address the needs. Plans might include coaching support, online learning opportunities, guest experts modeling and co-teaching with staff, professional readings, and recording themselves teaching a lesson for further study.

In each building, the teacher teams examine student data, engage in lesson studies and planning, and work together to improve their practice for improved student outcomes. They may observe each other to further their learning. Their teams are comprised of like content teachers as well as English language teachers, special education teachers, and other professionals who support the students in their classrooms.

Academic Writing

High school educators (including principals) come together to learn about academic writing and examine the content and literacy standards to identify what students are expected to know and be able to do. Rubrics are developed for assessing student writing based on the agreed upon conventions around tone, style, content, organization, etc. Exemplars are presented and collected over time from across the district.

This work is facilitated by experts within the district who nurture the work over the years or by an outside expert or a combination of both. Like content teams meet periodically to examine model lessons and learn from peers more about teaching academic writing in their content area. Each school identifies staff needs for teaching academic writing and develops professional learning plans to address the needs. These plans might include coaching support, online learning opportunities, guest experts modeling and co-teaching with them, shared professional readings, and recording themselves teaching a lesson for further study.

In each building, the teacher teams examine student data, engage in lesson studies and planning, and work together to improve their practice in academic writing instruction for improved student outcomes. They may even observe each other to further their learning. Their teams are comprised of grade-level teachers as well as English language teachers, special education teachers, and other professionals who support their students.

Building Plans

Each individual building will have their own plans as well. Their plans should align with the district's goals as well as their own individual goals. As you read through the examples, you can see that each building has a role in providing ongoing professional learning for its staff around literacy. There are portions that are led by the district to ensure that outcomes are the same across the district. However, once the expectations and requisite outcomes are established, each school will have various strengths and needs to reach the goal. The individual buildings will plan for and develop additional professional learning as needed.

In addition, each building will most likely have additional plans separate from the rest of the district. For example, if a school has identified student management concerns as a factor in their student literacy outcomes due to the amount of time lost either managing students or students being out of class, then the school will want to develop goals and plans to attend to these issues as well so that time spent on literacy learning is maximized.

Buildings also have different focus areas. One school might be a dual immersion school while another might be a STEM school or an arts school. They will want to make plans that allow them to continue to develop professionally in these focus areas as well as improving literacy outcomes. They may want to examine and improve how they teach literacy in multiple languages so that expectations are high in each language. Or they may want to select texts for reading instruction that support the STEM units that their school also uses. They will want to ensure that literacy is a part of their STEM or arts instruction so that students are developing literacy in these content areas as well.

An important component in professional learning is learning communities or teacher teams. Professional learning is sustained learning and growing together that results in improved learning outcomes for students. Professional learning communities are key to sustaining learning and incorporating it into daily practice. Dufour et al. (2016) define a professional learning community as a "collaboration [which] represents a systematic process in which teachers work together interdependently in order to impact their classroom practice in ways that will lead to better results for their students, for their team, and for their school" (p. 12).

Individual Plans

Many states and districts also expect educators to have their own professional learning plans. These plans can include action-based research that they intend to engage in as a part of their practice, professional readings, graduate classes, online seminars, conferences, etc. Often, these plans align with the district and building plans as educators focus on improving their practice that will contribute to accomplishing the district and building goals.

We described earlier how professional learning plans may be developed at both a district and building level with an overarching goal of developing student proficiency in literacy. Individual teachers may decide that due to the number of limited English-speaking students in their class, they would like to improve their ability to support English learners. Therefore, they embark on earning their credentials as an English development teacher. They may never take a position as an English development teacher, but they will use the skills gained in their classes every day.

District Role in Building and Individual Plans

The district's primary role in developing professional learning plans at the district level, the building level, and the individual level is to ensure expectations for student learning and what students are expected to know and do is clear. The district, collectively, identifies the strengths and needs and sets goals to address the needs. They also set the metrics that will be used to determine progress toward the goal.

The district has a role in supporting building plans by providing resources such as in-house experts and/or outside experts, materials for various study groups, and time for professional learning. It is also critical that the district help the community understand the critical need for professional learning by educators and ensure educators are compensated for any required professional learning that is outside their contract. The community needs to see time taken by educators for professional learning as an important component for success, not just a time when students may be out of school.

Districts can also provide individual teachers with funds that they can use for their individual professional learning such as conference attendance, visiting master classrooms at other schools, or graduate classes tuition. This tells educators that their professional growth is important and valued. Schools and districts can also provide graduate classes in areas of need at no cost to teachers right on the campuses where they work.

An elementary school with 80 percent of the students identified as limited English speakers began offering classes on a rotating basis each semester that fulfilled the state requirements for an endorsement as an English learner teacher. Teachers could participate in the classes free of charge as long as they agreed to continue their employment beyond the class by the number of semesters that they had participated in the free classes. This resulted in nearly every teacher earning an English learner endorsement and increasing their position on the salary schedule while remaining in the regular classroom supporting their students in learning English and academic content at the same time.

Ensuring school calendars and weekly schedules include time for professional learning is another way districts support professional learning plans. Developing these schedules are a test of creativity, but they provide big rewards. There is never enough time. However, districts and schools can increase the amount of time available for professional learning by tightly focusing improvement efforts to only two or three goals, reducing the number of meetings that do not involve professional learning around the agreed upon goals, and working with the community to add professional learning time to the school calendar.

Educators learning together is an important component of building a strong school and district culture that is focused on ensuring every student is educated to the highest level, graduating high school college and/or career ready. As educators learn and work to improve their practice together, they solidify shared values, beliefs, and norms. They learn to value and trust their peers, and their students see their teachers modeling continuous learning and improvement.

Appendix B
Reflections and Next Steps

This section of the book is intended as a space where you can collect notes from your reflections at the end of each chapter. Once you have completed the book, you can review your reflections and identify possible next steps as well as priorities. Remember, not everything can be a priority at once, so select just a few. Select those issues that you think will give you the greatest change in student outcomes in the short term. Once you have successfully begun the work to address those areas, you can then tackle another area that provides an opportunity for improving equity in our schools so that all students achieve to the highest levels and graduate high school college and/or career ready.

Table B.1. Reflection and Next Steps

Building Cultures That Support Equity			
Reflection	Response Notes	Possible Next Steps	Priority Area
Who are the marginalized students in your school? How do you know this? What are you doing about it?			
When a team of educators discuss individual students who are reading below level, what types of reasons are identified for this issue? When a student's home is blamed for their lack of reading ability, what do you say? How do you use the student's strengths to improve their reading abilities?			
What do the unspoken messages (symbols, celebrations, displays, etc.) say are the most important things or values in your classroom, school, or district? Why do you say this?			

What is your school or district plan for nurturing a positive culture throughout the school year?

Reading: The Basis of Equity in School

Reflection	Response Notes	Possible Next Steps	Priority Area
What fraction of children in your school/district leave third grade as below-level readers? Why? Be careful not to blame the children and their families. What it is about your district or school system that causes students to leave third grade as below-level readers?			
How is reading instruction provided in your classroom, school, or district? Does it follow the science of reading and use proven programs? Why or why not?			
Is reading instruction in your building based on equality or equity? How do you know?			

Literacy in the Content Areas

Reflection	Response Notes	Possible Next Steps	Priority Area
How many different types of Algebra I classes are taught in your school? Why?			
What will you do so that all students graduate from your school proficient in algebra?			
How do you support mathematical thinking throughout your school?			
How do you help students learn the characteristics of literacy in your content area?			
Is the rigor in your classroom what you want for your own child? Why/why not?			

Highly Effective Instruction

Reflection	Response Notes	Possible Next Steps	Priority Area
Individually name your students' strengths, interests, and concerns.			
Who are the students you still need to develop individual relationships with?			
What state standard(s) are you teaching in your current lesson? What higher-level thinking is involved? Is the complexity of the text used appropriate?			

If a visitor asks your students what the target for learning is in the current lesson, what would they say? Do they know how they will demonstrate their learning?

How do you ensure that you are providing interventions immediately when needed in class and not the next day after grading papers the night before?

When you have students work in cooperative groups, how do you structure the learning so that teams are held accountable for each student learning? How do you hold students accountable for their individual learning?

Student Supports

Reflection	Response Notes	Possible Next Steps	Priority Area
Who are the students not mastering grade-level standards in your classroom? Are they included in appropriate Tier 1 instruction? What scaffolds do they receive?			
What do you need to do to ensure at least 80 percent of your students are successful in Tier 1 grade-level instruction?			
What percentage of your students take at least one advanced level course in high school? Are some of your student groups underrepresented? Why? What can you do about it?			
Do your special programs provide equity or do they continue the marginalization of students? If students are still being marginalized, what will you do about it?			

Social Services

Reflection	Response Notes	Possible Next Steps	Priority Area
How does your school or district support social emotional learning for your students?			
How do you access resources for your students that are struggling with mental health issues?			
What are your students' most critical social service needs? What agencies or non-profits could be helpful partners with these concerns?			
When a student's living situation is blamed for the lack of success in school, what do you do?			

Allocating Resources for Equity

Reflection	Response Notes	Possible Next Steps	Priority Area
What would be the result of a time audit in your classroom, school, or district? What would it indicate are the priorities? How could you improve your use of time?			
When hiring personnel for your school or district, how do you ensure new hires want to serve your students?			
How does your classroom, school, or district allocate resources through an equity lens rather than an equality lens? What more could it do?			

www.ingramcontent.com/pod-product-compliance
Lightning Source LLC
Chambersburg PA
CBHW022012300426
44117CB00005B/142